"Camp Pain"

"Camp Pain"

Talking with Chronic Pain Patients

Jean E. Jackson

PENN

University of Pennsylvania Press

Philadelphia

10 9 8 7 6 5 4 3 2 1

Published by
University of Pennsylvania Press
Philadelphia, Pennsylvania 19104-4011

Library of Congress Cataloging-in-Publication Data
Jackson, Jean E. (Jean Elizabeth), 1943–
"Camp pain": talking with chronic pain patients / Jean E. Jackson.
p.   cm.
Includes bibliographical references and index.
ISBN 0-8122-3526-6 (cloth : alk. paper) — ISBN 0-8122-1715-2 (pbk. : alk. paper)
1. Chronic pain—Psychological aspects.   2. Chronic pain.   3. Pain clinics.   I. Title.
RB127.J23   1999
616'.0472 21—dc21   99-043392

To Louis, with love

Contents

Acknowledgments

First of all, my appreciation and gratitude to Ethan Bernstein, M.D., Kevin Jefferson, Ph.D., and the rehabilitation hospital that housed the Commonwealth Pain Center (CPC) for permitting me to carry out the study. (These, like all names of CPC staff, are pseudonyms.) Although Dr. Bernstein and Kevin read my research proposal, they nevertheless took a risk, for a substantial amount of my methodology was "seat-of-the-pants" and none of us knew whether participant observation would succeed in such an environment. Things turned out surprisingly well; I had a wonderful time, the vast majority of patients and staff members said my presence was an asset, and the research has resulted in several publications. I hope they find that this book partly repays them for their enthusiastic support of my project.

I am extremely grateful to the CPC staff. Most of them knew very little about my project or me, yet they extended every courtesy during our fine-tuning of the conditions of research and during the fieldwork itself which, being intensive, made me a nuisance at times. Yet I was never made to feel unwelcome. Their work was often difficult—certainly work that I could not do myself—and I admire their dedication and compassion. I especially enjoyed our interviews at the end of the study, when the distance between us decreased a bit. Staff members contributed in a major way to an absolutely fascinating experience and made me think a lot about the meaning of the word "professional."

My greatest debt is to the CPC patients who participated in the study. A flood of powerful feelings comes over me when I remember how patients welcomed and trusted me enough to reveal their innermost sorrows, confusions, and joys. Those who were initially suspicious had every right to be so; here was one more professional—a very nosy one—who wanted them to sign one more form and answer one more set of questions. When I read through my fieldnotes and interviews, I reexperience those days, those calamities, those faces, those jokes. Being with them enriched me as a scholar and as a person. The patient community contained so much variety and provided so many lessons about the human condition, that I feel that *they* somehow wrote this book, flawed and partial though it is.

Thanks also to the National Institutes of Mental Health (grant 41787) and the Office of the Dean of the School of Humanities and Social Science at the Massachusetts Institute of Technology for supporting the research with sabbatical funds and small grants. Publication of the book was also supported by a grant from the Office of the Dean.

The following people have been extremely helpful during this book's rather long gestation. For technical help during the research and writing, thanks to Alison Salisbury, Priscilla Cobb, Abby Moser, Kathleen Spinale, and Judith Stein. Peter Solomon, Patricia Flaherty, Alan Huisman, and Joyce Nevis-Olesen provided invaluable editorial help. Stanley Holwitz at University of California Press has been enthusiastic about the project from the beginning, and Mary Murrell at Princeton University Press made invaluable suggestions at an earlier stage. At the University of Pennsylvania Press, special thanks to Patricia Smith for her wholehearted enthusiasm about my project; thanks also to managing editor Alison Anderson.

For overall support, I am indebted to the late Martin Diskin, Michael Fischer, James Howe, Judith Irvine, Louis Kampf, the late John Liebeskind, and Sharon Traweek. Rayna Rapp offered excellent advice at proposal writing time. For help in thinking through ideas, thanks to Paul Brodwin, Thomas Csordas, Ann Gamsa, Byron Good, Mary-Jo DelVecchio Good, Cheryl Mattingly, David Napier, Leah Robin, William Ruddick, and the late Irving Zola. For reading earlier versions of the book, thanks to Paul Brodwin, Mary-Jo DelVecchio Good, Louis Kampf, Francis Keefe, Arthur Kleinman, Tanya Luhrmann, Ronald Melzack, Lorna Rhodes, Amélie Rorty, Judith Spross, and several anonymous reviewers.

I am particularly grateful to Arthur Kleinman, who supported this project from the very beginning. Complete strangers when I made that first appointment, during the past fourteen years he has been unfailingly good-humored, and generously critical. A very busy man, he quickly read and commented on everything I sent to him and always gave me the impression that he really *cared*. My lowest point came when a sociologist reviewing the manuscript for a publisher seemingly could not comprehend that I wanted to analyze pain sufferers' discourse, rather than "create typologies and theories which are logical and substantially supported by data," as Joan Cassell, who had a similar experience, puts it. (See the Preface, to her superb 1991 book on surgeons at work.) After writing three and one half single-spaced pages of criticism, untempered by even one positive comment, the reviewer, who chose not to remain anonymous, recommended that the manuscript not be published. This was especially dismaying because this person also studies chronic pain centers. Arthur was marvelously sympathetic, writing me a long letter with mordant comments about disciplinary boundaries and very needed words of encouragement. Arthur has trained many students, and although we are the same age and he would disagree, I count myself very privileged to have been one.

Chapter 1
A Baffling Phenomenon

"All of us here are rather desperate people"
                                    —a Commonwealth Pain Center (CPC) patient

Teresa, a sculptor and body building instructor, had begun having severe back pain after a motorcycle accident fourteen years previously. Hospitalized several times with a herniated disk that nonetheless worsened, she ultimately found herself with degenerative disk disease, bone spurs, arachnoiditis (nerve damage), and arthritis. Wanting to avoid surgery, she went to a pain center and back school. She also tried acupuncture, spiritual healers, massage therapists, crystal healers, mushrooms (which were purported to stimulate growth), hypnosis, and transcutaneous electrical nerve stimulation (in which an apparatus sends an electrical signal to disrupt a pain signal). When she found the prescription medicines she was taking for pain and inflammation were upsetting her natural harmony and not allowing her to focus, she weaned herself off the drugs. She felt that her body was "refusing the drugs—they were making me shake and vomit, they weren't working on pain at all."

When she became pregnant disks at two levels of the spine ruptured. Since the pregnancy ruled out any radiology tests, she was put on total bed rest and traction for six months. Three brutal days of labor produced an oversized baby that needed open heart surgery. Following the birth, Teresa had spine surgery.

She was subsequently admitted to CPC because a laminectomy had re-ruptured a month after surgery, making her, as she put it, "psychotic with pain." Her account of this experience included complaints about the bad things that can happen "when medicine and law cross each other," about "sloppy medicine," and about physicians who refused to help her.

Teresa also struggled over the issue of self-acceptance. "I have been told in many of these [therapy] groups to love myself and accept myself in this condition, and I refuse to do that. I do not love myself in this condition, and if I chose to love myself in this condition, I would never get better." She disagreed with other patients who had come to believe that fighting pain was the wrong approach. However, Teresa did want to learn to "work with [the pain] so I can at least call the shots." She spoke of needing to be patient, brave, and in control and maintained that chronic pain sufferers needed to get their bodies as strong as possible "because it is going to be this way for the rest of your life." She knew she was going to have lifetime pain and coping with it depended on self-discipline.

Teresa changed remarkably during her stay at the pain center, returning to the high-energy, flamboyant, and outspoken person she had been earlier in her life. For example, at her discharge planning meeting she sang a song to the staff, accompanying herself on the guitar.

However, her pain did not diminish in any significant way and a darker side emerged from Teresa's talk. Commenting about the high suicide rate among spinal cord and head injury victims, she said that, while she would work hard at finding other channels through which she could become a happy human being again, if this did not happen she would "take other measures that would change that." A week after discharge, while at a nearby hospital to undergo a procedure, she took the elevator up to the roof and jumped off.

Why? I do not know—I did not know her well enough. But in the pages that follow the voice of Teresa and others like her will put forward many of the reasons why they can become so desperate.

Severe chronic pain, which can so deeply affect the sufferers' existence as to erode personal identity and take precedence over other aspects of their lives, vividly illustrates the difference between disease as a biological phenomenon and disease as a lived experience. Pain is not merely an aversive sensation produced by physiological processes. It also partakes of sensory, motivational, emotional, and cognitive components, and these elements are all profoundly influenced by the cultural and social milieu of afflicted individuals. Families, the clinical community, and other social units participate in numerous ways and constitute some of the multiple threads of discourse about pain.[1] Severe chronic pain is often poorly handled by conventional Western medicine because of a tendency to ignore significant psychological, social, and cultural factors in its etiology, diagnosis, and treatment.

The daily agony of individuals with chronic pain is often intensified by the way this larger society views their predicament and attempts to deal with it. People disagree about the nature of pain problems and the proper ways to treat them, and the controversial issues relating to pain treatment are reflected in the heterogeneity of therapeutic approaches.

The unending suffering of chronic pain patients is compounded by these often conflicting elements; that something which dominates one's life so totally can be so full of uncertainties adds bewilderment and anguish to an already difficult situation. Moreover, chronic pain sufferers often have poorly diagnosed, complicated problems that lack the legitimacy of well-established pain-causing disorders such as arthritis or sickle cell anemia. More than one sufferer has remarked "I would rather have cancer"[2] for just this reason. It is little wonder that some pain sufferers assert that learning how to manage their pain can be as much of an ordeal as the pain itself.

This book does not attempt to resolve these uncertainties and conflicting opinions but rather aims at enhancing understanding of the wider implications of chronic pain by focusing on what chronic pain sufferers themselves have to say about their pain-filled lives, how they try to explain their distress, and their reactions to various attempts at providing relief. A critical issue relates to the additional psychological burden imposed on many sufferers when they are not seen to have "real" pain. Pain is not recognized as "real" when it is viewed as serving a function other than communicating about tissue damage or some organic malfunction; when this happens, there is a tendency to conclude that the sufferer is not entirely entitled to it. Grappling with how to describe "reality"—confronting and dealing with all that impedes the accurate and non-judgmental depiction of the nature of intractable pain–is a major focus of this book.

The Magnitude of the Problem

Pain specialists estimate that as many as 97 million Americans have chronic pain.[3] A 1994 Harris poll found one in five Americans suffering from pain lasting at least six months that led them to seek a doctor's help.[4] Pain is the most frequent cause of disability in America; in a given year perhaps as many as 50 million Americans are on short- or long-term disability. It is also costly; Frymoyer and Cats-Baril estimated that low back pain alone costs the United States from 50 to 100 billion dollars annually.[5]

Attempts at Definition

Pain is surprisingly difficult to define. The International Association for the Study of Pain (IASP) provides one of the better definitions: "an unpleasant sensory and emotional experience associated with actual or potential tissue damage, or described in terms of such damage."[6] This is a far cry from an earlier attempt by the distinguished physician Walter Alvarez (1884–1978) to classify kinds of pain: "Real pain, especially severe pain points to the presence of organic rather than functional disease. On the other hand, a burning, or a quivering, or a picking, pricking, pulling, pumping, crawling, boiling, gurgling, thumping, throbbing, gassy or itching sensation, or a constant ache, or soreness, strongly suggests a neurosis."[7] Similar examples of the desire to tightly restrict "real" pain abound in the literature; but pain defies such attempts.

One way specialists distinguish chronic pain from acute pain is in terms of duration; for many years, six months was the somewhat arbitrary cutoff point used to differentiate between the two.[8] However, nowadays specialists recognize the need for flexibility in classification with respect to duration; different kinds of pain merit different time periods. Chronic pain differs from acute pain in other important respects and resists efforts to normalize it to the latter. Unlike acute pain, which either disappears or gets worse, chronic pain is not necessarily grounded in a pathology producing rapid deterioration—the source of the pain probably will not kill the sufferer.[9] Another basic distinction is that chronic pain is no longer biologically useful. (While we may not like experiencing pain, it is crucial to survival.) In fact, some writers simply define chronic pain as any continuing pain that has lost its biological function.[10] These definitions do not go very far in explaining why some pain persists, nor do they help predict who will become a chronic pain sufferer, but we must understand why pain treatment clinicians make the acute/chronic distinction if we are to understand their recommendations for treatment. Chronic pain sufferers, their families, and non-pain specialist physicians probably founder more because of the problematic nature of this distinction than any other.[11] A final distinguishing feature is that chronic pain reflects some kind of failure of medicine.

All authorities on pain define it as an experience. Harold Merskey states, "whatever the physical basis for a pain it can be known to an individual only through his consciousness. Thus pain is only and always a psychological experience. As such it can be discussed only in psychological terms."[12] One must be conscious to have pain: anesthesia, properly administered, eliminates pain by making the patient unconscious. In general, the anesthetized patient who looks and sounds as though in pain is registering chemical and electrical activity, not pain (although there are gray areas with respect to some kinds of anesthesia[13]). The very phenomenologically based definition that "pain is whatever the sufferer says it is," while virtually useless for most experimental or medical purposes, has the advantage of stressing the subjectivity of pain.

Earlier explanations of pain linked a tissue-damaging cause (e.g., a lighted match) fairly directly with a pain experience. Known as "specificity theory," such explanations do not account for several kinds of pain.[14] For example, central nervous system pain (e.g., post-herpetic neuralgia, thalamic syndrome), associated with injuries to the nervous system, is characterized by the *absence* of something wrong where it hurts.[15] Nor can specificity theory explain phantom limb pain, in which an amputated limb hurts. Specialists used to classify phantom limb pain as "hysterical"—totally imaginary. No tissue damage was involved, so the phantom limb pain was not "real." However, changes in our models of pain have resulted in an explanation of phantom limb pain that sees it as a result of normal brain function. Indeed, the puzzle of phantom limbs stimulated some of the research that led to the formulation of these new models.[16] Nonetheless, as many authors point out, the ghost of specificity theory lingers in the pain literature and in how all of us think about pain.[17]

Most definitions of pain take as a core meaning an association with tissue damage, although the IASP definition does not require that there actually *be* such damage. These will, of course, exclude unembodied pain—that is, pain not felt in the body, what we might call emotional pain. As pain specialists are concerned with discovering the physiological processes producing a given pain (what medicine calls nociception), many typologies of chronic pain distinguish embodied pain associated with lesions from embodied pain accompanied by no discernible lesions. One possible explanation of the latter kind of pain is, of course, that tissue damage exists but has not yet been observed. But specialists are not satisfied that this possibility explains all the instances of "nonspecific" chronic pain they encounter; phantom limb pain is a good example. That medical classifications of pain depend on the presence and nature of lesions illustrates another of the anomalous qualities of pain: although its core meaning involves physical processes, it itself cannot be measured or directly observed.[18] As pain specialist John Loeser points out, "pain is not a thing; it is a concept that we impose upon a set of observations of ourselves and others. It has many attributes and dimensions, but cannot be measured directly."[19]

Pain as a Research Topic

Chronic pain as a topic leads one into myriad domains, from linguistics to literature to philosophy to religion to economics, as well as medicine and psychology. To understand chronic pain requires thoroughly rethinking our notion of pain. Such an effort involves exploring Western concepts of disease, health, mind, and body; experience and the way we describe it; assumptions about cause and effect; stigma, shame, and guilt; Western medicine (in particular, how illness is culturally constructed, and orthodox versus alternative approaches to restoring and maintaining health); legal and insurance systems; and popular psychology. The treatment of chronic pain involves the intersection of various medical, legal, social service, and insurance institutions, within which deeply held, but sometimes contradictory, values are embedded.

Intractable chronic pain, also called chronic pain syndrome, with its lack of response to traditional treatment, its tendency to generate hostility between physician and patient,[20] and the need to rely on subjective reports rather than physical indicators, is a fascinating research topic. The characteristics that make the diagnosis and treatment of such pain so difficult are the very ones that provide revealing glimpses into the workings of medicine and into our views about the body and mind, health and illness, and moral responsibility for one's actions.

The Research Perspective

This study specifically focuses on the experience of pain sufferers in the setting of a chronic pain treatment facility and the often conflicting perspectives and values that occur in such clinical institutions.[21] The idea of a multidisciplinary clinic devoted to the treatment of chronic pain emerged in the early 1960s, one product of a growing consensus that conventional treatments for acute pain—immobilization, opiates and heavy tranquilizers, surgical and other procedures—were often ineffective for many chronic pain patients. Pain centers were also a response to increases in funding, much of which was allocated to such centers in the belief that their programs were generally less costly than many of the alternatives open to chronic pain sufferers.[22] As of 1996 there were some 1,400 pain centers in the United States.[23]

The first pain centers were structured around a predominantly medical approach; pain was conceptualized in terms of tissue pathology and efforts were directed toward alleviation.[24] Subsequently, behavioral[25] approaches for dealing with chronic pain focused on several fronts: eliminating the source of pain when feasible, improving pain control through conservative methods, relieving drug dependence, and treating underlying depression and insomnia. These programs also tried to improve family and community support systems and in general worked at returning patients to functional and productive lives. Currently all centers follow a mixed course: even the most medically oriented require a psychological evaluation of patients and many centers offer a variety of therapies representing a range of approaches to the body and mind. The institution that was the focus of this study, here called the Commonwealth Pain Center (CPC), offered multidisciplinary treatment in a hospital setting with emphasis on conservative, noninvasive therapies.

The Institutional Setting

When I began my study in 1986, CPC had been functioning for fourteen years. It started in 1972 as a twelve-week program, but later added more staff and accelerated into an eight-week, then a four-week program, in response to pressure from insurance companies. Some other changes over the years reflected the growing knowledge about chronic pain. As time went on, patients entered pain centers earlier in the course of their difficulties—that is, with fewer surgeries and less life disruption. Moreover, shifts in attitudes toward the use of medication meant that patients arrived using far less medication.

Ironically, as the multidisciplinary pain center treatment approach gained greater acceptance, insurance companies began to show a preference for outpatient pain programs, and in recent years the number of inpatient centers has decreased. This meant that patients referred to inpatient centers like CPC were medically and emotionally sicker than previously, and many who might have benefited from the community component of an inpatient program no longer qualified. The continued viability of inpatient centers came into question, given this policy change on the part of third-party carriers. These factors were reflected in the history of CPC: in 1988 the facility moved to another town and began operation as an outpatient center.

Another reflection of the lack of consensus with regard to appropriate treatment of chronic pain was that, at the time of my study, CPC was shifting from a mainly behavioral approach to offering a somewhat eclectic range of therapies. Important staff conflicts arose as to just how far this shift should go. And, as we shall see from their comments, chronic pain patients themselves disagreed about the value of different approaches and their means of implementation in terms of increasing their understanding of their pain, the ultimate relief provided, and the degree of improvement in their ability to cope with their debilitating conditions.

Because severe chronic pain can dominate one's life and, if not seen as a "real" condition, can carry such moral opprobrium, it can easily threaten the ability to maintain identity. As conversations with patients at CPC show, pain sufferers must attempt to reconcile these powerfully negative impacts on personal self-esteem with their understanding of themselves.

CPC attempted to guide this reworking in certain directions by offering definitions and explanations of pain in parts of its program. In reality, however, patients received so many contradictory and confusing messages that I came to the conclusion that a mystification of pain was taking place. This was not explicit CPC policy, and I believe most staff members would disagree with the notion that such mystification was in fact a feature of its program.

Pain was mystified at CPC for two reasons. One is based on the Durkheimian notion that institutions reproduce and make ritual statements about the ideology and social structure of the larger society and culture—which, in this case, was the source of very conflicting concepts about pain. In addition, the mystification of pain was a component, albeit largely unconscious, of CPC's psychotherapy program. Parallels drawn in Chapters 5 and 6 between CPC's approach and initiation rituals and religious conversion illustrate how such mystification works. In some intentional communities, especially religious sects, mystification of a target population helps further their impression that confusion and disorientation mark their lives; the resulting disequilibrium makes it easier to create shifts in the inductees' thoughts and feelings. In the specific case of CPC, the message was something like: "Pain is mysterious, ultimately unknowable. During your stay here you must realize this and go beyond dwelling on pain and letting it run your life." In a sense this was an anti-intellectual and anti-rational message; while one may sooner or later have some insight about various aspects of one's pain, one can never gain a comprehensive understanding of it. Furthermore, a person's understanding might not resemble that of fellow sufferers.

However, patients had to learn this particular truth for themselves because CPC promulgated such a message covertly. Although its stated policy was to provide explanations for why patients had such severe pain and describe specific ways of dealing with it, in reality very few truly clearcut formulas existed for dealing with severe chronic pain. Some patients improved by moving from a passive stance toward fighting pain while others moved in the opposite direction and came to speak of accepting pain. Unlike the situation with chronic conditions like diabetes or alcoholism, the path of chronic pain management was not clearly marked on any map, and very different paths could and did turn out to be appropriate for different people.

In sum, the milieu itself did not necessarily produce improvement at CPC. Rather, its power to pitch patients more deeply into the ambiguities led them to affirm the pain paradox, which is that one's pain is absolutely real but must be treated as in the mind. This is what really made the difference, and it had to happen this way because of our Cartesian legacy of radical mind/body separation. CPC worked (*when* it worked) because patients confronted and dealt with the pain paradox on an individual basis. Some patients did report profound changes in the meaning pain had for them at the end of their month-long stay. The substance and method of these changes are a core concern of this book.

The Methodological Approach

This book is based on a year of participant observation and interviewing at CPC as well as on my own experience as a patient there in 1984. The research focused on CPC patients' life experiences before they were admitted to the center and the changes they underwent as participants in the program.

My approach to this research evolved over time. Originally I planned to take a fairly straightforward positivist approach, employing the conventional format of hypothesis-formulation, analysis of results, and interpretation. My main hypothesis was designed to test the correlation between a patient's positive response to the program's ideology and increased overall well-being. Noting that conventional (biomedical, social psychological, psychodynamic) approaches to pain could not explain the effectiveness of therapeutic communities—"milieu therapy"—in inpatient pain centers, I argued that employing an intensive ethnographic methodology would increase our understanding of just what happened in such settings.

However, the constraints I faced from the hospital's Institutional Review Board (I was denied access to patients' medical records) and the situation I encountered once I began research on the unit meant that I could not carry out the study as planned (see Coda for further discussion of how my approach evolved during the research). Although initially frustrated at having to alter my project substantially, I soon came to feel that the change of focus was fortunate. Influenced by recent trends in anthropology, I found myself taking a discourse-centered, interpretive approach. Of course, I was still interested in explanation, but in the sense of discovering how and why meanings were created, as opposed to discovering correlations between the variables spelled out in my research proposal. During the fieldwork it became clear that to demonstrate correlations convincingly, although an excellent goal, would require filtering out much of what I was learning, because it involved puzzles, ambiguities, and misunderstandings. I came to feel that a real understanding of what CPC patients were going through would emerge more forcefully if I paid attention to these ambiguities, contradictions, and unknowns.

For example, some patients reported being as puzzled about what was wrong with them when they were discharged as when they were admitted. Did this mean that they simply weren't "getting it," that they were resisting because they had something to gain by remaining in pain, or that something else was going on? Even many of those who improved or saw impressive improvement in others were not sure why the treatment worked. In short, I knew I was learning profound lessons about the experience and treatment of intractable pain, yet I did not have any clearcut answers to many of my (perhaps overly) clearcut questions.

The varied (sometimes completely contradictory) explanations proffered by staff members and patients at CPC all appear in the pages that follow. I present these ambiguous and conflicting opinions as vividly as I can. Rather than giving conclusive answers, this book challenges readers to figure out the meanings pain has for them; to discover that there is no single meaning, no single answer, or even single set of answers, at least at present. Pain is a quintessentially postmodern topic, and no master explanation accounts for it in its entirety. Many of the struggles at CPC occurred because the nature of the therapy required that chronic pain's contradictions be juxtaposed, at times dramatically, and their incommensurability graphically revealed.

Because I ended up looking far less at the social configurations of pain sufferers (e.g., demographic profiles or correlations between, say, gender and pain) than at their discourses about pain—meaning, talk, and practice—this study does not put forward any definitive scientific explanations derived from a rigorously followed research protocol. My answers are suggestive rather than conclusive. I hope they will complement those offered by the psychodynamic and behaviorist studies that dominate the field, which, I believe, downplay or outright fail to take account of key social variables in the clinical setting and the broader society and culture.

The interpretive approach argues that ethnographic description is an exercise directed toward the detailed elaboration of locally constructed social meanings. Social action is studied as though it were a text, needing to be read and interpreted. Rather than trying to explain, to answer *why* questions related to cause, I focus on what a set of behaviors *means* and how this meaning is socially constructed. The latter *how* question, it seems to me, is all too frequently given short shrift in interpretive analyses, which tend to be rather static depictions of a system of beliefs—of words, their distinctive features, and the contexts in which they appear.[26] Therefore, in trying to understand what various notions related to pain meant to pain sufferers, I pay particular attention to understanding how these meanings were constantly being constructed and reconstructed.

An ethnography is a write-up of long-term anthropological field research among a group of people, traditionally members of a remote, exotic culture. The people described in this book are not exotic, nor do they form a distinct culture (except in an extended or metaphorical sense). The term "culture"—now a very dynamic concept in anthropology and related disciplines—in this book refers not to a group of people but simply to the systems of symbols employed by CPC patients and staff members during the research. CPC was an institution embedded in other institutions that participated in larger cultural systems.

However, in one sense the book *is* an ethnography of an exotic culture, for it deals with the ongoing cultural construction of a new disease by those who have it and those who treat it. Thirty years ago, intractable chronic pain as a nosological category did not exist as it does today; inasmuch as chronic pain treatment is a new "culture" it is still in the process of working out its language,[27] values, rituals, and kinship ties to related disciplines and carving out its territory. A great deal of what occurred at CPC involved one group of people (patients) being authoritatively instructed by another group (staff) about pain, but paradox and ambiguity were inherent in these lessons, partly because comprehensive pain treatment was a new medical specialty.[28] I came to feel that how, and from whom, patients learned, and how these lessons were constantly being revised in a continuing dialogue with staff members and fellow patients, were just as important to therapy as CPC's formal educational and psychotherapeutic program.

At CPC there was a good deal of talk about "real" pain—that is, pain that is seen as organic and therefore legitimate, and also pain for whose onset or continuance the sufferer was not responsible. The chapters that follow ask readers to think about our discourse of the "real." Although I had read a great deal of the clinical literature on what is "really" wrong with chronic pain patients, I found myself in a fieldwork situation where the "real" often seemed to shift and was the focus of serious disputes between staff members and patients, among patients, and even within an individual patient.[29] Patients resented staff pigeon-holing them, and I did not want to be guilty of that. Staff members indicated from time to time that they, too, were mystified about certain patients and certain aspects of pain and pain treatment. The situation was confusing because several levels of truth existed, because truth shifted, because truth was contested—all limiting the degree to which one could specify what the truth was. The staff, of course, had far more authority for establishing the "truth," but, given the nature of pain, CPC could not operate like those institutions where those in authority have extensive power to determine the truth (as did, for instance, the prosecutors in Koestler's *Darkness at Noon* or the authoritarian Nurse Ratched's rule over a psychiatric unit in Kesey's *One Flew Over the Cuckoo's Nest*).

Early in my research I began to realize that my goal of presenting CPC from the patient point of view was unattainable, for by no means was there a unitary patient point of view. This was one of the sources of conflict at CPC. One reason for the profusion of quotes in the pages that follow is to remind readers that patients in pain centers are *very* heterogeneous, a fact that is not stressed enough in the pain treatment literature, which is by its very nature oriented toward making typologies and generalizations.

This book looks at illness rather than disease. Diseases are seen by biomedical practitioners as disordered biological processes. Illnesses are "experiences of disvalued changes in states of being and in social function; the human experience of sickness." [30] In this society, doctors are expected to decode illnesses, which, being experiences, are considered untrustworthy, and discover the underlying, authentic pathophysiology of disease. [31] Looking at chronic pain as an illness means focusing on the experience of a disordered body—a pain-full body—rather than on the disease or injury processes that began the pain—nociception.

Just as medical literature in general neglects the *experience* of illness, so the clinical literature on pain neglects the experience of pain. [32] Describing the chronic pain experience is not easy; as Elaine Scarry [33] so ably demonstrates, pain is difficult to express even first-hand. So I have made every effort to focus on how pain *feels*, how being treated for pain *feels*, what the mystery regarding pain and related topics in our culture *feels* like to someone grappling with it. In short, I focus on pain as a cultural construct, including the ways it is seen and felt to be a "natural"—biological—occurrence: the meaning of pain, but from the experiencer's point of view. This is not to deny the biological reality of pain, but rather to say that culture affects this biological reality and our experience of it in significant ways, and that we cannot entirely separate the two causes.

Earlier work on the sick role discussed the meaning of being sick, but in terms of how people take on illness-associated roles from the perspective of role theory. [34] This is not the same thing as a focus on the meaning of being sick for the person playing that role, and the authors' conclusions did not depend on verifiability by the subjects—far from it. A meaning-centered approach, as currently understood in anthropology, tries to understand an experience from the subject's point of view. [35] An example would be to focus on how chronic pain patients speak of their bodies in terms of objectification (describing the body as an "it") and alienation (speaking of the body in terms of disappointment, disaffection, or aversion). [36] Despite the difficulty of talking about the actual experience of pain, and despite our inability to discover a unitary, single set of conclusions about all pain patients, focusing on how pain patients talk about their pain in connection with their activities, attitudes, and expectations provides a rich corpus of information, with a surprising number of common themes.

The Clinical Versus the Patient-Centered Focus

Readers of these pages will come to see that the biomedical perspective as currently understood, while dominant and convincing, is not the only one; other paradigms and perspectives on pain are at least possible. Because pain in particular has an odd status in biomedicine, other perspectives and discourses are especially important. Suffering, misery, lament, affliction, and the other concepts in the linguistic domain of pain are so much a feature of chronic pain sufferers' experience that by ignoring them conventional medical and psychiatric discourses dealing with chronic pain can omit a great deal.[37] For example, intractable pain sufferers provide superb examples of what happens when the self, finding itself connected to an alienated body and deeply challenged, searches for a language to meet that challenge. But such searches are not documented in clinical reports. In part, these omissions reflect the fact that clinicians are most often concerned with treating pain, and treatment modes are perforce biomedical or psychotherapeutic. Omissions are also due to rather fundamental deficiencies in the present-day practice of medicine, in our conceptualization of body and mind, and in the lack of sufficient attention to the effects of the stigma attached to certain disorders—deficiencies that are more glaring in the area of chronic pain than in most other areas. In this study, the clinical perspective on pain and the assumptions behind it are not subjected to any comprehensive analysis. Through the ethnographic description of such a perspective in action, exposition is indirect. If, as a result, the reader can recognize the conundrums facing many pain sufferers because of the gaps, inaccuracies, over-generalizations, and institutional self-protection that mark the clinical discourses on chronic pain, then I will have achieved one of my objectives.

Because they suffer from from a debilitating, perplexing, and stigmatized chronic disorder, the subjects of this research lack some of the crucial qualities required for being granted high social status in American society. Yet, for the most part, they grant legitimacy to the processes that exclude them. These individuals talk of their exclusion in resigned or bitter terms; they may blame some parts of the system or certain individuals within it, but they seldom critically assess the system as a whole. This is not to deny the existence of a strong alternative (sometimes referred to as "complementary") movement opposed to much of the theory and practice of biomedicine, a movement whose influence on chronic pain treatment has significantly grown in the past ten years.[38] The biomedical system and, within it, the criteria used to exclude chronic pain sufferers from first class citizenship are examples of hegemony,[39] which can be defined as a dynamic process of domination in which those subordinated within it both accept it as just and proper, and resist it. The pages that follow offer many instances in which patients and staff members at CPC both bought into and struggled against the hegemony of biomedicine.

Interview transcripts and fieldnotes were so engrossing during write-up that they became squatters on virtually all my theoretical territory, and they occupy more of the manuscript than I had originally intended. But these materials do tell the story trenchantly, and some of the more reflective patients provide extremely insightful and sophisticated analyses. Many quotations from interviews and fieldnotes—minimally contextualized snippets of talk—appear throughout the book.[40] Such quotations allow readers to have a lasting impression of the patients and the community they formed, to imagine the conversations and meetings and appreciate the ironic humor that characterized many interactions. This format helps illustrate the ambiguity that surrounds the discourse about pain, as well as the variety of concerns, attitudes, responses, and ways of talking about pain characterizing this heterogeneous population.[41] The abundant quotes also give a sense of how patients' stories interacted with one another, often as dialogues.

In addition, presenting the material this way allows readers to feel more directly some of CPC patients' reactions to the unit: that too much was going on, that there were too many patients and staff members to keep track of, that the staff sometimes viewed patients not as whole people but rather as a problem—a body part, a disembodied complaint, a "case." Finally, the quotation format helps convey the point that pain is too complex to be comprehended using a single explanatory scheme.[42]

A related reason for choosing the particular presentational mode of this book is the goal of dislodging readers' assumptions and expectations about how these materials are being presented. Providing disjointed quotations of patients rather than employing the case study format favored by clinicians reduces the likelihood of being seen as adopting a clinical gaze toward CPC patients. Arturo Escobar argues that when a person is turned into a "case" the fact that "this case is more the reflection of how the institution constructs 'the problem' is rarely noticed." He also points out that the invention of and maintenance of labels are part of an "apparently rational process" that is in fact essentially political—and which can have devastating effects on the groups so labeled (stereotyping, normalizing, and fragmentation of people's experience).[43] I present the several paradigms explaining intractable chronic pain without specifying a correct one. Indeed, this would go against the main purpose of the book, which is to emphasize the unanswered questions in understanding and treating chronic pain. For the most part, patients' self-descriptions are taken at face value; I have kept my attempts to suggest what is "really wrong" with them[44] at a minimum. What was "really" wrong with CPC patients was the subject of daily passionate arguments about diagnosis, prognosis, and treatment. As I was not responsible for helping pain sufferers get better, I could focus on this arena of contestation without feeling a need to provide a clear diagnosis and treatment plan. Thus, for example, where the staff tended to see patient resistance as evidence of a defense mechanism and an impediment to therapy, I could entertain alternative explanations.

Such a heavily patient-centered approach is unlike much writing in the field of the social science of medicine, which, while it may offer a strong critique of the health care delivery system, nonetheless speaks from the authoritative, medically informed perspective of clinicians. Reflecting on this research, it has often seemed to me that some social scientists working in this area find it difficult to avoid seeing patients as their health care providers see them, even though their goals are to critically examine the beliefs, language, rituals, and social structure of the biomedical world.[45] In such studies the experiences of patients are often subordinated to the premises and perspectives of the various professional analysts who study or treat them, resulting in patients' discourses being distorted or decontextualized. Of course, I, too, have cut and shaped patients' discourse to fit my format and goals, but the basic concept of my presentation has been to let CPC patients speak for themselves. What they have to say is worth hearing and it should be given greater weight in the effort to understand the lived reality of severe chronic pain.

Another reason for my avoidance of a clinical perspective is that at times I find it disrespectful. Intractable chronic pain sufferers feel very frustrated by expert opinions that imply a "blame the victim" attitude. In addition, clinical approaches are sometimes so reductionist that they almost obliterate the totality of the person who suffers pain.[46] Finally, I am interested in exploring the clinical perspective itself and needed a vantage point from which to view it. Adopting an anthropological perspective toward chronic pain, those who suffer from it, and a particular treatment facility allowed me to see things a clinician could not. Such a perspective seeks, above all, to understand comprehensively, rather than understand enough to be therapeutically successful.

I am not saying that the clinical perspective is inaccurate, merely that it does not cover everything, that the biomedical paradigm is one among several. However, the clinical perspective is the most authoritative discourse we have, so much so that other ways of talking about pain are almost automatically considered secondary or even suspect. Therefore, from the beginning of this project I have faced a methodological dilemma: how to present, in authoritative language, an analysis of clinical material that does not uncritically accept the clinical way of perceiving things. This dilemma posed several thorny but worthwhile questions. Can I analyze something like biomedicine if I am forced to use the lexicon and paradigms that are themselves part of the very social reality I wish to examine? Byron Good asks, "if we deny the foundational claims of biomedicine, what alternative ways of thinking and writing are available to us?"[47] Even if other options exist, surely they are not as authoritative as the one I am examining. My solution has been to adopt a somewhat unconventional style of presentation, intended to remind the reader continually that the book's concerns are neither those of conventional case studies nor those of social science publications that model themselves on such writing.

The Dual Vision of the Insider/Outsider

Much of my work as an anthropologist has been among the Tukanoan people of the Northwest Amazon, whom I have been studying for over 30 years. This research and the present study, seemingly at the antipodes of ethnographic inquiry, have a number of similarities: problems translating Tukanoan language and culture on one hand; on the other, the challenging issues connected to discovering and representing the cultural components of pain at CPC; as Tukanoan concepts of the self differ from Western concepts, so pain patients' self-images often differ radically from those of people not in severe chronic pain. Many acculturated Tukanoans have acquired a "spoiled" self (in Goffman's expressive phrase[48]), which helped me to understand how pain sufferers' selves are also often spoiled—by diminished self-esteem and the confusion and frustration that accompany unending pain. Three major concerns emerged in this study as in my ongoing research on Tukanoans: first, an interest in identity; second, a concern with local discourses about what is "real" and "authentic" (in the Northwest Amazon, agreeing on the nature of authentic Indian tradition; at CPC, distinguishing "real" from "imaginary" pain); and third, a preoccupation with how one translates "culture"—in this case, how the researcher discovers and represents the underlying commonalities of CPC pain sufferers' thoughts and feelings about their existential situation.

Translating another culture, speaking authoritatively of another's experience, showing how identities change are difficult tasks. While at CPC, I tried to adopt the outlook of a naive and mystified participant, open to whatever patients wanted to tell me. Although I write in a knowledgeable, authoritative voice, I am aware that problems accompany any anthropologist's claims to authority. One example is the perennial problem of insider/outsider views—a concern of the copious recent literature on reflexivity (which discusses the merits of presenting the research process in the published results more comprehensively than occurs in conventional analytic monographs).[49] Chronic pain sufferers are "insiders" who claim authority based on first-hand experience of the pain-filled world; social scientists and clinicians who do not experience chronic pain are "outsiders" who claim authority based on extensive knowledge about numerous cases, arguing that this experience allows them to interpret a specific instance of pain-related behavior reliably. In this study I exploited the dual vision provided by my status as both former CPC patient and anthropologist, a position that incorporated aspects of both insider and outsider roles and that sometimes shifted rather rapidly from sympathetic former pain sufferer to detached anthropologist and back again during interactions with patients and staff members. This dual position certainly aided in achieving rapport and vastly enriched my reactions.

Partly because the epistemology of ethnography has interested me for many years, I originally planned a comprehensive discussion about this dual vision and about how patients and staff members dealt with me as both a former patient and a researcher. This seemed a unique opportunity to contribute to the current discussion on the anthropological construction of the "other." At times I felt like a "halfie": an ethnographer who is in some respects a member of the culture being studied and simultaneously in other respects an outsider. Lila Abu-Lughod uses this term to describe her identity as American, of Arab background, and Muslim, during her work with Egyptian Bedouins; Dorinne Kondo, an American of Japanese descent, uses somewhat similar terms to describe how she felt while doing research in Japan.[50]

Given these concerns, I must confess that I am somewhat perplexed at how little discussion this book contains of such inside/outside issues. Certainly I found out early on in the fieldwork that it was hard work putting my own previous experiences with pain into a kind of mental deep-freeze so as to avoid bias. But it is also the case that the logic of the writing drew me toward other concerns. Perhaps such an endeavor is beyond me at this stage. Given that I can preserve patients' anonymity but not my own, that one can never tell the whole story, and that the last thing I want to do is appear to be claiming some kind of superiority over the pain sufferers described in these pages, I find I cannot write of my pain problem except to say that for a period of three months I had severe low back pain and depression, both of which disappeared in the months following a stay at CPC. (I was seen as such a success story that the staff invited me to return and speak to a subsequent patient community.) That fact may disappoint some readers, but perhaps some will understand that my reflexivity has been transmuted into a more fundamental deconstruction of the problem of sense and nonsense at the heart of the experience of severe chronic pain and pain treatment. My experience gave me first-hand insight into pain as a sensibility, a way of being in the world that seemed to require, at times, that I pay near-total attention to my bones, muscles, and the like. This experiential grounding led me to ponder the cultural patterning and praxis I was realizing from within my body, including the accompanying moral implications, which I examine here. Meanwhile, readers are invited to engage in some interpretive deconstruction of their own attitudes toward mind/body interactions, how they construct Others, and the legitimacy or illegitimacy of a chronic pain condition, preferably many times while reading the book.

For many reasons, including the current scholarly attention being paid to the body,[51] interest in the larger contexts surrounding pain has recently surged, if an increase in publications that situate pain in these larger contexts is any indicator.[52] One could say a vast amount about pain—its history, how it is represented artistically, its ontological nature, how it is viewed in other cultures, and so on. I began writing this book in the hope of dealing with chronic pain in the comprehensive way the subject required. I soon reached 400 typescript pages and was still far short of reaching this goal. Thus readers will find topics not addressed, references absent from the bibliography, possible connections not made. There is no extensive discussion of such important issues as the physiology of pain in general or the history of pain treatment, no overview of pain centers, and no broad consideration of psychosomatic illness or of non-Western approaches to pain.

Two pruning rules have governed my choice of topics: first, to maintain, above all, an ethnographic focus—concentrating on CPC and those issues of vital concern to the patients I studied;[53] second, as much as possible to emphasize those issues that have received proportionately less attention in the clinical and social science literature on chronic pain. As indicated, most of the received wisdom about the psychological, social, and cultural factors contributing to chronic pain comes from clinicians. Some of their published work is based on case studies and generalizations derived from years of treating patients with intractable chronic pain. Other investigators follow the established research guidelines of experimental psychology and sociology. When planning my own research, I found scant comprehensive attention to the concept of pain centers as therapeutic communities and to the views of the patients themselves. Although CPC and a number of other clinics have considered the milieu feature a major factor in patient improvement, no study had focused on the therapeutic community as a component of a pain clinic's philosophy and practice, nor on how deeply it was subscribed to by the staff. I have concluded that, while almost everyone would agree that the role played by milieu therapy in inpatient pain centers is indeed crucial, the lack of attention in the literature can be explained by the fact that the research design required for such a study falls outside the research conventions of most clinicians' and social scientists' disciplines. My focus on patient discourse yields some insight into this neglected area.

Structure, Goals, Audience

To begin, I draw on accounts of newly arrived patients to describe the painful route that led to their coming to CPC and their experiences there during the first week. I then describe the CPC approach and patients' reactions to it and compare CPC to other kinds of therapeutic communities and intentional communities in general, examining why, even though the CPC community was a very artificial one, many patients found it to have a profound effect on their lives. Analogies in the literature on religious conversion elucidate how patients accepted or rejected CPC ideology. I also explore the ways severe pain erodes and destroys personal identity, looking in particular at the role of language. Finally, returning to the theme of our limited understanding of pain, I review the nature of the conundrums, the contradictions, and the contestation that remain.

A general objective of this book is to increase readers' appreciation of the usefulness of meticulously examining all the discourses relating to a societal problem, in particular those discourses that take place in clinical institutions.[54] In addition, I hope to contribute to greater awareness of the difficulties associated with the issue of personal responsibility in relation to an individual's pain problem. The problem of "free will" in psychosomatic pain (the term refers to both psychogenic pain and pain that had a medical cause at onset but is amplified because of psychological reasons) figures, explicitly and implicitly, in most writing about intractable chronic pain. CPC patients and staff members often talked about choices—conscious and unconscious, avoidable and inevitable—surrounding the onset and management of pain.

The free will issue is linked to another area that I hope may be advanced by this book: dismantling our rigid mind/body dualism while avoiding explanations based on the body's somehow "wanting" to be ill. Part of the reason why relations between chronic pain sufferers and their physicians are often troubled has to do with the mind/body distinction inherent in the Western medical model of human health and disease. If this book helps to ease some of these difficult interactions by showing just how exhausting, perplexing, and wretched a pain-filled life can be, I will have achieved a primary objective.

Finally, I hope that the book may increase understanding of the role American values play in the experience of chronic pain—their psychological effect on pain sufferers and their influence on lay and professional notions about treatment. For example, we feel that people in severe pain deserve sympathy. Yet another widespread view holds that being sick is a more acceptable way to avoid an undesirable work situation or a difficult task than to be seen as a quitter or lazy; certainly this notion often surfaced at CPC. Some authors suggest that many Americans assume that life should be painless.[55] The idea that pills can solve problems, or facilitate a psychic change of scene, has often been seen as contributing to our overdependence on drugs, legal and illegal; one very unfortunate consequence of this idea has been that they are underutilized in many situations involving severe pain.[56] Medications—which ones were beneficial and which were not—were a highly charged and much-discussed topic at CPC. A cultural predilection for invasive treatments such as surgery on the part of a physician, pain sufferer, or both, rather than more conservative measures, can be seen in the medical histories recounted by the patients entering CPC.[57] One pair of authors writing about chronic pain gives an example of a pain sufferer undergoing more than forty surgeries.[58] Such excessive use of procedures is not only often ineffectual but also can lead to iatrogenic complications, followed by feelings of frustration, regret, and guilt on the part of both physician and patient. A number of CPC patients had appalling stories to tell of such complications that produced or greatly contributed to their pain.[59]

Although the book is written for anthropologists, anyone who has a serious interest in intractable chronic pain—clinicians, social scientists, people who have experienced such pain or known someone in such a state—will find the issues addressed here thought-provoking.

Chapter 2
Summer Camp? Boot Camp?
An Introduction to CPC

"Every day is a surprise in this place. I had no idea what it was about, none whatsoever."

—a CPC patient

Immediately opposite the elevator was a suite of offices occupied by Dr. B,[1] the director, and his staff, as well as the nurses' station. Down the corridor to the right were the dining room, a consulting room, and various utility rooms. The semi-private patient rooms, a shower, and two physical therapy rooms opened off the left corridor, which ended in a solarium. Patient feelings toward this territory ran high: the dining room, used for so many activities, received the contempt familiarity so frequently breeds; the shower, serving twenty-one patients, was loathed as a breeding ground for fungus; the solarium, off limits (with some exceptions) to staff, was a refuge.

This was in no way an upscale clinic that placed its highest priority on clients' felt needs. The cramped quarters, the food, the chairs, the beds, the mattresses, the delays with things like getting toilets unplugged, all drew criticism from patients and staff members alike. One patient was shocked by the appearance of the place on her first day: "I don't know what I expected, but this wasn't it." Another patient compared the place to a detention center: "I was told: this is not a hotel, you have to do it yourself. Well, I knew it wasn't a hotel the minute I walked into the place, from the decor." Terence, a patient who was a doctor as well, commented that CPC was one of the dirtiest medical wards he had ever seen: "They just wash and wax the floors, they don't wash the walls. Thank God I'm here in the summer when there's less chance of infection."[2]

Patients' feelings about the unit were intense, almost palpable.[3] One recent arrival commented, "I can't believe how much negativity there is in the air, it's thick." Petty and major crises were regular occurrences. Someone was always doing Wagnerian battle with Dr. B or another staff member. Constant pain made many of the patients emotionally labile, and a goodly number of them were aggressive. A patient who suffered temporo mandibular joint disorder and faced major surgery to crack and reshape her jaw cried almost constantly during her first two weeks; she needed, she said, "to drain myself of the sadness I was feeling." To add to the tension, some patients were being weaned from narcotics and major tranquilizers, and others were worried about what would happen when their medications were reduced. Others were facing major crises at home that greatly affected their mood. And patients who were engaged in ongoing litigation or in struggles with a workers' compensation board were extremely concerned with how CPC would evaluate them.

The Daily Routine

The day began between 6:30 and 7:00 A.M., when the patients awakened, dressed, and went for medications. Patients with special needs were awakened earlier so staff members could help them shower and dress. Some patients got up early with the hope—sometimes dashed—of taking a shower before breakfast. Some were already up, never having gone to bed; insomnia is a frequent companion of chronic pain. Late at night one could always find a group of patients commiserating with one another in the solarium, talking, watching TV, drinking coffee, and smoking. Patients whose rooms were near the solarium would sometimes complain about the noise or the smoke, but most were sympathetic: they, too, had experienced sleepless nights and understood the need for distraction and companionship.

Medications were given out near the nurses' station before breakfast. Four times a day small numbers of patients would line up to wait for what some called the "candy cart," open for ten minutes. Those who missed the cart would get other medications but no pain medication until the next scheduled time. The doctors conducted group rounds in the dining room during breakfast or lunch; on Wednesdays, individual rounds were held in patients' rooms.

Patients were encouraged, and at times required, to tend to themselves and their needs. All meals were to be eaten in the dining room, and patients were expected to wear street clothes, make their own beds, do their own laundry, manage their physical therapy and relaxation sessions, and, to some degree, monitor their own medication. Being required to get their own cafeteria trays at meals, for example, perplexed—at times angered—new patients, who assumed that since they were in a hospital they were entitled to help. "People come in with the expectation that they will be relieved of their pain and it will happen by their laying in bed," a patient explained, "so they fight. They get uptight and their language is awful. I was just as shocked as anyone else trying to carry my tray, but I *did* it. If you can't, you'll drop your tray and they'll see you can't. People are fighting it, but this is what we're going to be faced with when we're at home. They're keeping a part of the real world here." Some patients would "cheat" and cajole fellow patients into carrying trays or pulling out the heavy chairs.

After breakfast and rounds there were various compulsory activities. Except for trips to other hospitals for medical procedures and a weekly visit to a swimming pool, patients remained on the unit during the day. Each patient had individual meetings once or twice a week with each member of her or his team—physical therapist, social worker, primary nurse, psychiatrist, and relaxation therapist. Group activities included "focus" (psychotherapy) sessions, exercise classes, relaxation training, twice-weekly meetings between the patient community and Dr. B, and classes on body awareness, self-awareness, and nutrition. On most Saturday mornings patients attended a workshop presented by a staff member. After the first week on the unit, patients could sign out on Saturday or Sunday, although they needed to return by midnight.

Of course, other things went on at CPC as well. Patients would congregate and chat near the nurses station while waiting—for a visitor, for medications, for the washer or dryer, for hotpacks and coldpacks. They would sign out to go to the hospital cafeteria or to take a walk. The solarium was seldom empty. The entire unit hummed with activity all day. Things slowed down after dinner, although there were evening sessions in psychomotor[4] and relaxation training; a Wednesday night outing, when most patients went as a group to a restaurant, museum, or movie; a family night on Thursday; and a Friday-night community meeting, workshop, and party, when patients would eat takeout or celebrate a fellow patient's birthday with cake and ice cream.

The CPC Program

The 21-bed CPC was housed in one wing of a private, nonprofit rehabilitation hospital. The staff consisted of Dr. Bernstein (Dr. B, the director since 1975, who had degrees in psychiatry and neurology); Rhonda, his clinical assistant (a registered nurse); three clinical psychologists; two social workers; four physical therapists; Naomi, the patient coordinator; seven registered nurses; seven patient rehabilitation associates (PRAs); and various clerical personnel. Consultants included a psychiatrist, Dr. Stevens (Dr. S); an internist, Dr. Oliveira (Dr. O); and a neurologist, Dr. Andrews (Dr. A).

CPC offered multidisciplinary treatment emphasizing conservative, noninvasive therapies: physical (exercise, whirlpool baths, ultrasound treatment, ice massage, and transcutaneous electrical nerve stimulation), cognitive (relaxation training, biofeedback), emotional (psychomotor therapy, group therapy, one-on-one psychotherapy), and social. For the vast majority of patients, treatment at CPC was paid for by third-party carriers.

A 1984 survey showed that 4,000 patients had been evaluated and half of these had been admitted as patients. The patients were 58 percent female and 42 percent male, their average age was 45, and they had been in pain for an average of six years;[5] 45 percent were receiving some form of employment compensation.

In 1986 the shorter duration of the program,[6] combined with the fact that many more pain sufferers were being channeled to outpatient programs than in previous years, meant that admission criteria were far less rigorous. A secretary in Dr. B's office complained that her job had turned into a struggle to "fill beds." The mushrooming popularity of the pain center concept also played a role. "We are taking people that would never have been accepted two years ago in this program, and it's because of the competition," said one of the nurses. CPC was in transition, dealing with changes in the larger system of health care delivery and also shifting from mainly behavioral therapies to more eclectic ones.[7]

By calling itself a therapeutic community, CPC sought to emphasize certain features of its program that distinguished it from treatment centers based on a medical model. In a therapeutic community participants are active agents of therapy, as opposed to passive recipients of professional and bureaucratized medical care.[8] Therapeutic communities emphasize "reality confrontation," giving verbal feedback to patients, and to their relatives, about patients' behavior as it appears to others.[9] A final characteristic is that any and every mundane event and activity in the community is potentially open to redefinition as therapeutic or countertherapeutic.[10] Many CPC patients, even at the end of their stay, did not understand that everything that happened on the unit was a potential opportunity for therapeutic work.

CPC staff members felt that patient interaction was crucial to the program's success; a social worker commented that patients did about 80 percent of the work on the unit. Getting patients to accept that they were the most important aspect of one another's therapy was part of the larger lesson they needed to learn about shifting the impetus for change from outside forces to themselves. Staff members saw the group setting as helping this process along, in part because patients were less defensive when they discussed their problems among themselves. New admissions were staggered at CPC (with one-fourth of the patients newly admitted every week), so patients nearing discharge guided and reassured (and sometimes warned) newly admitted patients.

Patients at CPC liked the community feature, remarking constantly on the feelings of solidarity they experienced; some likened the stay to a period in summer camp, "where you're living and working with others." (One patient labeled CPC "Camp Pain," thus providing the title for this book.)

In short, CPC stressed healing, not cure: patients needed to heal themselves, and motivation toward healing needed to come from within.[11] (Donna, a PRA, said one crucial CPC message to patients was, "you're not a victim, you're making a choice.") Pain sufferers needed to accept that they would always have pain and to accept certain related implications (for instance, that further surgeries or heavy narcotics needed to be avoided). Many incoming CPC patients were aware of this: a substantial number told me they had understood before being admitted that their pain would not disappear but that the program would help them cope with it better. When the CPC approach worked—and staff members differed remarkably about when it did and did not—patients left saying things like, "Well, I can't say that my pain is that much less, but I am coping with it better."

Patient Selection

According to Dr. B, pain sufferers with "uncomplicated pain" were generally not admitted to CPC. Staff members said that sufferers with "the greatest potential for being helped" were selected.[12] Some staff members believed that CPC patients were in more serious condition than either people in outpatient programs or the large number of people who have chronic pain but cope with it fairly well—people with "better resources, better coping skills maybe, maybe a better support system, less life disruption," as one of the physical therapists put it. Several staff members said that overall CPC patients were simply more desperate; however, there was no agreement on whether this was a sign that CPC patients were "the worst ones" or evidence that they were willing to take some action and therefore more enterprising than most other sufferers.[13] Matthew, a psychotherapist, commented, "I'm not sure that the difference [between CPC patients and people in pain on the street] is that great, to be honest with you. They say many people live lives of quiet desperation, so in some ways our patients may be healthier than that segment of the population out there getting through the day however they do it, whether it's on drugs or alcohol or in various stages of self-destruction. Not everyone who is out there is making it, and not everyone who is in here is not making it." His was not a unique opinion: four other staff members said they were not certain of a significant difference between CPC residents and those "on the street," except that the CPC patients had been identified in the system and were receiving services, whereas many people "out there" were in life-disruptive pain and had pain-prone personalities[14] but either did not know about pain center options or had no insurance.

CPC sought patients who not only would profit most from the program but also would not leave early against medical advice. At one point during my study, the dropout rate was 33 percent. CPC staff members did have firm opinions on who should *not* be admitted. One nurse said that patients who chose to come only because their wife or doctor or insurance company wanted them to were not ready and the program would not work for them. They would leave feeling very frustrated, sometimes early, sometimes discharged by Dr. B. Another nurse opposed admitting people in litigation, feeling that this kept them from making a commitment: "Naturally they are not going to make as much money" if their pain were to diminish. Furthermore, she pointed out, "They are scared: they don't know what the future holds, so they are afraid to really jump in. Their disability might be cut off, their workers' comp might be cut off." Pain sufferers who were in litigation for large amounts of money, she said, should not be allowed in the program until the claim was settled.[15]

The Multidisciplinary Team

The team approach is central to the pain center concept, a consequence of Melzack and Wall's gate-control theory of pain.[16] However, the makeup and activities of the team vary from center to center. Special training is also needed. For example, in certain respects the role of nurses at multidisciplinary pain centers differs from that in other clinical situations: CPC nurses concentrated on developing patient independence, counseling about drug dependency, and instructing patients on reducing the consequences of stress. Similarly, CPC physical therapists not only designed individual exercise programs and provided training on how to use therapeutic aids but also instructed patients about the CPC philosophy and did some informal counseling. In general, CPC patients approved of the multidisciplinary team approach.

In some centers the team evaluates patients over a period of time (this is sometimes called the "million-dollar workup" because it is so comprehensive) to decide who should be admitted to the therapeutic part of the program and what procedures to use.[17] Other centers, including CPC, concentrate less on diagnosis and more on multidisciplinary therapy.

At CPC each patient was assigned a team consisting of a physical therapist, social worker, nurse, psychologist, and PRA. Ideally, each patient developed a close relationship with at least one member of this team.[18] Donna, a PRA, acknowledged that the program needed "authority figures," but preferred her role, which she saw as being "really concerned about individual patients." She felt she had much better rapport with patients than most of the nurses. Given her goals as a therapist, she found the barriers between staff and patients frustrating and uncomfortable; her task, she said, was to learn how to be more responsive to individuals "and not get caught up in the way the machine kind of rolls here."

Although there were difficulties coordinating such a heterogeneous group, CPC staff members spoke highly of the team approach. One physical therapist said that the teams she had worked with on other floors of the hospital had been close but that CPC teamwork was tighter when it functioned well. She added that things broke down sometimes because dealing with chronic pain patients could be overwhelming, but that, when the team effort malfunctioned, it showed and became disruptive. Matthew, a psychologist, also commented on the need to work together more and worry less about protecting therapeutic territory.

A Diversity of Approaches

Individual staff members at CPC differed in their assessment of therapeutic approaches that departed from standard biomedicine. Because this was an inpatient unit, every staff person had ample opportunity to present to patients informally his or her own position about useful therapies. Overall, staff members seemed to value diversity. Rhonda, Dr. B's clinical assistant, said that if the overall philosophy was to help people find ways to distract themselves from pain and be more functional, then openness to approaches like therapeutic touch, movement therapy (therapy that attempts to place the person in direct contact with her or his implicit bodily-felt experiencing rather than verbalization),[19] and acupressure enriched the program. Nina, an evening nurse, believed that Western approaches that teach about how the body functions and about medication, as well as Eastern philosophies that teach about achieving control over oneself, were needed. Neil, the psychologist who headed the psychology unit during the later part of the study, felt that the Eastern emphasis on the spiritual side of things—meditation, self-discipline—was valuable, adding that most biobehavioral and psychosomatic programs had progressed to offering training in meditation, providing nutritional counseling, and emphasizing physical and mental exercise. Matthew approved of a heterogeneous staff because they exchanged information about new therapies, like energy work (a holistic therapy that claims to work with the electromagnetic energy field [sometimes called an aura] surrounding individuals), visualization and polarity, and bioenergetics. He said he approved of anything that worked, that was helpful, that inspired hope.

Although the staff generally favored having many options, some, like Kenneth, a physical therapist, were ambivalent about "soft therapy—the sixties kind of stuff." He did not think it was necessarily wrong, because he had heard good things about some of these new therapies and "that's the bottom line—if it helps people get better." He criticized his own attitudes, saying he sometimes felt "Teutonic" and was working on taking in, listening more. His own biomedical approach "where you kind of perpetrate things on people" bothered him sometimes.

In general, younger staff members were the most enthusiastic about alternative approaches. Linda, a nurse, although in her late forties, spoke for most of them, saying that, although such an approach was very unscientific, it worked because people wanted it to work. "I mean, I've seen the therapeutic touch, and maybe there really is something to it, that there is a force field around your body, and the negative energy can be worked out through your feet." She said the mind was probably the most powerful part of the body and controlled many functions: relaxation could lower blood pressure and pulse rate. Nicole, a young movement therapist intern, also approved of therapeutic touch and cognitive therapies like guided imagery. She disapproved of "the powers that be" (Dr. B and Naomi, the patient coordinator) for not appreciating these new perspectives.

Internal criticisms resulting from the multidisciplinary nature of the program fell along these lines: Naomi spoke of "sibling rivalry" and "territoriality." Georgia, a PRA, thought there was too much testing (lab work, EMGs) and too much emphasis on medication. Evelyn, a physical therapist, worried that therapies that concentrated on the body might encourage a patient who was already too somatically focused to continue to justify a my-body-is-the-problem analysis. The underlying basis of the CPC program, she said, was that you have to move on, stop being wrapped up in every little bodily sensation. She also worried that staff skepticism about some of the newer therapies would become apparent to patients, who would then drop out and not participate. Others shared her concern: Nina commented that when staff got frustrated they tended to blame alternative approaches, saying they were "a bunch of baloney."

During my study, biofeedback, autogenics (a relaxation practice), hypnosis, acupuncture, therapeutic touch, movement therapy, pain imaging, and reflexology (foot massage to alleviate pain in another area of the body)—all somewhat marginal in mainstream medicine—were practiced or at least discussed favorably during formal sessions with patients. Dr. B was not persuaded of the value of some of these therapies (he dismissed acupuncture as a form of hypnosis[20]) and apparently did not know of others (e.g., reflexology) that were practiced in the evening. Intern Nicole criticized his attitude: "He's very attached to his mode of interacting with patients, which is, of course, the confrontative style and really rarely even acknowledges some of the other people who are doing more alternative sorts of things with the patients. And I think that's really too bad, because he has the beginnings of something very powerful in terms of a really well-rounded treatment team. Yet, because he never deals with it that way, he kind of sabotages them—basically everyone has to do things behind closed doors." Staff turnover during the year of study brought about an increased emphasis on alternative therapies.

To sum up: despite some problems, staff valued the diversity they collectively represented, and, for the most part, shared in a commitment to make CPC an example of holistic medicine. For them, holistic medicine meant looking at the big picture, at an entire life rather than a body part; trying to handle the problem without narcotics or surgery; and looking to the body and the mind for healing ("working through some of the energy in the body") rather than depending on conventional medicine—in other words working *with* the mind and body rather than *on* the body.[21]

Another interesting division was evident between day and evening staff members. Beverly, a young evening PRA, said the evening atmosphere was more laid back, which permitted getting to know the patients better. Evening staff members felt they had it better, she said; evenings were less hectic, patients liked the evening staff better, and activities —ice massages, Wednesday night outings—were more leisurely, "nothing too reprimanding." To evening nurse Nina, the days were "kind of pushed," whereas evening was a time to unwind, a time when, if patients needed extra nurturing, they could get it. Donna, a day PRA, seemed to envy how evening staff members could get close to patients, going on outings with them and engaging in long conversations.

For Naomi, the patient coordinator, the day/evening contrasts presaged the world patients would face when they returned to their everyday lives. The daytime involved one's nine-to-five job, with demanding bosses, arbitrary rules, and regulations. Evenings were more relaxed; even though some activities were strenuous, it was more of a "nurturing atmosphere."

She noted that day staff members did not see themselves as community members and that, while she had once seen this as a problem, now she approved of the division. If the staff participated too much in the community, they would become its leaders and patients would expect to

be taken care of rather than do things for themselves. Thus staff participation would actually be disruptive, impeding community formation.
Beverly, a PRA, agreed that separating staff and patients ensured that
staff members would not get sucked into taking care of whining and
complaining patients. Still, like some other evening staff members, she
was critical of certain aspects of the difference, noting that patients complained that during the day they were not treated with respect; simply
asking a question might trigger a dismissive, abrupt response.

One division of labor patients were not explicitly told about involved
Dr. B playing the stern parent, challenging patients to examine their
feelings, and Dr. S, the consulting psychiatrist, playing a more supporting, affirming figure. Dr. B saw his role as that of the "tough guy" who
insisted on compliance, dealt with rigid defenses, and confronted maladaptive behavior; Dr. S saw himself as more sympathetic, establishing
an alliance with the patient and dealing with intrapsychic dynamics related to how the patient had adapted to pain. Dr. B stated that he needed
to "resist a multitude of dramatic and aggressive manipulations," and
tried to challenge the patient's rigidity by employing a "degree of skepticism in interpreting patient communication." Such challenges made
patients angry, agitated, or anxious, providing entry points into their
system of maladaptive behavior and beliefs. In practice, this partition of
therapeutic labor did not seem to play out quite as Dr. B and Dr. S envisioned, because Dr. B was by far the most important presence at CPC
and Dr. S, who was on the unit only for weekly appointments with only
some patients, had a distinctly minor role. Patient comments suggested
some of them definitely noticed this "good cop/bad cop" routine, and
that it had little effect. One said, "I come from the corporate world, so
I can see their little games. One person is the heavy; it's like salesmen,
how you get a customer to buy." While other pain centers might not set
up this particular division of therapeutic labor, many do mention having
staff members play similar roles. One clinic director, for example, mentions doctors in his clinic playing parental roles similar to Dr. B's.[22]

I use the phrase "tough love" here to refer to CPC's efforts to get
patients to be more autonomous, self-directed, and physically active.
Many steps were taken to encourage independence and to wean patients
from expecting that their problems would be taken care of because they
were in a hospital receiving medical treatment. Since they were in fact
in a hospital, this atmosphere produced confusion at times, anger at
others. Some patients objected to sloganeering—often-repeated phrases
such as "get on with your life," "get into the program," "be responsible
for your pain," "see the connection between stress and pain"—saying
they felt they were being brainwashed. Almost all patients at one time
or another objected to the confrontation and manipulations employed

by the staff (discussed further in Chapter 4). These features of the program elicited strong reactions; patients used terms like "boot camp," "like a nursery school," "detention center," "torture chamber," "POW camp," and "concentration camp" when they realized that what they had thought was a hospital was a radically different setting.[23]

Stresses and Strains

CPC had never stopped changing: improving its program, adjusting to personnel turnover, and responding to developments in medicine and in the larger society. During the period of research, however, it was undergoing deeper and more substantial changes, including an attempt to respond to society's increasing interest in alternative therapies. Those who favored such innovations complained that CPC needed to catch up with promising developments in pain management and pointed to other centers that were making extensive commitments to these new approaches. Nicole chafed at the divisiveness over this issue, pointing out that since these approaches were increasing in popularity, those in charge should acknowledge them and integrate them into the program. Matthew also favored the new therapies, but said that since insurance companies dominated everything and did not want "fringe therapies," the established therapies would continue to prevail at CPC. Vera, a physical therapist, felt CPC was something of a "dying floor," feeling the pressures of depending on third party payors. It toyed with alternative methods as only lip service, and would continue to provide "safe," mainstream therapies.

This sort of discontent was behind the most visible sign that CPC was in transition: extremely high staff turnover.[24] During my year of study, four secretaries, two social workers, two PRAs, one physical therapist, one nurse, and two psychologists—including the head psychologist—left. Sonia, a nurse who had been with CPC since its beginning, felt the staff had been more dedicated during the first four or five years of the program. She thought the principal reason for the defection was an inability to work with Dr. B, although she thought he did an excellent job. Other reasons included deciding to return to school for more training or feeling one was not going to advance at CPC.

Kenneth offered a somewhat different analysis. Teamwork, which needed to be very strong and engaged in by people who shared the same goals, was being subverted by the two new psychologists and two new social workers, who were "doing their own thing." The result was fragmentation, made worse by lack of leadership.

Some complaints concerned inconsistent treatment of patients: Linda, a nurse, said, "Well, I think a lot of patients do need confrontation, but there's a double standard. Certain people are confronted heavily, and other people who need to be confronted heavily are not, if they fit into certain categories. For example, with one of the people who works on this unit, if you're a young female, blond, seductive, you're not going to be confronted. If you are a man, or anybody who's overweight, has teeth missing, has tattoos—a loser—sometimes you are not listened to as much, you don't have the credibility."

Georgia complained that Dr. B was very often absent: "It's actually like the absent father coming home and dictating to the children what they need. And so often he doesn't know enough about what's going on with patients to be making particular decisions with them. His approach is very often heavy-handed, his philosophy is generally, I hit him over the head and the staff will pick up the pieces for me. That's another feature of the absent father: Wait till your father comes home! So then all the patients get all ticked off at daddy and they spend hours, sometimes, in various psych groups focusing on [Dr. B] and how angry they are at him instead of focusing on their own father or their own psych issues." Nina concurred; because Dr. B was seen as a parent, "it's like Dad went away on another business trip and he's not available again." If that was the role he was going to play, she said, then he needed to spend more time on the unit.

Staff members, especially the younger ones, also complained about their personal interactions with Dr. B. "I've had two conversations with him since I've been here," Beverly said. "You want someone to acknowledge the work that you do, and as I see with other people, he just doesn't acknowledge it. The staff goes through different phases here; they feel that they aren't getting any feedback, they're not being geared in any direction because the director of the program really has no contact. He just doesn't really get involved at all with the people who work here. But then again, that's just his personality." Nicole wished that Dr. B were not quite so attached to his persona. She said she did not agree with Matthew's opinion that Dr. B was destructive, but she did see him doing inappropriate, "out-of-bounds stuff all the time, just confronting people for the hell of it. And he does it with staff—he's a riot. During rounds I'll say something to him about a patient doing such-and-such in group yesterday. He'll sort of say, "you're just the intern, shut up." And then he'll go in and use the piece of information that I gave him to confront the patient."

Do these complaints indicate that CPC was undergoing such unique and extensive problems that any analysis would not apply to any other pain center? I think not. Although CPC became an outpatient unit two years later, the change was mainly in response to the effects of nationwide shifts in third party payment policies. Similarly, CPC was not alone in adjusting to shifts in attitudes in mainstream medicine with respect to acceptable pain treatment therapies. Pain centers today face an uphill battle in demonstrating to insurance companies, workers' compensation boards, and the administrators of managed care companies that the pain center option makes good medical and financial sense. These third party payors play a significant role in determining who is admitted and in evaluating patient progress.[25]

Without denying the significance of CPC's ending its identity as an inpatient unit or of the marked staff turnover that occurred during the study, it is important to remember that people in all institutions have gripes and that one as complex as CPC, facing so many pressures from the outside and trying to do such difficult work, would be especially vulnerable to such complaints. Members of institutions always have problems with their hierarchy, and there are always complaints when an institution seems slow to respond to changes in the larger society. My interviews with staff members provided an opportunity for them to vent, but for the most part they did not use their time with me this way. Hence, despite some of the younger staff members' comments that Dr. B needed therapy himself and despite the long-term staff's bemoaning a lessened dedication on the part of younger staff, my overall impression was that CPC staff members worked extremely hard, were very committed to patients and supportive of one another, and respected and admired Dr. B.

Chapter 3
The Painful Journey

"I'm just a guinea pig."

—Harry, a CPC patient

Like sufferers in pain clinics everywhere, CPC patients had encountered any number of problems in addition to pain, among them difficulties with medications, work, finances, interactions with friends and family, the health care delivery system, and their emotions. Arrival at CPC brought challenge, hope, and new difficulties.

Medication

About a third of those admitted said they were dependent on medication of one sort or another (some of it in extremely high doses). For some, the side effects of pain-relieving medications and the dependency that developed had proved more troublesome than the relief was worth. One man, suffering from ten years of complications from a penetrating ulcer, said he was digging his own grave: "I hate my dependence on this, to be able to talk, walk, only with pills." Others commented that pain medications became ineffective over time, in spite of stronger doses.

About half the patients who said they had a problem with drug dependency also admitted abusing drugs in some way. Ursula said her medication problem ruined a lot of things in her life, including her marriage. She had never been honest with her husband, hiding the number of drugs she was taking and even writing her own prescriptions. "I'm embarrassed to tell people I'm a nurse because of the drug history I've had. You'd think I'd have known better."

Some patients spoke of "doctor shopping" until they found one with a liberal policy about prescriptions. Helen, in her fifties, said she had been active all her life until multiple medical problems produced pain she could not deal with. The death of her husband had also been a factor; she had nursed him for years, then found herself without anyone to take care of. Following his death, she "started doing the meds heavy; I had three drug stores prescribing, three doctors."

A few patients saw a two-way connection between pain and medication dependency. When Ursula experienced difficulty with her crutches, she would "pop a pill" to take care of the increased pain—and then wonder if she just wanted an excuse to pop a pill. Other patients felt they had been overmedicated; one woman reported she was taking thirty-eight prescription medications when she was admitted.

Work and Money

Most CPC patients' work lives had been severely disrupted; some had not been employed for years. One woman had survived the breakup of her marriage and gone on to raise her children, obtain a college degree with honors, and create a satisfying career. She was forced to stop work when she developed severe bladder interstitial cystitis. She complained bitterly that she could not think of working, even part time, though she had no disability insurance or workers' compensation. An aide in an emergency room said she had to quit because she could not concentrate and concentration was crucial in her job. In her new job as a mental health aide she found herself resenting listening to patients' problems, because she felt she was experiencing more agony and pain than some of them. And Toby, an assistant professor at a state university felled by a bungled surgical procedure, complained about watching someone less qualified, with fewer academic and pedagogical credentials, get the job he lost.

Many spoke of how much they had enjoyed work, or at least part of it. Edward, a manual laborer, commented that while the breadwinner aspect of his job had given him a sense of accomplishment, he derived a great deal of sheer pleasure from the physical end of it: "There's a good friend of mine—we have laughed and joked about it, how ridiculous it is, but we'd almost be happy shoveling shit against the tide. Just as long as there was shit to shovel." However, not all spoke of work with such longing. Kurt, whose job injury was followed by difficulties with his employer over disability payments, said, "When you say 'comp' to a doctor, they treat you like welfare. They don't care for shit, they sent me back to work."

Some who continued to work found they could no longer perform adequately. Others said they worked in constant pain. A migraine sufferer who sold clothing in a department store reported going to the bathroom, throwing up, and going back to work. She was proud she could manage to do her job without letting her problem show. Some used medications to be able to keep working. One nurse complained that her doctor-employer knew she was "addicted" but kept giving her codeine to keep her going.[1] Others reported losing jobs because of the effects of heavy medication.

While some could disguise their conditions on the job, others found they could not. "The spasms would come, just come, I never knew when. It's excruciatingly painful when it happens," said a woman in her thirties with a mysterious condition involving pain and weakness in the arms and hands ("some kind of myopathy"). She was embarrassed when this happened in public, and concerned about her participation in a nuclear medicine technician training program. Told that her condition would prevent her from continuing in the program, "I lied and said I was doing fine."

Interestingly, work had analgesic effects for some patients; one man, whose difficulties began with a combat injury during the Vietnam war, said that work was a distraction, even working 90 hours a week. It was staying home that caused problems.[2]

Finances were an area of great concern, especially for patients who had lost their jobs and were trying to deal with medical expenses and hiring caregivers. Many talked of problems with insurance companies or workers' compensation boards, and a number powerfully resented suggestions they were faking to receive compensation: Edward said he felt bad when someone who had heard he was on disability as a result of a work injury would say, "Aw, you got it made: there's nothing really wrong with you, you can just sit back now and collect your money and lay around all day in the shade."

One man who had worked in a paper mill in Maine became involved in a protracted workers' compensation claim and had to get a lawyer because his doctor said his problem was not a result of the accident but rather a birth defect. He felt this doctor was "in cahoots" with the company, which sent all their workers to him.

Patients acknowledged that compensation programs are subject to abuse. One man, injured on the job and then laid off, said that people who showed no proof of damage on their X-rays yet kept insisting they had pain were "phony." He continued: "I know I wouldn't fake an injury like that. I'm too strong of a person to do something like that." The paper mill worker said he could not imagine how a malingerer seeking money could go through "all the grief and aggravation," but was "sure it happens." In fact, he said, if the insurance system did not contest claims so vigorously, there would be "more slipping and falling" and "a whole world of people out there with million-dollar settlements."

Interactions with Others

Many CPC patients said they felt they were sometimes not accorded the social recognition usually provided to someone who is ill. Those who were told "We have found nothing wrong" felt that either people saw them as crazy or the doctors had simply not yet discovered what *was* wrong. Either conclusion produced anxiety, which probably helps explain why some patients provided rather bizarre lay diagnoses, and pursued alternative treatment paths such as faith healing.

The constant need to decide how to communicate the experience of pain can be demoralizing because to decide consciously how to show one's pain is in itself suspect.[3] Those who moan and groan constantly elicit negative reactions because such behavior is acceptable only temporarily. They are likely to hear, "You should take it like a man," or, "Keep a stiff upper lip." One CPC patient said that one sister told her that "we all have our own problems" and the other sister told her to ignore the pain. Those who exhibit no overt behavior signaling pain—"pain behavior"—come to realize that many people find it hard to believe someone is experiencing severe pain if they do not cry out, grimace, or complain. One carefully groomed woman's question, "Why should I look as bad as I feel?" illustrates the expectation that inner state will be reflected in one's appearance; looking absolutely normal tended to make one's problem less believable. Many patients said they wished they had a problem that, if not actually visible, was at least well recognized. A woman with back problems said they resulted in her being seen as "just a kvetch. But if I had a pacemaker, my friends wouldn't ask me to go jogging."

Clearly, one *must* engage in some sort of pain behavior or eventually no one will pay attention; those who opt to "suffer with dignity" find their pain is forgotten or diminished in importance by those around them.[4] Because chronic pain sufferers are concerned with maintaining control of their pain and of their behavior in general, they often try to appear normal when interacting with others. This choice (usually encouraged and to a great extent rewarded by those around them) may actually increase their pain and perhaps reduce their control. Although pain's invisibility brought certain advantages, success at hiding pain came at a price. One woman said, "I'm such a phony, I laugh, I smile." Those who did have visible signs of a problem used them to demonstrate its authenticity.

However, visible aspects of pain ("I looked horrid then") also brought a set of problems. Many worried about how they were perceived by others even though they did not intentionally disclose their pain. A conversation with one man reveals the weave of suspicion and defensiveness that mark the search for a legitimate way to show pain:

"On the outside if you hear somebody talking about pain, they're complaining all the time, you don't know how much of that is in their head or whatever, or [if] they are just trying to get out of work."

"Are you talking about yourself, too? Have you felt when you are on the outside that people have suspected you or . . ."

"I never discuss my pain with other people."

"So, nobody knows that you are in pain?"

"They know I am by looking at me sometimes."

A few CPC patients reported receiving extraordinary understanding and sympathy. One man said he would have gone insane if he had not had the support of his wife and children. He had seen ten different doctors, all of whom told him that the pain from his work injury was in his mind. But his wife kept telling him not to give up; she had been married to him for so many years she knew he would not make it up.

But in most cases patients said their problem had failed to inspire understanding from those closest to them. As a consequence, some had tried to go it alone. "I felt isolated, no one understood me," one woman commented, "even my kids." Others mentioned the frustration of trying to explain chronic pain to people who had never experienced anything similar. A man said his family thought he had something like a morning backache and could not fathom what he was going through.

Some felt they had been dismissed. A woman said her husband did not allow her to talk about her temporo mandibular joint pain. "I was very resentful and hateful toward my husband, I still am. I wanted to kill myself." Another woman said that her husband did not believe she had a real problem—she was just lazy. "So I'm wondering, does everyone think that?"

Many said they socialized far less than before the onset of pain, did not go out, felt bad about asking friends to come over, because "they all have something to do." Several made comments about finding out, as several put it, "who your friends are and who your *real* friends are." Eleanor said, "they drop you like a hot potato. You are no longer enhancing their lives. And what do you do? Do you call up and cry on the phone and say, 'Please come over'?"

Many reported feeling abnormal in everyday interactions, using words like "invalid" or "cripple," sometimes in response to the urging of family members. One woman reported that her husband worried she would do further damage. When he would come home and ask her how she was feeling, she would say, "Not too good." When he asked what she had done that day and she told him, he would say, "Do *not* do that again!" She commented, "One month of that, and I turned into an invalid!"

Families were the focus of tremendous guilt for some patients. One man said his children were definitely affected by seeing him in pain all the time, going to the hospital all the time, not going to work like other daddies. As a consequence, his daughter was "picking up behaviors" that made him wonder whether she was sick or not.

Guilt also came from not being able to provide, and from incurring debt. A man commented on how discouraging being unable to work was to someone who had been raised with the idea that the man works and supports his family. Women were more likely to talk of feeling guilty about being so involved with pain that their family life was totally disrupted. And many were aware of becoming burdensome to their families. One woman said she had asked her husband whether he could accept her being away from home in order to go to CPC. He had replied that he was not sure he could accept her *not* going.

Some patients were also aware at some level that their families caused or exacerbated their pain. One woman who suffered from neck pain complained that, although her husband needed counseling he would deny it, saying she was the sick one; her husband was "a pain in the neck." Another woman with a disabled husband said that, ironically, caring was a big part of her pain problem: "You try so hard, you care so much, you don't realize it causes pain. You can't believe your body's capable of letting out such signals, because your mind can't control it." People had suggested that she was causing her pain or taking on her husband's pain.

Interactions with the Medical System

With a few exceptions, medical practitioners and patients in pain generally collude to maintain a conceptual separation between the mind and the body and search for objective evidence of an underlying organic condition.[5] Loeser, a pain specialist, is extremely critical of many of these practitioners, stating that their highly specific diagnoses for chronic pain "commonly legitimate the type of therapy the provider is licensed to utilize. . . . The offending broken part has been identified as lying everywhere from the limbic lobe of the brain to the intervertebral disc, to small ligaments of the back to chronic, recurrent strain/sprain of muscles, to the role of environmental factors at the home and workplace." With respect to low back pain, he states, an accurate diagnosis can be established in less than 15 percent of the cases. Many pain specialists question assumptions about mind/body dualism and deny the distinctions between "genuine" and "false" pain,[6] "physiological" versus "psychological," or "organic" versus "functional." However, in clinical practice mind/body dualism constantly emerges. Everyone involved (including the patient) is eager to know the cause of—and, by implication, the best treatment for—pain. And the implications are vastly different if the cause is seen as organic rather than emotional.

Pain specialists do have criteria for concluding that pain is psychogenic, including repeated workups with no organic findings, reported pain inconsistent with what one would expect from a diagnosed condition, indications of major unresolved life stress, and signs that the patient is pain prone. But such criteria are not conclusive; this is why many chronic pain sufferers worry that doctors have missed something organic: a bone chip, scar tissue, anything. There are many gray areas and much contention.[7] For example, a director of a pain clinic that treats psychogenic pain does not seem to see the logical difficulty in his remark: "Unsuccessful treatment or regression after discharge would imply that the severity of the emotional disorder precluded a successful outcome, but it need not call into question the accuracy of the diagnosis."[8] One proponent of behavioral approaches to treat pain evades the issue of cause by maintaining, "If there were no pain behavior, there would be no pain problem."[9] Another states that only improved function (i.e., behavior changes) matters, not whether the amount of pain has changed following therapy.[10] Taken literally, these statements mean that treatment does not depend on diagnosis and subsequent alleviation of pain but on extinguishing behavior patterns—in other words, what the patient feels is of no consequence, as long as those feelings are not made apparent. Other pain specialists,[11] and certainly most patients, would disagree.

Physicians' self-image is of crucial importance in chronic pain, because so many roles are available to (and at times demanded of) them: they must be clinical healers with an appropriately sympathetic manner, scientists and technicians diagnosing with CT scans and the like, authority figures who decide whether someone is eligible for disability,[12] and parental figures insisting that a patient behave in a particular way. That physicians' own feelings come into play can be evident at pain specialist conferences.[13] Sympathy, exasperation, hostility, rejection can sometimes be read between the lines in conference reports and case histories.

Genuine disagreement occurs among physicians themselves in those specialties that most often deal with chronic pain, ranging from the very mechanical (orthopedists), through neurologists and neurosurgeons, to psychiatrists.[14]

The vast majority of CPC patients spoke of unsatisfactory—at times extremely unsatisfactory—interactions with members of the medical profession. Most strongly criticized what they saw as bad medical treatment: doctors had misled them, did not understand pain, provided no diagnosis, demoralized them, did not do enough, responded slowly, or prescribed ineffective, unnecessary, and inappropriate treatments. Others charged that physicians were intimidating and purposely confusing, practiced sloppy medicine, ordered procedures that produced more pain and introduced new complications, got patients dependent on narcotics and major tranquilizers, did not take responsibility for the whole patient, hid information, were dismissive, sarcastic, and snide, blamed the victim, thought they were God, did not believe the patient, did not follow through—in short, were not healers.[15]

A number of patients were suing a member of the medical profession, and many more felt they had grounds for such a suit. A few said that when they indicated to a physician that they were involved in litigation, they were given the brush-off, seen as clearly difficult cases, a classic "crock."[16] Several spoke of difficulties finding a new doctor under these circumstances.

For some CPC patients, lack of a firm diagnosis or a reasonable prognosis was a consistent source of upset. One man explained how frustrated he felt when his physicians said they could not find anything. He would go for tests hoping fervently that something would show up, and after a while he did not care what it was. A young woman with migraines said that she had been through a lot to discover that there was nothing medically wrong. But if there were a cause, perhaps perhaps something could be done: "If it is my hormones, a chemical imbalance, correct it. My veins or vessels are too small? Widen them."

Patients often became especially incensed if a doctor implied their pain was not "real." Being advised to see a psychiatrist was often interpreted to mean that claims about having a medical problem were unfounded. A woman who suffered severe vertigo and headaches following an ear infection said she became alarmed when told there was no medical reason and therefore the cause must be psychological. But she could not buy that; her pain was so excruciating, it could not possibly be in her head, so she figured she was misdiagnosed. An elderly woman with pain and numbness in the genital-anal region said her surgeon said she had "phantom pain" because there was no reason for her to have pain.

Quite a few patients criticized the entire field of medicine. One man said that when physicians implied "it's in your head," they should be more humble and admit they did not know what was wrong. Several patients spoke of wanting to transfer their pain for a day to the doctor so that he or she could see exactly "what the hell it's all about."

Complaints about hospitals and other health care institutions spewed forth—echoing the bitter recriminations found throughout the literature on chronic pain sufferers. But while relations between chronic pain patients and physicians are among the worst in medicine, many patients reported warm, trusting relationships with their physicians and believed their doctors had done all they could and should not be blamed for a failed surgical procedure or for not knowing why the pain was so severe. A former expert ski instructor spoke gratefully of a doctor who, after giving her "every test in the world," looked her "straight in the eye" and told her there was nothing they could do to ever change the way her back was: it was going to be that way forever. She added that other doctors "will never really tell you anything." Others said their physician taught them about mind/body connections, at times in a gentle way. One woman said her doctor told her that when you are in pain for a long time, your body goes into a depression. He reassured her that he was not saying *she* was depressed, it was her body. (The issue of whether one's pain is seen as part of oneself is discussed in Chapter 7.)

Emotional Consequences

"Watching my life flip through my hands" is how Toby, formerly an assistant professor at a state university, now jobless, homebound, dependent on others for care, put it. Emotional problems such as depression often accompany chronic pain: feelings of isolation and emotional lability ("I'm so moody!") were frequent laments. Those who could not work especially had ample time to brood about their pain. Others spoke of frustration, boredom, feelings of helplessness and hopelessness; many mentioned fears about getting worse or never getting better. Feeling dependent on drugs contributed as well.

Patients spoke of giving in to feeling sorry for themselves though they knew it was not a constructive attitude. Some attributed their depression in part to "living a lie" about their pain, disturbed by the discrepancy between their inner state and the way they presented themselves. A few were ashamed at having conned professionals.

Anger, guilt, defensiveness, feelings of inadequacy, impatience, and bitterness frequently surfaced in discussions. A major topic was loss of self-esteem, to the point of actively disliking the person one had become. A young woman with temporo mandibular joint disorder spoke of the last seven years during which her whole life fell apart; the confidence and self-assurance she had had disappeared. She did not know who she was, and she wanted the "real me" back. When she went to a psychologist who said it was never going to be the same again, she became more depressed. And Ethan said that he had become defensive since hurting his back, in the sense of not wanting to let go of anything that felt good. He had never been that way before; he had always said, "this has felt good for a while, let's find something new that feels good." He projected these worries onto his daughter, finding himself "doing things that were not conducive to making my child grow—I would get worried about her falling down from the jungle gym."

Some spoke of frank self-hatred. Mary, a nurse, said: "I'd fight myself, and that's where the hate grew, not even realizing that I had learned to hate myself just by separating myself into so many people. I had trouble even combing my hair in the morning; I'd look at the mirror and sometimes I would spit at myself in the mirror. That's how disgusted—I can't even say I was, because I still am like that with myself, you know, you stupid bastard, and everything you could think of, you know, cockroach, snake, leech, is the first thing I would think of, in the morning when I looked at myself." (Some saw disapproval of the current self as a first step toward improvement. Teresa, for example, said she did not love herself in her current condition, and if she did, she would never get better.)

Feelings of guilt came from many directions, including comparison with other pain sufferers. Yvonne, a psychotherapist who suffered from cluster headaches, considered herself more responsible for her pain than those who had experienced something like a car accident that resulted in a total transformation of their world. But, she added, her depression at its worst had very much the same effect.

One woman, hit from behind while driving a car on an errand for her children, said she had always sacrificed herself and put everyone else's needs ahead of her own. Her friends and family had said, "Well, if you hadn't gone that night, if you'd stood up for your needs, it wouldn't have happened." She did not think they were trying to make her feel guilty, only to point out how hard she made things on herself; the accident could have been avoided if she had "let the kids get their own construction paper." In fact, her friends and family *were* saying she should feel guilty. Her own response is not unusual for someone whose pain originates in an avoidable event: even though logically there may be no way one could be held responsible, the idea that a purely chance event could so totally disrupt one's life is so upsetting that seeing someone—even oneself—as responsible is easier to bear. The utter absence of an answer to the pervasive "Why me?" question was indeed very hard to bear. One man reported that he kept wondering "What the hell did I do to deserve this?" To be sure, sufferers of all kinds often lack an answer to this question, especially in modern, secular societies where many misfortunes are "explained" as random occurrences. But this question has special weight for chronic pain sufferers because pain is so often associated with punishment.

Declines in mental and emotional functioning troubled many patients. Toby, the assistant professor, said he found this distressing, as he always had to use his mind for his living: "It's one thing when your body goes to pot, but when your mind's following it, oooh." Some began to doubt their own sanity: "Mind you, mentally I had lost my mind at that point." "I was so absorbed with pain I was becoming psychotic with it." "I was a crazy person when I walked in here." Sleep disturbance, inability to concentrate, and lack of energy were common complaints.

A research scientist said that in the later stages of a severe pain attack she could not even think through sentences or do addition. CPC staff members told patients that these were all expectable consequences of depression, but since one area of conflict between staff members and many patients was over just how depressed people were, patients tended to attribute these symptoms directly to the pain.

But if some patients resisted suggestions about the link between depression and pain, others would readily talk about it. The most disruptive aspect of the pain for one migraine sufferer was in fact a slow buildup of depression. Over the previous six months she had cried and slept a lot. Although diagnosed as a hypoglycemic, she had come to believe it was simply depression and pain. Ethan said that, although feeling is part of being human, he had spent the previous year and a half trying to keep himself from feeling anything in order to distance himself from his pain and his body.

Some contemplated suicide; one, Teresa, did kill herself. "People were nice," a woman said. "but I was thinking of ways to kill myself. I was such a bitch." Ethan said that at one point he had been suicidal, and the only thing that had kept him from "checking out" was his eight-year-old daughter, who would much rather have a cranky, nasty father around than have no father at all. A man said that when he was admitted to CPC he looked at the windows and thought, "Damn, they're too small.'" Several told of hoarding medications with suicide in mind. Yvonne said that she was afraid to go home because of the "black bag" waiting for her—yet she did not have the strength to throw it away.

Overall, most patients knew that not working increased the risk of depression, that wanting to be in bed all day was a bad sign, that "giving up" was not good, that thinking of suicide was an indication that they needed help. But, having "tried everything," they saw no options.

Emerging Themes

Several themes recurred during my intake interviews with patients. (Intake and discharge interview questions are listed in Appendix 2.) Despair is not too strong a word for one of them; despite some upbeat, bootstrapping talk along the line of "don't let the bastards wear you down" or "mind-over-matter," a large number of incoming patients said they were extremely discouraged.

"It doesn't go away" was one of CPC patients' most frequent responses to the question, "What's the most frustrating thing about your pain?" They had learned that chronic pain's very persistence creates a deep gulf between chronic pain sufferers and those who have experienced only acute pain, for many people find it hard to imagine any pain can be as long-lasting or as intense as sufferers claim. "After a while, no one believes you," said one man, "not even my wife." Richard Hilbert, a sociologist who has written on chronic pain, holds that chronic pain is "outside" culture because its meaning is so problematic; it is difficult to think of pain as unending because a key feature of the term is the notion of temporality.[17] Clearly, many non-sufferers find the notion of severe unending pain simply too threatening to contemplate. To think of unending pain is to think of hell, and, indeed, a parsimonious definition of hell is severe chronic pain. The metaphor has additional force for sufferers of intractable chronic pain: those consigned to hell are there because of sins committed, and some lay and clinical thinking about chronic pain ascribes moral responsibility to some of those who suffer from it.

Another theme was confusion: all patients were puzzled about one or several aspects of their current pain-dominated lives. This emerged in accounts of past attempts to find relief—many of which showed a willingness to explore mind/body connections. One man said he had tried "everything, including suicide: acupuncture, chiropractor, acupressure, neurosurgery. You name it, I've tried it." A migraine sufferer also said she had tried everything: the Christian Science Center (without telling her husband, as they were Catholic), acupuncture ("an awful lot of money for nothing"), Headache Center, stimulators, electrodes. Nothing did any good.

Many patients were also confused about just what sort of physical therapy was appropriate and particularly frightened of further damage. A woman who had undergone thirteen back operations had a constant fear of creating a new problem or undoing the (temporarily) successful results of previous treatments. A man talked of having to decide whether to use his painful arm; maybe it would not hurt later if he did; sometimes it did and sometimes it did not. Even if he did nothing, sometimes it hurt later anyway. Patients strongly resented critical remarks about these confusions: one man said that at one point he had been afraid to do things, which provoked comments from people that he was afraid to get well. But he was not afraid to get well: he was afraid he would hurt his back more if he did things.

Another theme was choosing whether to fight pain or accept it. Some said they intended to keep on fighting, or at least "not give in." A woman put it this way: "There's a lot of attacking the enemy. When the pain wins for the day, it's, well, This time it won." For some people, fighting pain was definitely the wrong approach: they spoke of knowing that they needed to accept the fact that they would always have the pain, and hoped CPC would help them do this. One woman said that fighting the pain meant you were just "stuck with it," which kept stress at a maximum. Rather than continually asking Why me? Why this? one had to accept that this may be the way one has to live.

A variation of the acceptance theme involved the harmful effects of denial and the need to acknowledge the presence of pain. Several had tried to deny that the pain imposed any limitations. Mary commented that her fear of becoming an invalid was so great that she ignored signals to slow down and not overdo, which, in fact, made the problem worse.

These concerns were related to the theme of control—of one's body, one's future, and one's environment, including social environment. Some patients seemed to like the idea of focusing on the pain, but many seemed to think this would mean giving in to the pain and losing control. Franklin, a young man with a bad back, summarized the control problem well: "Where do you draw the line? Do you pretend it's not there? You have to learn to listen to your body, but then again, you can't let your body dictate everything to you; there's a fine line."

Finally, some patients mentioned punishment. Rebecca, hit from behind in a "freak type" car accident, ended up feeling as though she were "the bad guy." And a man in his sixties frequently wondered "What have I done wrong?" during his years of suffering with pain following a stroke.

Views on the Mind and Body

While the very notion of psychosomatic pain asserts the presence of psychological and sociocultural inputs, note that the term covers a range of causal theories.[18] For example, the bleeding ulcer that worsens because of stress is somatically quite different from stomach pain diagnosed as hysterical—that is, with no peripheral involvement.

Phrases we all use, such as "pain in the butt," contain the notion of somatization. "Stress" is another term currently used to talk about conditions that bridge the mind/body divide. "Neurasthenia" once served such a purpose: its downward mobility and eventual extinction demonstrate how a fairly neutral term, when associated with a stigmatized condition involving emotional processes, eventually becomes stigmatized. So far "stress" has not fallen, perhaps because it has such a plethora of meanings that the relatively few with negative connotations do not drag down the term as a whole. Also, in some senses an overstressed life can be seen in positive terms—as long as the stressed individual has high status (e.g., a CEO or rock star), it is "life in the fast lane."[19]

Incoming patients varied so much in their level of self-awareness that it is impossible to generalize about their views on the respective roles

of mind and body in their pain, other than that in their initial interviews, they all first described their pain in physical, medical terms and
discussed its cause. They referred to falls, automobile accidents, complications following a medical procedure, and the like; most spoke of
scar tissue or improper body mechanics (e.g., favoring one side) that increased pain, swelling, or spasms. For example, a young man with costo-
chondritis (Tietze's syndrome), a condition involving cartilage swelling
and hardening in the chest, explained it had been under control with
steroids, but it "just went berserk" after he was hit in the chest and
thrown through a wall by a very angry body builder. He said his doctors
thought that the increase in pain was a consequence of his reaction to
the event—after all, he was a tense person and tension causes pain. But
he argued that tests showed damage and hardening of the cartilage, and
that the disease was not well understood.

Some explanations were rather fanciful. Fred, a young migraine sufferer, said doctors had told him he had too much electricity in his head,
resulting in the frontal and temporal lobes bouncing against each other.
Ethan had concluded that some of his nerves were misrouted, making
certain motions impossible.

Some patients held contradictory views. Ethan, for example, described his pain in entirely physical terms, saying his mechanistic descriptions reflected his "pretty firm mind/body split." Yet he had tried
hypnosis and shamanism; since his assumptions were not working, he
explained, he needed to explore alternatives.

After first describing their pain in terms of sensations produced by
physical causes, most patients moved on to broader concerns such as
how they felt about their transformed, pain-full selves. However, many
found it difficult to talk explicitly about links between mind and body.
The tendency to stress the physical derived in part from their struggle
for legitimacy and in part from the problem of finding adequate language. All patients certainly accepted *some* mind/body interactions—
that the body informs the mind of a need to urinate, say, or that the
mind interprets an image and the body becomes sexually aroused. The
struggle involved accepting the mind as at least a partial cause of their
pain. Suggestions that depression or "pain proneness" can bring on
pain frightened many patients; they resisted—often vehemently—the
idea that prior psychological attributes can bring on pain. "The pain
causes the depression," said Davie, who suffered migraines after an ex-
plosion at work and several brain surgeries, "Anyone with pain will be
depressed, pain takes over your life. You don't want to do anything because it hurts." [20]

Issues of responsibility and guilt often came up in patients' responses
to psychological-sounding explanations. A patient complained that Dr. B

and CPC psychologists blamed him, but whereas responsibility is an issue in alcoholism or drug dependency, in his case, which involved several surgeries for bleeding ulcers, "I was chopped up for nothing. I'm a victim of the medical establishment."

The suggestion of psychogenic pain can have a striking impact on self-esteem. A young woman commented that she felt a lot of her pain was "psychological, I mean, a lot of it is up in my head." Responding to a question about how that made her feel, she said, "like shit."

Several newly arrived patients indicated that they had considered a more comprehensive approach to their problem. Certainly most, especially headache sufferers, saw a connection between stress and pain. Mary was "always aware" that being irritated increased pain: the minute she would raise her voice or get angry, terrible pain would result. "And I would say, why did I do that?" Another woman, feeling very ambivalent about her marriage, talked about handing responsibility for anything technical, like loading a camera, over to her husband, making him feel "ten feet tall" and making her feel as though she had lost her dignity: "You're churning inside. It ends up in pain."

A young woman traced a link between her pain and early childhood; in her family expressing emotions was not allowed, and given that they had to go somewhere, they went to her body. Unlike having something emotionally wrong, she said, having something physically wrong was accepted. She also felt that her pain was the only way her mother was ever going to pay attention to her. A woman in her sixties who had been abused as a child also made a connection with her past: as sitting or lying down produced pain, whereas standing up relieved it, the pain was obviously "brain directed" because "the enema was given that way." Terence, a patient who was also a doctor, said he accepted that peripheral pain became centralized (routed into the central nervous system) after a while, which meant the brain's inhibitory and enhancing mechanisms, linked to emotional state, affected the level of pain. Pain could be amplified, he said, if "someone bugs you."

One final sign that many entering patients recognized mind/body connections came from responses to a question posed at the end of my initial interview: why was there such a range of outcomes at CPC? The vast majority referred to factors such as attitude, secondary gain, and psychological stress. Seeing such connections is apparently easier when one is not looking at oneself.

Getting Admitted

Most CPC patients had heard about pain centers, or about CPC in particular, from physicians. Some of these recommendations had not been very specific. They were "vague," Ethan said, "simply, 'others have been helped who look like you.' "

Some of these physicians had stressed particular aspects of the program, like physical therapy. Ethan said an orthopedic surgeon told him that whether or not he needed surgery, his body was so out of shape from having spent a year in bed that his next step was to get some muscle tone, and CPC would do that for him. Some physicians had suggested CPC specifically for help with a drug dependency. One patient's doctor gave him an ultimatum: go to CPC or "I'll give you another doctor, who'll give you all the drugs you want." A few referring physicians had mentioned the benefits of milieu therapy.

In a number of cases, however, doctors either were misinformed, had dissembled, or were misunderstood. One man complained that his physicians had led him to believe that CPC did surgery and medical procedures; no one had told him the emphasis was on *coping* with pain rather than *treating* pain.

Patients who already had a negative view of pain centers had resented their physician's recommendation. One recalled being hospitalized for a bad back, but they could not find anything wrong. When his doctor said he needed a pain clinic, "I told him he was a jerk and I signed myself out." Conversely, some patients came despite opposition from a medical professional. One patient's physician thought the problem could be resolved through counseling, "but it takes more than seeing a priest." Terence, the patient who was also a doctor, said his orthopedist had told him he had too much insight for CPC to be of much benefit. When Eleanor told her orthopedist that CPC was the next step, he said, "Oh, my God, don't do that!" but did not elaborate. She thought it was just "the same old thing of doctors trying very hard to make the person better, being disappointed if they aren't, and wanting to be the only one who does it."

Whatever their sources of information, most patients reported having very little hard knowledge about CPC prior to admission.

The Evaluation Interview

The evaluation interview with Dr. B and his assistant Rhonda prior to admission evoked mixed reactions. Many found it too brief and short on explanation of what they would be getting into. Others complained about "hype." One patient told Rhonda, "That was an excellent sales pitch, I'm really sold. Does it include parking and conjugal visits?" Other aspects of the interview also drew criticism. Yvonne reported that she "felt bizarre" in Dr. B's office, and put off by the interaction: "Then he came in and sat down, barely introduced himself to me. [Rhonda] sat next to him and talked in the third person about me: This is a 34-year-old female, she has had blah blah, and I felt very put off, very unsafe, like, Where the hell am I? I want to get out of here!"

Others had no complaints about the evaluation interview.

The First Week

Every CPC patient found the first week confusing and stressful.[21] In part, this was because CPC operated under less-than-optimal conditions—space limitations, staff turnover, and so on. However, some surprises were intentional, calculated to shake patients up, to make them more open to the CPC experience.

Being poorly informed about the program's structure produced some of the confusion. Many patients were dazed by the admissions procedure. One recalled her confusion on her first day: "I had all kinds of papers, and they told me, 'Read them and you'll know what's going on,' and I couldn't read them all. And I still don't know what's going on." Another woman said, "I don't know what I expected, it was all surprises. I'd had it, I was so down. I imagined my husband was putting me into a psych unit—that was my fantasy, with doctors in white coats running around with long needles and the bride of Frankenstein for my nurse and steel doors that shut behind you." Some were simply homesick. One woman said she felt so lonely the first day that she cried whenever anyone said anything to her: "They put me in here, I didn't know anyone."

Yet there were those who had been pleased as well as surprised. Helen, who had arrived in an ambulance, said that although she had expected to go to physical therapy, she had never heard of "focus group, psychomotor, the patient community." Talking with others got her out of her "poor me" frame of mind.

Clearly, a number of patients did not hear, or forgot, some of what they were told about the CPC program prior to admission. One of the social workers felt that since patients were not ready to hear what they had been told, they had not heard it. But it was also clear that referring physicians and CPC staff were not fully forthcoming in presenting the nature of the program to potential patients: eight staff members stated outright that patients were not adequately informed. One of the PRAs said that if people realized how much work they would have to do on themselves, significantly fewer would come. A physical therapist spoke of a "catch-22": if you informed people fully they might decide not to come, but if you did not inform them enough they might leave.

Matthew was also bothered that incoming patients were not adequately prepared. Recently admitted patients, hearing the word "diagnostic," expected physical, somatic tests, and were shocked when they found out how heavily psychotherapeutic the program was—suddenly to have to air your dirty laundry and lay yourself bare was difficult if you were not psychologically minded—or even if you were.

However, like several staff members, some patients approved of what most agreed was insufficient preparation, and saw it as an intentional part of CPC's efforts to attract those who might profit from the program. Fully informing patients at the evaluation interview, one woman said, might result in your "lying at home worrying you can't do it."

The inadequate communication about the nature of the program had several negative consequences. One was the already noted high dropout rate. Another, according to Linda, was the first-night shock patients experienced when they found they could not have the sleeping pills and narcotics and tranquilizers they were taking at home.

But some patients said they had been adequately informed. A man commented: "I knew that they weren't going to diagnose your pain and fix it; they were going to teach you how to deal with it on a day-to-day basis."

The Brochure

Some patients blamed their early disorientation in part on the CPC brochure, which Toby described as "a joke, it's like a travel brochure." Ethan talked of "a little glossy brochure that has no content." Many said the brochure should be "more honest."

One man who suffered from migraines was blunt about how misleading the brochure was: "Lies." Asked for details, he said that, although the brochure said medication would not be reduced until later on, the first day he was given only one Fiorinal and one codeine, which was a reduction of 90 percent. When he talked to Dr. B the next day, he was told, "Take it or leave it."

The much-maligned CPC brochure did, in fact, state that the program, unlike other hospital programs, was designed to expose pain sufferers to resources for dealing with a pain problem other than those available through medical treatment alone. The brochure also noted that minimal attention would be given to diagnosis, for usually it was not the diagnosis that was in question, but rather the patient's failure to respond to therapy. This somewhat cryptic language is characteristic of CPC's approach—namely, to focus on the patient, more specifically on the *patient's* failure to respond to conventional biomedical and psychotherapeutic treatment.

Although psychotherapy and family meetings (run by the two social workers) were given separate sections in the brochure ("since we believe that pent-up emotions aggravate pain, talking out the feelings that may make you tense can help to relieve your pain and thus lead to new ways of coping with tension-producing situations"), they appeared in a group of technical-sounding topics dealing with medical rounds, biofeedback, physical therapy, thermography, and transcutaneous electrical nerve stimulators. This tended to give an overall impression of a state-of-the-art biomedical approach to pain similar to that of more medically focused pain clinics.

The brochure also introduced CPC's theories on the cause, maintenance, and amplification of pain in a statement about the muscle tension that produces some kinds of pain, saying that there was no simple explanation for the build-up of muscle tension, which tends to come from a combination of factors, some of which might be physical while others might be related to various life stresses. It also stated that stress often complicates illness and disability by adding to anxiety and depression as well as by causing medical, neurological, and hormonal effects, leading to the conclusion that pain has both physical and psychological implications. It added that the CPC program was designed to help chronic pain sufferers explore the sources of their muscle tension and ways in which tension might have been contributing to their pain. This section did bring up the notion that psychological factors can cause or exacerbate pain, but it is not difficult to see why patients, after a few days of hearing CPC staff members hint that at least some of their pain was psychogenic, felt the brochure had not adequately informed them.

For the most part, new patients did not seem to object to psychotherapy and family meetings per se (unless they were extremely suspicious of CPC or very resistant to any such approaches), but they disliked what they saw as misrepresentation in the brochure and evaluation interview. Indeed, a substantial number of patients who had already had psychotherapy said they welcomed this component of CPC's program (although some still had complaints about the nature of the therapy), and some of these individuals were comfortable with the notion of somatization. But others—who might have agreed with a statement like "pent-up emotions aggravate pain"—did not at all accept the notion that one had pain in part *because* of one's psychological makeup.

The brochure also discussed the therapeutic community feature of the program, mentioning that the presence of other pain sufferers could be productive and helpful. It noted that increasing social interaction could relieve depression and that patients who had become reclusive could begin to use rusty social skills and find meaning in their lives beyond preoccupation with medication and physical dysfunction. This section of the brochure also hinted at what is here called CPC's "tough love" feature. Noting that many people with chronic pain spent the day in bed, with resulting sleep problems, it said that at CPC patients were encouraged to be active, despite pain. Patients who could not walk to therapies went in wheelchairs, or even on stretchers if necessary. Regardless of an individual's condition, he or she went, and received encouragement from the staff and fellow patients.

Another hint of CPC's tough approach appeared in the section on family meetings, which noted that a pain sufferer might have become very manipulative without realizing it and that his or her family might not be aware of the most helpful things to do. One last hint concerned efforts to lessen "pain habits" (i.e., excessive or inappropriate pain behavior) developed over the years: CPC staff members believed patients' pain was real, but also believed that repetitive discussions of pain were not helpful.

Not all patients felt they had been misled; some (who were quite positive in their initial response to CPC) said that, since the brochure was supposed to attract as many prospective patients as possible, it would of course have an upbeat, medical tone. In general, those patients who complained about misrepresentation in the brochure did so because they had not grasped the *implications* of various CPC policies—public rounds, a rigid approach to medications, mandatory attendance at all activities, and so forth. Only a very few patients had foreseen the nitty-gritty implications of a rehabilitation program for chronic pain.

Public Medical Rounds

Even though the fact that medical rounds (meetings between the staff and a patient to assess progress) were held in a public setting was explicitly mentioned in the brochure, most patients were surprised that rounds were held during breakfast or lunch. One woman liked neither that rounds were public nor that they occurred during a meal: if you were constipated, it was very hard to discuss it under those circumstances. Asked whether she thought the policy had a purpose, she replied, "Probably to make you more outgoing and assertive. I could use a little of that." Wednesday rounds in the rooms also met with displeasure—one woman found "all their whispering stuff" unprofessional: "If they have something to say to you, say it."

Doctor's Group

"Doctor's group" was the twice-weekly meeting between Dr. B and patients. Mondays he would talk about things related to chronic pain: medications, depression, advances in treatment, and so forth; Wednesdays he reviewed the progress of the four or five patients about to be discharged. A description of doctor's group in an orientation packet given to patients began by reminding patients that the therapeutic community was an important part of treatment, and went on to say that, although the details discussed in the psychotherapies were confidential, the therapeutic community needed to know about their fellow patients' basic problem areas in order to be helpful. A public presentation of the problems that were complicating pain allowed each patient's support network to get an *accurate* understanding, not the distorted view some patients wanted to convey. This message was also posted on the patient bulletin board (in part for legal reasons: doctor's group did in fact break patient confidentiality). This was one of the more vexing areas of the program for many patients, and those sitting in on their first doctor's group session were often dismayed to hear how much of a patient's personal life Dr. B. revealed. Fred, when asked what the doctor's motives might be, speculated it was to scare people and get them "bullshit" (very angry) at him so they would take care of themselves more.

Kurt definitely did not like doctor's group. When a fellow patient's marriage was brought up, he wondered, "What the hell does that have to do with me?" He worried about what Dr. B would say about him, especially given what Dr. B had said about some patients coming to CPC just to increase their insurance settlement. But, said Kurt, if he thought this, "why did he let us in in the first place? I'm still new, I don't like him."

Most patients rejected the idea that it was necessary to broadcast "hard truths" to the patient community and staff. Some spoke of calling their lawyers and ascertaining whether they had signed away their right to confidentiality.

A woman protested that doctor's group publicly humiliated people: "There must be a better way; there's a difference between public embarrassment and getting tough. I haven't participated in labeling people, insulting them, I think it's unnecessary. I've been very uncomfortable seeing people treated that way and identifying with them. It's not a safe, comfortable place."

Patients also worried that doctor's group might prove harmful to patients from different cultural backgrounds—for example, the possible impact on a young patient from a strict Chinese family that stressed saving face.

Several patients pointed to an inconsistency in this regard: they were not supposed to talk about confidential matters discussed in group therapy, but staff members were apparently free to relay any information about patients. Many were upset to learn that something said to a staff member in private had become part of their record. "The nurses hash over everything you say in meetings; they squeal on you," said one man. Kurt complained that the staff used this information "against you."[22] Ursula, the nurse who had abused medications, also felt ambivalent about this policy, because people would say, "This one's a druggie" and look down at her for having failed. She was not sure to what degree confidentiality was respected at CPC nor "how much it *should* be."

Medicine Downplayed

The policy of downplaying diagnostic work and medical treatment was something many recently arrived CPC patients were apparently unaware of, if the number of complaints about promised-but-not-delivered diagnostic procedures is any indication. Harry said he had assumed they would have some "decent doctors" to "check you up to a T to find out what was the matter with you," rather than insist on psychological explanations.

The process of coming to understand CPC's nonmedical approach elicited many comments, well captured by a patient's distinction between treating pain and teaching how to cope with pain—"They're *physical* here, but not medical." A patient said he had got the impression that staff members thought you could adjust to any level of pain, but he disagreed: "If you're having surgery, you can't do it without anesthesia."

Initial Medical Exams

Some patients were pleased with the medical attention they received the first day or two on the unit. A paraplegic told how Dr. A had told him his pain was very common among paraplegics, whereas he had been told at a rehabilitation center, "It's crazy, you're paralyzed."[23] But most were unhappy about the exams by consulting physicians. Kurt spoke of them as handpicked, in Dr. B's pocket. Another complained that his "complete physical" had been so perfunctory he could have done it himself.

The vast majority of complaints were about initial encounters with the attending internist, Dr. O. Basically, his role was not only to examine incoming patients but to convey the tough love message that encounters with physicians were going to be different. For example, one patient, who suffered from a chronically inflamed pancreatic duct, reported that Dr. O told him he " 'didn't see any inflammation, so what's wrong?' I was in such pain I thought I'd have to leave."

A woman commented that Dr. O would be fired anywhere else, but that Dr. B "papered over" the problems and always excused him. "A bad day. Every day he has a bad day. His behavior is just ridiculous. And yet he does greet each patient the first day, he's part of the greeting committee. Quite an introduction to the place!"

Another patient was standing with his back to the door when Dr. O walked into his room for the physical exam, "and as I turned around, he grabbed my arm and tried to flip it over. I raised hell with him. He didn't even have the courtesy to say 'Hi, I'm Dr. So-and-so.' " Asked what the doctor's motive might be, he said he sometimes had the feeling that staff members thought his pain was "upstairs," and that Dr. O was trying to surprise him to see if he was making believe. At one point, according to this patient, Dr. O had said, "Some day I'll catch you."

An attending neurologist, Dr. A, while less abrasive than Dr. O, communicated a similar message and often elicited similar reactions, as this exchange with Harry shows:

"He hits you on the knee, hits you on the leg, bottom-of-the-foot tickle."

"*Neurological exam?*"

"If that's what you want to call it. Call it whatever, my dog's had better exams than that. 'Yeah, you'll do all right, just tight muscles.' "

A pretty young woman who had put on about fifteen pounds after becoming inactive from a bad back reported that during her encounter with Dr. S, the consulting psychiatrist, he had told her she was a bit overweight. "I was *going* to discuss it. If he'd waited a few minutes, I would have brought it up myself. I don't look that bad—and he doesn't look so hot himself. It's almost as though he's trying to get me really hostile to him. The way he said it, it was very condescending; I hate that, it drives me crazy. If you're short, blonde, somewhat attractive, you're talked down to. They think you're stupid, and I'm not stupid."

She did have an inkling that his behavior might have been deliberate but, like most patients, did not immediately see it as a part of her therapy. Asked why he might act that way, she said that he had probably wanted to see her react, but then speculated that "maybe I didn't bring it up soon enough for him, I don't know. He really caught me off guard, I said, 'Well, I'm on a diet.' Dumb-dumb, I felt. My first day, and I was kind of out of breath."

Kurt, too, had a glimpse of the strategy. "They test you a lot. The shrink here, he's told some people some real derogatory remarks just to see what their reactions were. I don't know how I would do under that. If he ever made a derogatory remark about me—his suit might get wrinkled up a little. But he doesn't do that with me." Kurt said Dr. S had "jumped on" Edward, Kurt's roomate, about his beard.

Conclusions

Patients had encountered any number of problems prior to coming to CPC. When they arrived, they had mixed reactions. A few features of CPC were approved of by everyone—ice and oil massages are an example. But patients questioned the usefulness and appropriateness of most of the features of CPC's program. All patients found one or more features surprising. Some of the surprise came from patients' being inadequately informed about what they were getting into, and both staff members and patients had opinions about why parts of the CPC brochure and evaluation interview were overly brief and oblique. But many of the surprises were due to patients' unfamiliarity with CPC's therapeutic goals. That medicine was downplayed was one; the advisability of manipulating, shocking, and disorienting resistant patients was another. And that therapy was going on all the time, that any issue could be an occasion to engage in "reality confrontation" (the repeated reflection back to the patient by both staff members and fellow patients of their view of his or her conduct) to provide the impulse toward change,[24] was so unexpected that many patients never figured it out. Much of CPC's approach derived from the ideology and practices of the human potential movement, which blossomed during the 1970s. For example, confrontation and manipulation characterized self-discovery programs of that era such as EST (Erhard Seminar Training),[25] as well as the therapeutic community movement. What was unique about these features at CPC was that they occurred on a purportedly medical unit.

Chapter 4
"Getting with the Program"

"They're trying to teach you to walk down the corridor with a smile on your face, regardless."

Because CPC's approach required that the patient be seen as a whole person, the goal of changing that person's behavior and attitude toward pain—and perhaps diminishing the amount of pain—could be achieved using several approaches.[1]

The Educational Component

A significant part of CPC's program involved educating patients—about pain itself, about various pain-managing modalities, about depression and other emotions, and so forth. Some of this education took place one-on-one (e.g., during a daily session with a physical therapist), some in classes and workshops on topics dealing with the body (biomechanics and biomechanical therapies), nutrition, sleep, medications, and the like. Most patients were receptive to this part of the program, and many said the CPC experience helped them learn valuable lessons. Some of these were difficult to learn—for example, how to let go of anger at hit-and-run drivers or physicians who had no business practicing medicine. As Matthew put it: "There is a lot of injustice in the world. Unfortunately all of that flailing and thrashing about doesn't really do people much good. I can understand it, but it's not growth-producing, it's not life-giving, it's destructive."

Many patients were taken aback by CPC's lessons about doing exercise even though pain was increased, of "working through pain." Thus, although many patients had looked forward to physical therapy, there was fear as well, and most were relieved to find out that damage could be avoided with proper supervision. For example, one woman, with a history of back surgeries, recalled hearing of things she would be doing—such as stairs—that made her very leery. "But I realized after a few days that they know a lot more about it than I do." Staff members also taught patients to recognize and respect limitations. Almost all patients approved of the physical therapy program.

Exercise made Ethan almost lyrical: "To feel the blood flowing through my veins as something bringing oxygen to muscles that I am working, rather than as something bringing drugs to soothe sore muscles, it's the nicest feeling. I lie here, sometimes, and I giggle about how good I feel." Yet for some this was one of the program's most difficult features, at least for a time. Umberto, a meat packer with a bad back, complained that his physical therapist, Fredericka, a tough-mannered Israeli who seemed to be assigned more than her share of resistant patients, was "commanding" him to do things he was not able to do. And she was "without pity." But by the end of his stay he had nothing but praise for her.

At first a number of patients were suspicious of the relaxation training. Barry recalled thinking, "This is like hypnotism and no one's going to hypnotize me, I'm not that suggestible." A woman said she liked relaxation, but not in a group on mats in the dining room. Although she liked people, she felt that lying on the floor so close to others was not very nice. "So I shut out everything and I fall asleep, and then they get sore at me." (Her snoring did indeed irritate both patients and staff members.) But many liked relaxation from the start.

In the course of their stay, most patients learned relaxation techniques well enough to see results. Mary told of growing tense while driving during her weekend leave of absence, "but, the minute I got stuck in the traffic I just started doing some relaxation and I was fine. I started noticing the trees and different things that I had never even noticed. It really worked; I had strangest sense of calmness, such peace—something I had a longing for for years." Fred, the young migraine sufferer, said, "What helps me is sitting around like a Buddha, zonking my head off. I could have thrown the pills away at home if I'd known about the ice and the relaxation."

By the end of their stay, the great majority of patients were happy about relaxation techniques, whatever their overall evaluation of CPC. One young man in a wheelchair who had been told his back pain was "impossible" because he was paralyzed, despite ending up with an extremely negative opinion of CPC, valued relaxation. It had taught him that some of his pain was due to stress. When the pain got bad he would now use relaxation techniques three or four times a day, whereas previously he would get into bed and that would be it for the rest of the day.

Some patients learned that simple distraction helped control pain.

Barry said: "My wife calls, 'How are you?' 'Fine.' 'Why?' 'I've been doing lots of things.' 'But that used to make you worse!' It's hard for me to say. It's the community—maybe it distracts me." Barry talked specifically of the pain that occurred during transfer from bed to wheelchair. He had been doing this cautiously, guarding himself, but discovered that if he moved around in bed before the transfer—causing himself pain—the transfer was easier because he was choosing to cause pain; this meant he was no longer anticipating pain but rather relief of pain. Of course the mechanical effects of moving around helped loosen him up and the activity was a distraction, but Barry was interested in the discovery that a change in cognition—seeing movement as a solution rather than a problem—affected his pain perception. Barry apparently shifted the locus of control to a more internal one, achieved a greater sense of mastery over the pain, and perhaps experienced less pain as well.

He pursued this issue during a workshop with Kevin, the psychologist, during the first part of the study: "You say 'Let the pain take care of itself.' I'd rather think of me being able to take care of the pain." Kevin responded that he may not have used the right words; he had meant to say that, while one can practice techniques that *may* control pain, it may not be a good idea to focus on controlling pain: since one cannot totally control pain, focusing on it may make it worse.

This anecdote not only illustrates how CPC's approach could succeed, but gives some sense of the semantic minefield involved: here, focusing versus over-focusing, and purposely causing pain seen as a healthy approach.

In workshops on the nature of pain, Kevin would distribute a handout that described organic or tissue damage—something with physical presence that "you (and others) can see or touch"—and then go on to discuss how pain differed from this: "While physical damage can contribute to pain, physical damage is not the same thing as pain. Pain is not, by nature, physical." The handout went on to state that some pain "is in your head because you are alive, you think, feel, and breathe." Kevin was attempting to draw the useful distinction between nociception—tissue damage that brings on pain—and pain itself, an experience. However, asserting that pain is not physical, with no further explanation, is misleading because the logical conclusion is that pain is being described as imaginary.

Clearly, any attempt to educate along these lines could touch on other areas of concern. Responding to Kevin's workshop, a young man said he had made the staff a little uneasy because he disagreed with their "big philosophies," in particular Kevin's statement that pain, although it was real, was not physical. He had replied to Kevin that pain was analogous to electricity: "You can't see electricity, but you grab the end of a wire in a machine and it'll hurt you." A conversation about the workshop with a woman who disliked many features of the program was instructive:

"Did anyone actually say 'your pain is in your head' or 'your pain is imaginary'?"

"When they draw a picture on the board, and say, 'this is your brain and this is this'—well, what is your brain? It's your head, right? In other words, they're not coming right out and saying it to you, because they could get into big trouble there."

"What do you mean, 'big trouble'"?

"If they came up and said to you, 'I feel like your pain is in your head,' that it's all psychosomatic, right? Ok, I could prove them wrong, so I could sue them. So they never come out and say it, but they do say, 'the brain does this, the brain does that, and the muscles are connected to the brain, but it all starts here.' So, what is it? It's your head."

Some heard Kevin's message quite differently. One woman called it "the lecture saying your pain is real," noting that she and others were grateful because "a lot of people felt that they were going to tell us we were crazy." Such different interpretations are evidence for my argument that staff members' messages did not form a well-synthesized set of lessons. As Beverly, a PRA, put it, "One part of the staff will say one thing and the other will teach you something else. Like, half will teach you not to focus on your pain, and then you'll have the workshops to look into your pain—to feel it and explore it, which can be very confusing for the patients."

Although most patients initially resisted attempts to teach them about the role of emotions in the pain experience ("They're fanatics! They totally subscribe to a state-of-mind explanation; when they point out how tense I am, I get pissed. Of course I'm tense!"), at the end of their stay, most patients said they had learned some useful information about psychological factors that contribute to pain. For example, one woman said she was amazed at how people could surmount their pain and in some cases apparently erase it with the proper image of it. Another woman, who had complained that CPC staff members "really pick your brain, they tell you it's all in your mind," came to accept that the pressure she felt from her father did affect her pain.

Workshops included discussions of depression. Patients often defined depression in terms unlike those used in standard clinical definitions. In response to a question, one woman said that she didn't think she was depressed because "I don't feel like killing myself—usually when I feel depressed to me is when I want to kill myself." Many patients saw depression as a "down," temporary mood; for example, "They're telling me I'm depressed. I'm depressed today, I'll admit it, the pain is very bad."

Patients resented staff members teaching that pain was caused or amplified by depression. "Some people have simplistic models," a man pointed out, saying that staff members *say* they didn't say "depression causes pain," but they did. Barry resented being "force fed" the program's message about the links between depression and severe chronic pain; he thought the staff stressed depression so strongly because if patients were to come in and not suffer from depression, the need for them to be at CPC would not be very great, given the near-absence of medical treatment.

Further evidence that depression was a highly contested issue at CPC appears in the struggles over the antidepressant doxepin—a major reason for resisting it was the stigma attached to taking a drug for depression. Indeed, a few patients steadfastly refused to take the medication, even though the staff told them that a common side effect was alleviation of pain and insomnia. Some patients engaged in a kind of competition to see who was on the lowest dosage.

Patients accepted "stress" more readily than depression as a cause of pain, in part because many people seemed to link depression with a personal failing, but saw stress as due to exogenous factors. Most patients also rejected formulations about pain and depression stemming from childhood experiences: "You just don't stay depressed for sixteen years."

However, many valued the lessons about depression. One man thought patients resisted the label because they couldn't accept that their life was "a flop." Several came to see themselves as having been depressed but not aware of it.

The word "psychological" was often used by patients to characterize the psychogenic explanations more vaguely. For example, Harry, who had neuropathy in his arms and back pain, asked Dr. A how the swelling in his arm could be psychological. Dr. A had replied that "if you think about it long enough it will swell." "I don't believe that. I didn't think for years I was going to fall down and hurt my back, and all of a sudden one day—I hadn't really planned it." The day before, a pain in his back had come on during a trip to the pool:

"Why in hell would I be doing one thing, then all of a sudden say, 'oh, gee, now I'm in the pool, I'm playing volleyball. Gee, maybe I ought to have a back spasm now.' Do I think of this and send it to my back?"

"Well, they say it's unconscious . . ."

"Well, I think they are full of shit."

But Edward did come to agree somewhat with the message about psychological predispositions, concluding that his bad body mechanics at work when he got angry meant he had set himself to get hurt "a long time ago." He admitted that if anyone had told him that, "I would have taken a swing at them because it would have been like saying 'you did this on purpose.'"

Uneasiness about returning to work was heightened by CPC's insistence that patients wean themselves from pain habits and overdependence on the medical system. Edward, apparently thinking about his roommate Kurt, pointed to what he saw as a deliberately threatening aspect of the physical therapy policy: one's performance would demonstrate that "there is nothing wrong with you, you can go back to work."

Kurt was indeed worried about this issue (staff members seemed to think it explained his resistance and some of his depression). Thus at his first interview he praised his physical therapist, Tracy, and said flexibility and rotation in his neck had increased. However, toward the end of his stay he talked of a report Tracy was writing and worried he might lose his pension as a result: "I told her, 'If I lose my pension I'm going to end up going right back to where I was, working three jobs and running myself into the ground.'" This possibility had made him increasingly morose, negative, and resentful. When Tracy told him there were going to be no restrictions, that he was ready to go back to work, he tried to talk to her, but: "She's got her mind made up. I've resigned myself—if that's the way they're going to write it down—because I don't have the pen. You can't argue with somebody that's got the pen, they're going to write down what they want to write down."

This aspect of CPC's program led to some rather curious ideas about its financial dealings. One man was convinced Dr. B was benefiting directly from workers' compensation:

"I'm sure he gets so much if he gets people back to work. I'm almost sure of that from what he's saying."

"You think there's a kickback if he can get people back into work?"

"I'm sure of it."

Any interactions with staff members that involved being evaluated—information "going on your record"—clearly brought up issues connected with earlier experiences with authorities for many patients, as evidenced by the abundance of complaints about being treated like a child. In fact, patients sometimes did sound like children wanting "a good grade" or lying because they were worried about the evaluation. A young man complained that he was reluctant to go in and talk to Dr. B, because "even if I had something extra hard eating at me, I could beg them to not reveal it, but it'll go on your record."

Several patients thought CPC's own concern with success pushed staff members to make patients return to work. But, as Harry noted, "success" could be an ambiguous notion: "They want you to be the big success, to walk out of here and say, 'Oh, I'm totally free.' It's like being in the military and they're training you to go into combat. They're brainwashing you, is what they're doing. They're telling you you're going to survive. Look at the Vietnam war, there weren't too goddamn many survived out of that."

But others said they understood and agreed with the idea of sending people back to work and teaching them to be free from the medical system—people needed to feel normal and productive, not disabled and sick. Franklin said: "The more doctors you go to, the more you think nobody can help you, and that you can't even help yourself."

One common complaint was that CPC "goes by the book," "textbooks us," "treats everybody the same." A woman said, "and for some of the staff I feel they have this little cookbook that says, 'in order to get rid of the pain you just mix this, that, or the other thing'—you read what to do and then you do it." But, as another patient put it, "You can't say to a whole group of people, 'well, you're all depressed and you're all suffering from anxiety.'" These objections reflect the discomfort many people feel about statistically based studies that categorize people using some kind of negative valence—especially if they themselves are being so grouped. Patients were not unaware that some of their number did have pain habits, were hypochondriacal and overly pain-focused, did benefit from pain in some way, or may have had early experiences that could contribute to their current pain problem, and this doubtless increased their anxiety about how they were being seen.

To some extent the complaints about "textbooking" reflected the distance between patients and some staff members. Several patients noted that staff members who worked more intensively with patients knew them as individuals, whereas for the "professionals" patients were "a chart, a form, something out of a textbook. They pigeonhole us: You're type A, B, C, or D."

Some staff members also found this a problem. Nina was especially concerned about making sure the program was individualized; given that certain approaches do not work for everybody, they should not be "crammed down their throat." And Donna said that while some patients needed limits, not all did, yet everyone got put into the "same barrel."

The Psychotherapeutic Component

Psychotherapy at CPC, like the educational component, was designed to enable patients to achieve insight into their pain problems, but in a way that was at once less direct and more individualized, and required a more engaged response than workshops or classes. It was intended to give patients an opportunity to become more aware of possible psychogenic aspects of their pain experience and to see why they were not managing their pain and limitations as well as they might.

Several patients noted that the confinement, small living space, and locked-up medicines reminded them of a psych ward. An interesting twist on this came from Yvonne, herself a psychotherapist, who was told that CPC was *less* psychological than it appeared to her. "The brochure stressed the importance of the psychological component, but when I talked to [Dr. B], he told me it was not a psychological unit—I already knew it was not a psychiatric unit, but he told me that psychological terminology meant nothing here, that this was a medical unit, and words like 'termination' were irrelevant. I was very angry."

Staff members did take pains to emphasize that CPC was not a psych ward. Sonia, a nurse, said she got "really upset when I hear people refer to this as a psych ward. I always make it very clear, even if it's doctors or nurses that are just coming here, it's not a psych unit, it's a pain unit." Polly, a PRA, concurred, adding that if by chance someone was admitted who needed psychiatric facilities, he or she was transferred. Nina said that no psychosis was involved with CPC patients; rather, they were just situationally depressed or simply needed some guidance getting back on the right track.

As we have seen, most patients both welcomed this feature of the program—at least some aspects of it—and disliked it. Some patients appreciated the psychological emphasis almost from the first. A woman remarked, "Within three or four days my condition improved. That's when I began to believe the psychological diagnosis. Because yesterday and today my condition is not terrible. For the first time I stopped saying 'I'd rather die, I've suffered more than Jesus Christ on the cross'—I said a lot of foolish things while in that state of mind."

A young woman reported experiencing changes during the first week. Although she knew she was anxious, she didn't think she had problems. But so much had come out (including a "bad experience" when she was ten or eleven), she felt as if another person was surfacing, almost to the point of feeling possessed. She added that not everyone wanted to give up the goodies that go with pain. In the last months she had had a lot of attention from her husband and family, and it had been nice: "It may not be the attention you *want*, but if you didn't have any before, it's OK." The trick for her was to get her husband to keep it up after she got better.

Although many patients appreciated exploring their feelings, they still resisted some of the implications. As we have seen, one of these was the supposed link between present and past pain. A patient said, "I've really had to open up here. If I didn't have a 14-karat childhood, that has nothing to do with what happened to me now." He continued: "I can't buy that what is going on [in his arm] stems from the past. I sometimes feel that they don't believe you—'you're not really in pain, it must be something that happened to you a long time ago.' They're saying, 'Hey, it's not this, it's what happened to your mother and father.'"

Furthermore, recalling unhappy events of the past was painful:

"I have put them behind me, forgotten, a thing of the past. Well, now they're all back. When you talk about these things, it brings back the tears."

"You don't feel better when you cry?"

"No, not if we're discussing when I was a little guy."

But some found the difficult delving into the past ultimately worth it. An elderly woman who remarked, "They try to get me to go back to my childhood, and it's painful, you know? (In Yiddish we say 'pouring salt into an open wound')," experienced a release when she "broke down and cried" in her focus group because others had gone through the same thing.[2]

And some simply found psychotherapy unnecessary and invasive. One woman said, she didn't like having her brain picked, and feeling she was constantly being watched was making her "a wreck." She had taken courses in psychology and did not like being on the other side. Nor did patients like staff members' redefinitions of their behavior; one said that if patients were having fun and laughing staff members would say they were hiding behind their humor.

However, patients who said they were not helped believed it had helped others. Thus Kurt, who ended up very unhappy about the program, admitted he had seen it work for Umberto, who when admitted wouldn't smile or talk to anyone. "Now he's always joking. This guy, he's come a long way, I'm very happy for him."

Umberto—almost a stereotype of a person lacking self-awareness—entered CPC very embittered about not being able to work and about his home situation. Early on he compared the center unfavorably to a hospital he had stayed in previously, where "there were groups but you weren't treated like a piece of dirt being swept under the rug." But in his second interview he said, "They made things come out that I was holding inside—it seems I was holding things inside for years. I never socialized or communicated with anyone."

Umberto was a CPC success story; he had entered sullen and bitter—as he said, "with a bad attitude." His wife and daughter were apparently at their wits' end; I had been afraid to approach him. By the end of his stay he had completely come out of his shell and was universally adored—when he gave his good-bye speech his fellow-patients presented him with a cake.

(However, we all wondered how long it would last. Kenneth, a physical therapist, said this was a general concern: "I just wonder if it has carry-over and what happens when they get out of here, is the indoctrination long enough?")

Reactions to focus group therapy were extremely varied. Some found it hard to talk. Some saw very little purpose: "How much of that stuff can you listen to? Soon you only block it out of your mind and think of the trout in the old fishing hole." A woman complained that she heard horrible, "nutty" stories, which would build up in her and she "wouldn't know how to handle it."

But sooner or later most patients, even those initially reluctant, responded positively. One man reported that in focus group he heard someone pouring out *his* story: "I didn't have to ask, the things I wanted to say were already being said, and I'm sitting there going 'wow!'"

Experience in focus group certainly played a role in the strikingly different opinions people had about the program by the end of their stay. Franklin, who described his initial response to the program as, "What? They think it's all in my head?" came to appreciate the groups, where "people sort of held out a psychological mirror to me: this is what's going on, this is what we see is happening. Gives me a chance to hear myself talk, too, and see the reaction of other people—see whether I'm far off base or whether I've got something there."[3]

Some patients definitely did not like or understand psychomotor. Ursula said she liked all the groups except that one: "The leader is as flaky as a $3 bill. Last night she tried to stir up trouble, picking at you. The last time there was a major war for two people because she pitted them together. I can't understand why they don't get rid of her."

Linda, a CPC nurse, said, "I have seen how psychomotor works. I can see where combining talking with movement is much more effective, not only for the person that's doing it, but for the persons watching it because they get attuned to watching body movements, and how we have a whole other language we can use with our bodies. And becoming more aware of speech; somebody says, 'I have the weight of the world on my shoulders,' and where is the pain? It's on their neck. 'I have a pain in my throat, I can't swallow, I'm being suffocated.' I mean, this is when they're talking about their mother or their father. You start putting connections together and it's amazing. And if we can educate them to just break their consciousness enough to be attuned to what other people are saying, and how they are saying it, they will be more attuned to what they're doing—to their own feelings and behavior. That's the whole thing."

Predictably, problems arose in a month-long program that encouraged intense psychotherapy when, as often happened, the end of the month did not coincide with therapeutic closure. For example, a migraine sufferer had at first not wanted to open up. But she eventually felt safe enough to "get things out in the open that I didn't even know were bothering me." However, at the end of her stay she said unhappily, "I mean, they got me to talk about a lot of things that I never talked about before, and then they just left it like that. So now I've got to pick up and put it all back together myself. And I have absolutely no idea how to do it." Another woman made a similar complaint: "I'm scared. The dysfunction in my arm, I believe there's nothing neurologically wrong. So the failure is in making recommendations I can act on. Maybe for some people, the program is helpful; I understand the manipulations. But why open something up and not give any actionable advice to even *begin* to deal with it?"[4]

Some patients continued to approve of how they had kept things bottled up before. A young woman said: "I don't know how to explain it. It's like trusting someone to bare your soul to, and you get all these things out in the open, and then it's time to go home. And what do you do with all this stuff? I was able to keep it back before, because I knew I didn't want to deal with it at the time because I had too much to deal with."

She did in fact have a lot to deal with: her pain, an extremely rocky marriage and three children, trying to finish training for a new career, and her mother's malignant brain tumor. She defended her strategy of repression: "Your mind has these defense mechanisms so that it knows when there's too much to handle. It's better to deal with it in a way that won't be hurting or damaging to you."

Staff members recognized the legitimacy of these complaints, advised some departing patients to continue with counseling, and invited some to join a weekly group run by Dr. B. For Nina, the evening nurse, this was connected with CPC accepting a sicker population than it once had. She felt a six-to-eight-week program would be more effective, as did many other staff members.

Confrontation, Tough Love, and Psychological Manipulations

Confrontation therapy at CPC was targeted at reducing maladaptive, self-defeating behavior. Dr. B said he "simply and directly" confronted patients with the fact that "they must give up life-styles and identities built around full-time suffering."[5] Confrontation and manipulations, along with more straightforward operant conditioning,[6] are used in pain centers for many of the same reasons they are used in substance abuse programs. An example of confrontation would be telling a patient, "If you're paid to be in pain [receiving disability or awards from litigation], you won't improve." Manipulations are attempts to dislodge the patient from a point of view or pattern of behavior by actions that are deceptive in some way.[7]

Confrontational approaches were used when the staff determined that a patient needed to be directly and strongly challenged about an attitude or behavior. This could mean simply being extraordinarily blunt; for example, during a workshop discussion of psychological contributions to pain, a patient asked how someone like himself, who had been hurt after his car was hit from the rear by another car, could have "all in your head" pain. Thomas, the psychologist leading the workshop, replied that he, too, had been in a car accident, but "mine healed, and yours didn't."

Dr. B was the lightning rod for much of the exasperation around confrontation. For example, a woman with a medication dependency said that Dr. B had made her cry and said things to her that "just floored" her. But, she added, what he had said was accurate and she had cried "because it was the truth and I didn't want to hear it. He lays things on the line, he does not bullshit; he is a very blunt person." Any number of patients spoke of coming to admire Dr. B for his ability to get past their defenses.

One man, in his last week, told of an encounter with Dr. B. during group rounds: "It was good for two weeks, three weeks and then this week's been all bad. Like he asked me today, 'How are you doing today?' I said, 'not good, it's the weather.' He said, 'Oh, it's because you're going home.' I said, 'what kind of statement is that?' And he didn't reply."

Harry had heard this exchange. "The guy in there this morning that said, 'well, it's a rainy day and I don't feel so good,' well, I don't think the guy's lying. I don't, because boy, on rainy days and damp, cold days, some days I *hurt*. And so what does [Dr. B] say to that? 'You're getting ready to go home, so you'll feel pain again.' That was his response. Now, for a physician, that's not logic, that's a bullshit story."

Even patients who disliked confrontation sometimes wondered out loud whether it might be effective. Fred thought it worked better than "the sympathy approach. In the psycho hospitals, they say 'go in and yell and scream, you'll feel better.' Here, if you go into a room and yell, staff says 'we're going to throw a rope around your neck and pull you up.' The second or third day I was having a real big headache. I was running around, cowering in the corner. [Dr. B] said, 'it ain't going to do you a bit of good. You want sympathy, you're not going to get it.' The next time I didn't yell and scream and I sat down and relaxed. It lasted twenty minutes, but it wasn't so bad."

Although some CPC staff members felt that confrontation conflicted with their training and self-image as sympathetic caretakers, all agreed that confrontation was appropriate in certain situations. "I actually think it's good to have somebody—and I don't know if it's necessary to have the good-daddy and bad-daddy sort of set-up—but I think it is good to have someone who is confrontative for these people," Georgia said. "I've heard it put this way: in this pain unit patients are motivated by getting them angry and in others they are motivated by getting them to feel some sort of positive feeling, some sort of positive emotion." Naomi thought confrontation would "mobilize some of their anger and give them some energy to fight, to prove you're wrong. I don't think there's any of us that at one time or another hasn't gotten a little extra energy to prove somebody wrong, and worked a little harder to be able to say, See?"

All staff members also agreed that confrontation was tricky. Naomi noted that they had to be pretty skilled at determining who needed hard confrontation and who needed gentle persuasion and that they did not always guess right. Several PRAs disliked the division between staff and patient that confrontation encouraged.

Staff criticisms of confrontation in the main concerned how it was handled. Tracy, the physical therapist, commented that at the same time one was being confrontational there also had to be a backup support system. Beverly, the PRA, felt that confrontation implied a lack of respect for the patient. Matthew found the tone of the unit too rough: one had to both confront and affirm; furthermore, confrontation was much more effective if an alliance had already been established. He said he struggled with knowing when to accept that a patient knew what needed to be done and simply needed encouragement. He also thought confrontation should be used only by someone trained in psychotherapy; when he saw nonpsychologically trained staff members confronting out of anger, he was troubled. (Matthew had decided to leave CPC, and the frequent use of confrontation was one of the reasons.)

Others objected to an apparent division among staff members with respect to confrontation. When only one person confronts, said Vera, a physical therapist, other staff members can believe the fantasy that they are the good guys. Yet the "bad guy" sometimes does more good for the patient than the good guy. Many commented on Dr. B's prominent role in this regard. Naomi put it delicately: "We very often depend on [Dr. B] to do the confronting." Rhonda was more abrupt: "The big boss is the big confronter, [he delivers] the one-sentence confrontation, and then walks away and leaves an angry patient." She went on to say that if other staff members were to confront to the degree Dr. B did and then walked out of the room, it would usually be counterproductive because they were the ones that had to continue with the therapy. She compared her style with Dr. B's: "I think I respect more how he does it and doesn't discuss it further, because I find that I'm more of the discusser. I was, in fact, given the award of The Perfect Bitch when he was away, and it was really funny because I thought, uh-huh, so that's the difference. He can do it, and I'm sure there have been a million terms for him, but it's different. The patient will keep me going and going with explanation and I won't get any further."

The younger staff members openly questioned whether Dr. B played the confronter too much and in an appropriate manner. Nine staff members stated outright that, while confrontation was necessary and the staff did it well overall, they had problems with at least one aspect of Dr. B's confrontational style. Nicole said, "I think he does it to the point where it makes people just run away—it's 'Yes, I'm fine, Doctor,' every morning on rounds and, in fact, they're not getting their needs met and they just slither out of the program and they'll go back to what they were doing. For some people, it does really push them right up against the wall— they break and they're willing to then pick up the pieces, take care of themselves, put the puzzle parts together in another way. But I think for a lot of them, it just sort of scares them to death, they just sit here and say, 'Yes, I'm fine,' and don't deal with it." Georgia said that sometimes Dr. B sounded downright cruel. Even Neil, a recently arrived psychologist who was extremely careful about what he said to me, disliked Dr. B's way of confronting patients; if it occurred in front of others, it violated a boundary and threatened the patient's self-esteem, confidence, and willingness to change.

First encounters with CPC's combination of strict discipline and enforced independence, here called tough love, displeased many: A man with post-herpetic neuralgia and a host of other problems recalled his first day. "I was very angry; in fact, I felt like going home. I don't mind fixing the bed, but it looks like a self-service over here. I came here to find if they can find out something to alleviate my pain, not to teach me how to be self-dependent. I'm self-dependent, I can cook, I can do anything."

The regimentation struck new arrivals forcefully. One man said, "Let's put it this way: I thought you'd get help and sympathy; when I got here I got help and regimentation. It's like the army. For me, I'm seventy-three, I can take it, but these others crack up and [drop out]—three out of ten, that's what I've heard."

Yet some approved of the tough approach from the first. "No more consoling hand holding," said Toby. "No more of the nurturance that many people were used to getting. And I agree with it, it's either go or no go." Another described the therapeutic effects of CPC's toughness on another patient: "From the outside it may look cruel, but it helps the most to help her the least."

Recall that the staff saw its task as manifold: to rehabilitate patients by training them to become independent; to address long-standing psychosocial difficulties that affected the pain problem; and to move patients away from excessive reliance on drugs, the medical system, and "pain habits." Tough love was meant to help in these goals by weaning the patients from passive and manipulative approaches to their pain problems and to caregivers. In one form or another, it figured in virtually every part of CPC's program. Manifestations of tough love ranged from a stony-faced insistence on continuing physical therapy exercises despite increased pain to day nurses ignoring patients' requests for help. Many patients found staff members' actions along these lines disagreeable and as often as not unnecessary: "They are snobbish and rude people, and I don't see the sense of it," a woman said, "Are they this way at home?" To find such people, she added, must have required searching far and wide. Patients expressed bafflement at what they saw as lack of compassion, unprofessionalism, deliberate disregard of the Hippocratic Oath, or simple meanness. Although the vast majority of patients praised at least some staff members for being supportive, lack of sympathy on the part of staff members was a constant (and unresolved) topic of conversation. Some patients noted contradictions between the educational and tough love components: "We're told to be assertive," one woman said, "but when you are, the response is disdain."[8]

CPC injected tough love messages in the way medications were handled. Patients who voiced displeasure regarding doxepin provided numerous opportunities for "reality confrontation" with staff members and fellow patients.[9] These patients were given a lecture: "It hurt my feelings," Kurt recalled, "him saying I'm going to sabotage my treatment and recovery if I don't take the Sinequan [brand name for doxepin]." A young man said he was not sure how to describe CPC's attitude toward medications — "fascist or what." Discussing medications in public was stressful, and Dr. B decided what to do without discussion: "He has changed mine four times; when I tried, one afternoon, to talk about it, he missed the appointment."

Medication decisions were indeed implemented without any discussion. (During the evening workshop on the topic, patients would howl with laughter when the discussion turned to taking responsibility toward medications and educating oneself about side effects.) Nor did patients always agree with the policy of administering medications on a fixed schedule. Yvonne, who had many headache free days, reported that Veronica, her primary nurse, had said she was manipulative because she had asked Dr. S to put her medication on prn (as needed), whereas Veronica felt she should be taking it on schedule like everybody else. Her justification was that it was a drug that was not good for her body, so if she did not have to take it she would rather not.[10]

Tough love involved encouraging self-sufficiency in virtually every activity, in part to develop lasting attitudes and habits. "It's good," one woman said. "You need strict discipline. My husband did everything." Her own story illustrated how family members can become involved in an individual's pain problem in a maladaptive way. Her husband had spent several years nursing his first wife before she died of cancer and had indeed "done everything" for his second wife after she developed several pain problems. He clearly mistrusted CPC's approach; she said, "the more I tell him about this program the more he gets really upset."

However, exercising "strict discipline" could mean conflict with such values as respect for one's elders or extending sympathy. Edward told of an encounter involving an elderly woman after group exercises. "She was having a lot of trouble getting up from the mats, no doubt in horrible pain, but the program is structured so she had to get up herself. I don't fault the therapist, she's doing her job, but I couldn't do her job."

Part of the message of self-sufficiency was that one should know when to ask for help and when to be assertive. One woman practiced this lesson at home during a leave: "The other day I said, 'Please stop that bickering, I don't need this right now.' They stopped. It was because I focused on my needs. They apologized. Before, I would have interrupted the conversation I was having and tended to them."

The emphasis on self-sufficiency brought surprise and anger when it was used as part of the efforts to get patients to focus less on their medical problems and the medical system. One man angrily told of an incident during group rounds when a fellow patient said, "I have a lump, I'd like you to look at it," and Dr. B replied, "just because you're in a hospital doesn't mean you can have everything looked at."

In their final interviews, patients were asked just how much of the tough love approach was consciously intended as part of therapy. Many remained unclear about the policy and continued to explain their experiences in terms of individual staff members' personalities, describing them as authoritarian, insensitive, or condescending. Some saw no purpose for tough love except to be "firm." Others attributed Dr. B's saying things, like "winner," "loser," and "here if you succeed, you'll succeed in the outside world" to his personal style rather than a consciously practiced technique.

One patient said he thought Dr. B probably had been "pleasant at one time" but learned he could help people more by being hard: "I think he's a great man in terms of professionalism and knowledge, and a compassionate man." Toby criticized the "contempt" many people had for Dr. B: "I could see them being angry, frustrated, maybe mad on a situational basis, but he has become symbolic of not only this place, but of the medical community in general. And I keep telling them, 'the guy's a drill sergeant, but he's no fool; if it were more appropriate for him to act like Mary Poppins, and if that were more effective, then I am rather confident he would.'"

In sum, few patients saw tough love and confrontation as conscious policies to the degree they were, although some entertained the idea. Even fewer figured out its purpose of lessening or eliminating dysfunctional adaptations to pain acquired over the months and years; and, occasionally, of provoking patients enough to force long-standing conflicts into the open so they could be addressed.

It would not be fair to say that all patient complaints about staff members reflected resistance to tough love and confrontation; bad chemistry certainly existed between certain pairs, and both staff members and patients undoubtedly made mistakes. Furthermore, staff members' personalities fell along a continuum; I heard no complaints about some staff members (Nina was one) during the entire research period. In addition, staff members did sometimes deal with patients as patients, not as people.

Manipulations—when staff members acted in a way that was duplicitous in some manner—were also intended to provoke patients into healthier attitudes and behaviors. Talking about her discharge planning meeting (held in Dr. B's office by the patient's team toward the end of a patient's stay), a woman described a technique some patients called "reverse psychology." Despite her good record, Dr. B closed her meeting saying, "I'm quite certain you'll go back to drug taking or doctor shopping." She said, very loudly, "No!" He said, "I think that's just what will happen." She replied, "You'll see!" She later commented that Dr. B "gives you the brush-off; you feel as though he doesn't care. But he wants to give you a final push, to get you over the hump, so you can focus on something else. He tries to out-psych you, to antagonize you, just to get you to do the opposite, to put you in a rage to fight back, get you out of the stuck position you're in."

Several patients quite clearly saw the deliberate technique behind such behavior. Eleanor noted, "[Dr. B] does an awful lot of stuff that you *know* he is doing on purpose." Edward found that figuring out this part of CPC's approach helped him adjust: "And the more I understood, the easier it was for me in the program; I found it easier to roll with the punches in situations that at first glance were totally irrational; but then you looked at it and you realized it was a set-up—a set-up confrontation designed to provoke a response. So you kind of stepped back a little and watched it for what it was, and accepted it for what it was, and then in turn watched some of the reactions. [Dr. B] uses it quite often with people to get them off their tails and get them rolling, doing something. It hasn't always worked, but I'm sure it wouldn't always work."

However, a very bright, psychologically aware young woman who understood CPC "set-ups" as well as Edward commented: "I don't have problems in general with rules and authority structures. Maybe I know too much. It drives me crazy; I find it very humiliating for that person when they're being manipulated."

Fred described an encounter with Dr. B during a migraine: "I had my first headache the third day. Usually I'd yell and scream and holler my brains out. He used reverse psychology and said, 'Go ahead, yell your head off, you're only killing yourself.' So I started thinking, 'who the hell does he think he is?' I walked up to him and said, 'Do you think that this reverse psychology will work? Well, I'm going to show you you're right and that I'm a better man than you are.' So two weeks later he said, 'You look like you're doing one hundred percent.' I should have had him go down on his knees and kiss my feet."

Patients usually noticed the kind of manipulation in which staff members made a concerted effort to send a message, loud and clear. This happened to Kurt, who resisted the idea that he was depressed and did not see himself as one of those "paid to be in pain." He complained of being continually "tested," that everyone had been "on my case" including Tracy, his physical therapist. When he mentioned Dr. B's sarcasm to her, she had said, "You must be depressed, you've got a problem because you're always complaining." At one point, Kurt said, he had "turned the tables on them" by asking Dr. S, "if you grew up in a depressed home, wouldn't you become depressed because of the situation?" Dr. S agreed. Kurt then asked, "then why is it when you come here, everybody tells you you're depressed?"—in effect arguing that this would make a person depressed even if they had not been before. Kurt had said he was worried about being discharged with no limitations specified in his medical record—and staff members had told him this was likely.

Kurt's roommate, Edward, who said manipulation had been effective for him, reported that it had simply made Kurt more belligerent: "I saw it as being done to goad him or to push him into thinking about retraining, about doing something with the rest of his life instead of just collecting his retirement and working on the side, you know, working under the table. And becoming more productive. And he was very, very depressed about that. And he had me scared because I had never seen him that down in the dumps. He withdrew, someone who was a very open, jovial, happy-go-lucky guy. I was keeping both eyes on him half the time because I just wasn't quite sure what to expect from him. And he pulled out of it, and it just was disquieting to see it pushed him that far."

Kurt's fellow patients thought he had made excellent progress in physical therapy. But he himself and his wife left very unhappy with the experience. On the day Kurt was discharged, staff members said he had some limitations after all. Edward said Kurt was relieved, but "more than being relieved, he was saying, 'the fools.' You know, he was quite put out that they had played a game with him, he really did not like the whole idea of playing a game."

Manipulation was also used in medication policy. A substantial number of patients complained that staff members used medications to punish assertive behavior. (This was denied by Dr. B.) For example, one woman was disgruntled with the way CPC had arranged her visit to another hospital for X-rays. When fellow patients suggested she go to Dr. B "one-on-one," she replied, " 'I can't do that, he'll just up my Sinequan."

Edward told of a woman who was "not thrilled" with the medication that she was on. "She was flat-out, upright honest, and she said that she wasn't feeling good and she hadn't slept well and [Dr. B said] 'just double it.' And if he had slapped her in the face I don't think he could have hurt her any more. Some of that emphasis, I think, was designed to provoke a response."

Patients complained vociferously about the large amounts of stress produced by tough love, confrontations, and manipulations. But staff members definitely considered this stress beneficial in the long run. Neil, a psychologist, commented that "if they can endure the program, they leave in a much more coping mode."

The Love and Acceptance Component

It is worth repeating that virtually all patients—including many who did not like CPC—praised at least one staff member, with Dr. B often heading the list, for being nurturing despite the tough love and manipulations that went on. (Indeed, most patients acknowledged that the staff was dedicated and supportive and had a difficult job.) A woman singled out Nina: unlike "the others on the swing shift, she's completely different, she'll hug and kiss you."

Beverly's description of CPC philosophy illustrates what I am calling the "love-and-acceptance" perspective: "We try to instill in people here a new frame of mind, which is good; self-esteem. People leave here knowing that they are worth something and that they can do something for themselves and make life better. That the pain doesn't have to control them, they can control the pain."

Georgia's description is similar: "It's very important to get in touch with oneself, with how to be true to oneself and one's needs, as a human being. And all human beings need nurturing, all human beings have particular interests and desires that have to be acted upon. In a way, [patients] are trying to give more of themselves, give themselves away to other people when they haven't given enough to themselves. I think that very often it's not necessarily their fault—I don't think it's their fault at all that they are the way they are, that it's very much a product of society."

In addition to "love and acceptance" from certain individual staff members, the program contained a few activities that could be characterized this way. Most of these occurred in the evenings. For example, patients reported feeling completely comfortable with the PRA who accompanied them on the weekly outing (usually Georgia or Beverly)— there was no pushing or prodding; everyone, for three hours, was an equal. Massage with ice and especially oil were also examples of nurturing and "loving" activities performed by staff members for patients.

Finally, while most of the discourse about pain at CPC was set in either standard medico-scientific or psychotherapeutic terms, a couple of the evening workshops drew on the understandings of alternative medicine and emphasized support and love.[11] It is noteworthy that, while patients sometimes found the material offered in CPC seminars and workshops incorrect, inconsistent, offensive, and unethical, no one ever complained about the "love and acceptance" workshops. For example, Georgia's monthly evening workshop on "love therapy" was a noteworthy contrast to the tough love dished out during the day, in part because it espoused alternative therapies and in part because it contradicted—perhaps subverted—some CPC policies. Georgia would begin by discussing books that emphasize the healing power of self-acceptance and a supportive environment.[12] She also talked of Norman Cousins's discussion of studies that showed increased patient improvement in hospital settings that were less institutional,[13] where there was good food, windows with views, artwork on the walls, and so forth, a listing that always elicited snorts of laughter from patients.

At the end of the workshop, Georgia would mention the guilt people suffering chronic pain often feel. Reflecting on this, one man said that probably everyone felt guilty when they started to improve. Finding out that with ice and physical therapy you could do the things you hadn't been able to do before made you feel bad. People had to deal with "years of waste, or certainly a diminished capacity." Or surgery they hadn't needed, which had been true for him—he said he had "surrendered" to his surgeon and should have gotten a second opinion. Thus CPC's message could feel empowering, or the opposite, because such guilt could be incapacitating. CPC's message was confusing, he continued, because patients were told, "accept yourself the way you are, but you have to change." This comment nicely captures one of the contradictions CPC patients played out when trying to put the program's philosophy into practice.

Patients approved of Georgia's performance (which included wearing a clown mask and handing our Hershey Kisses). But one extremely sharpwitted woman examined the implications of Georgia's message by asking, "what if you can't do that?" She was concerned about the possibility of buying into a "love and acceptance" idea of etiology and treatment and becoming even more demoralized when she found she was not getting well. Of course, many authors address this extremely thorny issue, including Bernie Siegel, also mentioned in Georgia's workshop, whose "exceptional cancer patients" do not necessarily see their cancer go into remission.[14] This issue was a very real one for CPC converts when they fully realized that, even though they had come to accept CPC's approach, they would still leave with serious pain; somehow, they hadn't been able to "love and accept" themselves enough to make it go away.[15] Self-help and inspirational books and articles, insofar as they suggest that disease is a direct reflection of mental state, are damaging, as they assign blame to those who "fail" to improve.

Conclusions

CPC addressed pain in a multidisciplinary, comprehensive way. In practice, the various components did not exactly form a seamless whole. CPC staff members' instructions to patients were often murky, at worst even contradictory, so patients frequently commented about how confused they were. Those who said they had the program's message all down would contradict themselves later. Simply being told they must stop being passive patients and wean themselves of an overreliance on the medical system was confusing in itself, given that most saw their problem in organic terms and were, after all, in a hospital.

Part of the effort involved teaching. Teaching about the "whole vicious cycle . . . pain, depression, anxiety . . . narcotics . . . teaching them how to take care of themselves in an emotional way" (as Linda, a nurse, put it); teaching them "a whole different way of trying to live," as Donna, a PRA, put it.

Part of the effort involved patients digging deep into their psyches, uncovering wounds that had not healed. Another effort was to make patients more self-aware. Donna noted that most patients found it difficult to "even notice what emotions they are feeling—just naming what they feel, that's the first one. And then once you know what you are feeling, you can choose whether or not to act out of that feeling or to act out of a different motive, a different potential." Getting patients to move to a more internal locus of control regarding pain and their approach to life was another goal. Neil spoke of this as empowerment over the way you live your life.

Tough love and the confrontations and manipulations created a kind of barricade between staff and patients. (A certain amount of disagreement between staff members and patients can be found in any rehabilitation facility, more in therapeutic communities, especially substance abuse programs.) We saw Naomi defend the barricade in terms of therapeutic goals: otherwise, the staff would do too much for patients. In contrast, Donna found it perplexing and felt it interfered with her cognitive therapy work. Yet in institutional settings characterized by a pronounced and rigid authority structure questions must be asked about abuse of power and policies that serve institutional interests rather than those of the clients. CPC patients struggled mightily with this issue. They were, first, *patients*, who were in a total institution so rigid that some compared it to a prison.[16] Also, they were in a program that, as PRA Polly said, was like no other and hence scared patients. What the program offered was not crystal clear, and there certainly were neither guarantees nor clear guidelines for successfully completing it. Furthermore, for various reasons (some of them at least ostensibly therapeutic) the program was, as Kenneth put it, "assault and battery" on a patient.

This little world presents us with a beautiful example of the dynamics of hegemony (a system of domination accepted as just and proper by those subordinated within it) and counter-hegemony (pockets of resistance in such a system). Power and authority were abundantly present in the metaphors patients used: detention center, school, mental hospital, boot camp—even, if one thinks about it, summer camp. CPC, being a pain center, was actually none of these, yet here, too, authority was very asymmetrically distributed and very inflexible. Few mechanisms existed for challenging the structure or contesting the ideology. Often dissent was redefined as further evidence of a patient's personality and emotional problems. Bloor and his coauthors found this to be a characteristic of many therapeutic communities; they call it "redefinitional work."[17]

Yet patients tried. Rightly or wrongly, they interpreted staff members' actions in terms of institutional self-protection ("every day they have to write down they took you off of something," "justifying their role by forcing you to believe you're depressed"); or in terms of putting what society needs foremost, as when patients complained that all CPC wanted was to get them back to full-time employment, or that CPC's notion of success was similar to "brainwashing" military recruits to get them ready to die in combat. A related issue was how the medical system shifted blame for a condition onto a patient when doctors failed to find what was wrong. Sometimes complaints were about individuals in authority who went against the program's therapeutic policies: told to be assertive, patients complained of subsequently "being treated like an idiot" or punished for such impudence by having their doxepin dose increased.

What was especially interesting about the exchanges at CPC was the interweave of opposing roles played by both staff members and patients. CPC saw itself as contesting received medical wisdom, yet it participated in perpetuating many of these structures and ideologies, sometimes un-intentionally and sometimes because it was powerless to do otherwise. Patients at times played the role of "good little patients," compliant, eager to please the authority figures to avoid having a "bad mark" on their records. Yet at other times, incensed, they resisted and emotion-ally acted out like five-year-olds, or sounded quite adult and quite con-vincing in their critiques. Also, although many patients wanted to avoid being the target of the program's confrontative tactics enough to mis-represent their condition, many others did not necessarily want to please the staff or look good in this fashion; some felt they needed to show they were *not* fine in order to ensure disability payments. And a few obviously wanted to prove that theirs was a hopeless case.

Clearly, despite younger staff members' efforts to promote the "love and acceptance" approach, the program did not try to be user-friendly; it provided a treatment approach that aimed at winning over patients by being successful. This, among many other reasons, made evaluating its success difficult. Matthew put it this way: "Ultimately, progress or lack of progress on the part of the patients here is as much their responsi-bility as the program's. And I know that in some ways that sounds like a cop-out, because it is our job to make people better. But you can't make anyone better who doesn't really want to get better, who has invested in being ill, invested in being in pain in some way." Is this an example of "blaming the victim" or describing a feature potentially present in all cases of illness? Matthew's comment illustrates the ambiguity—slipperi-ness, some said—of CPC's ideology, and why we can see it as a microcosm of the way chronic pain (and, sometimes, chronic illness in general) is looked on in the larger society.

Chapter 5
Building and Resisting Community

"Well, once in a while they'll say 'concentration camp,' or one group
of patients not too long ago called it 'Camp Lejeune' [a Marine boot
camp]. But usually it's associated with letting down their hair, being
themselves, fun, they'll pull pranks, short-sheet beds, do things like
that."

—Naomi

T. F. Main, a physician working with demoralized British soldiers after
World War II, first applied the term "therapeutic community" to describe a "spontaneous and emotionally structured (rather than a medically dictated) organization in which all staff and patients engaged."[1]
Maxwell Jones developed the idea further during the 1950s at Belmont
Hospital, on an inpatient psychiatric unit.[2] Today, however, most therapeutic communities found in hospital settings are not located in psychiatric units. Bloor and his collaborators discuss how "redefinition" is the
"motor of therapy" in such settings. Incoming patients are inducted into
a "new social world" emphatically different from their old world;[3] they
encounter new ways of seeing and describing social life and their place
in it. In this treatment setting, modification of patients' social conduct,
and with it their way of relating to others and their felt social identity, *is*
the treatment.[4] The therapeutic community is a mirror reflecting back
patients' problems, which are not considered to be abstracted biological
malfunctions, but part and parcel of patients' everyday understandings
and behavior.

CPC differed in certain ways from the original model of therapeutic community established and promulgated by Maxwell Jones. Robert
Rapoport, an anthropologist who studied Belmont House, characterizes
it as espousing democracy and permissiveness as well as "communal-
ism."[5] Permissiveness did not characterize CPC in any way, and democ-

racy was only paid lip service. Whereas at Belmont House and similar institutions everyone addressed everyone else by first name, at CPC staff members with M.D.s were addressed as "Doctor."[6] In addition, while the ideal therapeutic community is supposed to emphasize sociotherapy, for various reasons in treatment centers like CPC psychotherapeutic norms become strongly established, facilitating development of "sick roles," which the early therapeutic community movement sought to eradicate, emphasizing rather the creative and active side of the patient.[7]

With respect to CPC's qualifying as a community per se, neither the collectivity of patients and staff nor the one comprised only of patients succeeded in most senses. Even when compared to other therapeutic communities, CPC's was especially unusual, artificial, and fragile. At any given time the patient community was quite heterogeneous, due to differences in age, medical condition, social class, and so on.[8] The program lasted only a month, and staggered admissions meant that its composition changed every few days. The high rate of individuals leaving early increased the turnover rate, and some of those who stayed did so only because they feared they would lose benefits. Furthermore, pain sufferers' reasons for opting for the CPC program (to get help with a pain problem, hope for a high disability rating) had nothing to do with its community component. Indeed, some of them feared this aspect of it and chose to be admitted only because they "had nowhere left to turn." Some of the communal experience was imposed by the program's design, some of the language about community was part of the package of therapeutic ideology delivered to patients on arrival, and some of the cohesion and solidarity was generated by a manipulative and authoritarian staff who behaved that way in order to help construct barricades to foster such feelings. Finally, whatever the strength of patients' communal experiences while on the unit, it turned into a memory upon discharge.

Yet patients raved about the community, and staff members said it accomplished most of the therapeutic work. In order to reconcile this discrepancy, we need to employ a subjective, discourse-focused definition of "community": a group of people who interact intensively who feel they constitute a community—who, more than a random aggregate of people, feel they have a collective purpose, shared understandings about proper and improper behavior, and strong feelings about one another.

Staff members (and patients repeating the program) often commented that the effectiveness of the program varied directly with the strength of the patient community. The nature of a given community was mostly determined by several factors: individual patient personalities; intragroup dynamics—whether a strong core of patients formed because of good chemistry; patient-staff relations, in terms of both individual encounters and the entire patient community vis à vis the staff; specific events that galvanized or demoralized the community; and changes in CPC policy and the staff over time. However, these configurations were quite ephemeral because the composition of the community changed every three or four days.

Patient Reactions

For some patients, the community provided support by accepting them as they were: "there's nobody pointing a finger and judging." The contrast with home and family was sometimes particularly striking. A man who had known eleven years of pain following a stroke said that, whereas at home when he would talk about his pain people would laugh at him, saying it was imagined, at CPC people listened. A woman's husband "threw away all my medications, and I think he feels when I come home I'm going to be fine, even my blood pressure and my diabetes are going to go away." In contrast, fellow CPC patients knew what she was going through. Edward recalled that outside, the fact that he was in litigation had produced unwelcome comments, but at CPC nobody said "this is a good racket," or "you've got a good thing going." Sadly, everybody was saying the opposite, "this really stinks, it really stinks."

Some spoke about how quickly feelings of intimacy sprang up among community members. Here is Ethan, with his typical hyperbole: "When I leave here twenty days from now, I will never see another one of these people again unless it's casual or unless they initiate it. And yet, the relationships are as deep and as intimate as exist on this planet."[9]

Rebecca said that she and other women at times would hang out together: going downstairs to raid the vending machines when they were on diets and had no business there; sitting and talking about missing their children or boyfriends or husbands; being "just really silly and giggly." A couple of times she had found herself with three other women all on one bed, all trying to fit, talking and laughing. However, she added that they were not just trying to comfort each other all the time. There were little squabbles and gossip; being human, they would get angry and then make up.

Sometimes the support would be nonverbal. Rebecca commented on the unspoken language shared by chronic pain patients: "a look or a certain tone of someone's voice, and you just reach out and just hold their hand, and it makes all the difference in the world."

And laughter was not all that rare; one man found out that no matter how much you were hurting, you could sit around and "laugh like mad." He told of how an elderly woman, who was always going to the wrong place, went to psychomotor by mistake one night before Raquel, the leader, got there, and proceeded to sit in Raquel's chair and run the session: "It was hilarious."

Many patients also commented on a high level of patient solidarity; for example, right before meetings patients would round up everyone to avoid getting "black marks" for lateness. The feeling of being strongly supported prevailed even when it took the form of pressure. One woman described the "astounding" power of the community to motivate: "I guess it's like that of these Jim Jones fanatic religious groups in a sense. Ultimately it's being put towards a very constructive purpose." Linda, a CPC nurse, spoke of peer pressure felt by recent arrivals: if on their first morning they tried to "goof off" and run around in pajamas or act like guests in a hotel, they stopped, because they didn't want to be embarrassed or made to look like children in front of disapproving fellow patients.

Reactions to friends being discharged illustrate how many came to need the community. A woman said she was missing her three recently discharged friends more than she missed her friends back home.[10]

Some patients commented favorably on the variety of backgrounds. Eleanor, whose interests were sculpting and horseback riding, commented: "When I first walked in the door I didn't think I would find anyone I could relate to, and, of course, as time wears on, you do. The things I'm involved in are not things that a lot of people here are involved in, and I found that it's not those involvements you respond to, it's a whole other layer. The pain, and having children—I mean, there are other issues of being a human being that are a common ground. And when you are in a position where those things are very important, you talk about them, whereas in the outside world you might talk about what you do, rather than what you feel. You get to know people much more intimately; if you tried to get to know them that way at a cocktail party, they'd think you were crazy. Not that I go to cocktail parties."

Some were more ambivalent about the diversity. A life-in-the-fast-lane New Yorker said, "It may seem very snobbish, but I feel like a foreigner. I've never met people like this—living in a mobile home in Alaska, a construction worker. Some are fascinating, yes, as human beings some are great." Terence, the M.D., admitted, "these are kind and good people but there isn't much to talk about. I said to myself, 'I can be a snob and not associate with them, or I can relate at that level."

An elderly woman said, "It never occurred to me that, in general, the blue-collar person does not think in abstractions of any kind. I have heard no political discussion, except when I've introduced it and then it's been no discussion, it lies there on the floor. In other words, the whole pattern of socialization is quite different from anything I've ever experienced before—and very rewarding. It's interesting how pleasant conversation without abstractions can be."

And some were disapproving. One woman wondered why Dr. B admitted "truck drivers," whose "level was so low," or a woman "who swore" and whose "husband is a mortician."

Learning from one's fellows was another often-heard theme. Ethan said that, while he listened to what those he respected had to say to him, most of what he learned came from simply drawing parallels between himself and them, learning from what they said, how they moved, learning how much pain some people were in, and seeing them go on, even though they knew they would have it forever. Some saw warnings: "I could see myself on a downhill slide, it was getting harder and harder to push myself to do what I did. And after coming in here and seeing a few people, I said, 'yeah, if [my trajectory] had gone on for a while longer, that [depressed person] could have been me.'" Finally, a man said that after seeing what his fellow patients managed to do he had concluded that if he could not do it there was something wrong with his head. (Note he is saying that if he does not improve, even though other patients' progress motivates him, *then* there is something wrong with his head—a complete reversal of the view most patients held on admission.)

Many found just seeing others with worse problems beneficial. A man with severe complications from a blocked pancreatic duct said to Barry, a paraplegic with only partial use of his arms, "there's nothing wrong with me compared to you."

Not all the lessons learned seemed entirely welcome. One man felt his fellow patients were so tired of hearing his complaints that he would have to lie to them in order for them not to scatter into their rooms when they saw him coming down the corridor; he'd have to smile and say he was "dynamite."

Participating in the community produced other kinds of negative reactions as well. Some recent arrivals needed time to adjust. For example, Franklin said he found it a bit intimidating at first. The very variety of backgrounds and interests among patients that pleased many patients presented a problem for some. Mary explained that in addition to the stress of pain, she was dealing with personalities that were unlike hers, and being in a weakened emotional state heightened her vulnerability. Sometimes she did not feel strong enough to say, "I don't feel like listening to you" or "why don't you look on the bright side of things?" She also said she was leery about giving advice because, after all, she was living with these people in an already stress-filled environment. To risk eliciting reactions like "Oh, she doesn't like me," or "Who the hell are you to say that to me?" would be foolish. Patients did flock to Mary with their troubles; she herself said she was hyper-nurturant. (A staff member characterized many of the nurses admitted as patients to CPC as very invested in caregiving. Health professionals, whose job is to provide care, were over-represented at CPC.)

Patients complained about their fellows the way people anywhere do: about their personalities, their stupidity, their values, their habits. Ethan described a psychomotor session with "a bunch of people feeling threatened by talking about emotional stuff, but with no real emotional content. A bunch of people talking about emotional stuff not to work it through, but simply to be the center of attention. It's just what people do, it's no fucking different." [11]

People who left early usually objected to some aspect of the formal program, but some said they simply did not like being in a group of people in so much pain. Ethan read a letter from a woman who dropped out, though she had made progress, saying that being around so much pain was ripping her up emotionally. The staff's interpretations of this woman's departure were that the moment had come in her progress (she had been admitted in a wheelchair but had not used it at all during her first week) when she saw the need for a radical change in her life, and saw that she could have avoided or lessened much of the suffering she had gone through before being admitted. The prospect of these changes overwhelmed her and she opted to avoid them.

The single trait that drew most complaint was "negativity." Patients who thought themselves worse off than anyone else. Patients who were not motivated. Patients with one-track minds. A sort of "winners and losers" discourse appeared fairly frequently (as we have seen, encouraged by Dr. B), with remarks like: "It's like life. You have to stay with the winners." Yet "negative" patients enjoyed a certain solidarity as well. A young woman described how she and her friends would "sit around together and rip everyone on the staff apart." [12]

One woman who heard that others complained about her smiling all the time said she did not see why she should be negative; she was naturally cheerful. She was, predictably, given a roommate who was very negative, and her heartfelt, eloquent reaction was much like other reactions to difficult roommates: "I had to get out of there because it's too negative, I couldn't take all this negative. If there were to be a little pin drop at the end of that tunnel, I would have stuck it out. I was going to pack my bags and leave." After this roommate left she was assigned an equally difficult roommate: "If I talked to her, I was digging; if I didn't talk to her, I didn't like her. My husband came in and he knew, 'get out of this room.'" But she stuck it out.

Negative patients were especially hard on newcomers. One recent arrival said that some of the highly critical patients got her very discouraged because they sounded so sure of what they were saying. "But then I realized, I'm here for me; I have to get out of it what I can."

Excessively negative patients eventually became isolated. Davie said it was surprising how supportive the community was to anyone who was trying, but those who "sniveled and complained all the time" were ostracized and left early.

We have also seen that in a few instances patients not only felt no solidarity with others but found that comparing themselves to fellow patients made them feel bad, as did Yvonne, who felt more responsible for her cluster headaches and depression than patients who had been in car accidents.

A related issue was the idea that some patients were admitted simply because they wanted to be on the unit, unlike those who were there because they saw no alternative. Surprisingly—because virtually all patients found the CPC program extremely tough—every so often a patient would indicate that another patient was in the program because it was comfortable: "They have it cozy here, a little nest, their needs taken care of." Some patients thought this was impossible, but others, like Harry, agreed: "Another thing I've seen here, a lot of people fake it. They come here on the assumption that this is a good place to be, 'I can get along, I can work out real good.' And when they leave they have a 100 percent improvement, and that really looks good."

"Why would somebody come here and get pushed and shoved around and eat crappy food if they're faking it? What's in it for them?"

"To prove to themselves that they can be a success story and show other people how wonderful they are, like the doctors, 'Oh, you've done a great job.' "

For most of the patients who entered saying they had a medication problem, dependency involved prescription medications. For the most part their fellow patients were sympathetic; at times patients who had once had a drug or alcohol problem would become buddies with a person struggling with a dependency, supporting him or her through detox.[13] But some patients were intolerant; one man, describing such patients as "addicts,"[14] said they were partly to blame.

Over the period of research four patients appeared who were solidly into the recreational drug subculture and elicited a great deal of opprobrium when illegal drugs were discovered. These four were especially manipulative and untruthful; at times it seemed they needed to con other people as much as they needed drugs. The exasperated response to these patients contrasted sharply with the support patients normally extended to one another, despite defensive postures and mistakes.

One evening one of these, a young woman, became extremely abusive and violent after a fellow patient gave her street drugs, putting the entire unit in an uproar. The two were discharged the next day, shunned by their fellows, who had difficulty seeing any similarity between these young women's problems and their own. Several complained that such people destroyed the community and should have been sent to a drug rehabilitation center first (a point also made by several staff members during interviews).

After Ursula overdosed on illegally-acquired drugs (she herself was not sure whether she intended to commit suicide), her roommate said, "These people with the negative attitudes really bug me. They say, 'No one understands,' they think they're the worst off. They *can* talk up a good story about how they're feeling, and it's not so. I felt betrayed—I thought I *knew* her."

"Negative community"—a phrase heard quite often—referred to a perception of a collective negative attitude. Patients often spoke regretfully of the dissolution of the group they had helped form as its senior members were discharged, and of the new group as negative, failing to cohere, or forming in opposition to the staff because of the attitude of recent arrivals. A very embittered paraplegic who left the program extremely disappointed said that at first he had been with a good group, and that if he could have stayed with those people throughout he would have been helped. "But now, forget it. They sit around and argue about whose pain is worse." Another man said that when he came in he had met people he hated to see leave, but some of the new ones fouled up the atmosphere.

Indeed, this kind of complaint was so common, and its opposite so rare, it seems clear that the pattern has more to do with the dynamics of being a new patient versus an "old hand" than with any objective decline in the quality of the community. New arrivals tended to be evaluated in terms of personality rather than as people going through the difficult first week; patients seemed to forget that they themselves had been negative and withdrawn at first, and that most of them had, over the course of the month, come out of their shells and increased their participation in the community. Many thought that negative feelings in the community were partly the result of so many patients leaving early. It does seem likely that this made the first week even more difficult and more of a probationary period. Perhaps patients further along, together with their warm welcomes, were also taking a wait-and-see attitude: this person may decide to leave, so why invest?

Community and Therapy

Some patients favorably compared CPC to other kinds of inpatient units. One man had been in the hospital's substance abuse unit on another floor, where, he said, not everyone felt they had a common problem, whereas what CPC patients shared was abundantly clear to all. A patient who was also a psychotherapist with professional experience in other kinds of inpatient units found CPC patients to be more caring for one another than in other therapeutic communities.

As noted, most patients felt that being in a community had helped them improve. Many changes in thinking about pain, particularly about one's own pain, came from interactions with other patients. Fred talked about patients who had preceded him being able, at the end, to "stand up tall and say, 'I'm Ok, I'm hurtin' for certain, but no one can tell.'" (Note that this imaginary patient could teach Fred only by disclosing that he or she had pain.)

Individual patients often maintained that "my case is different," but toward the end of their stay many acknowledged, however, somewhat ruefully, that they had come to recognize similarities between their own previous behaviors and attitudes and those they witnessed in other patients, often recently arrived, and that this recognition had been an impetus for change. Franklin said being with some fellow patients felt like looking through a window and seeing himself before he came in: full of self-pity, withdrawn, feeling that his problem was worse than anyone else's. Edward analyzed this process from a very self-aware perspective: "We're all in the same boat, but it's easier to say that 'that guy has a problem.' And then half an hour later you say, 'that sounds familiar, I wonder why?'"[15]

The story of a young woman with migraines who left the program early offers an example of learning about psychogenic influences by watching others. A fellow patient concluded that this young woman's problem "is all psychosomatic—like they really feel the pain, but instead of physically, it's all kind of mentally. Like this one patient who lost her mother, and everything was dumped on her lap and I think this is when her headaches began. Her mother had been on a cruise and hadn't even gotten home yet and she got killed on the bus. And [the patient] had to handle everything, the poor kid. So I think this is when her headaches started." An older woman referred to this patient as someone who had had a really severe arrested development because of things that had happened to her at a certain stage, and that until she could work that through, her pain was very necessary to her, although another part of her certainly wanted to get rid of it.

Another patient with migraines, who was unhappy with her marriage and thinking about divorce but feeling very dependent on her husband, commented that since everyone was in the same boat she could study them. Asked why, she replied, "Pain—why they have pain. It's usually very similar, they lost control someplace."

Many felt that the community kept the difficult aspects of the CPC program from overwhelming them and impeding therapy. For Barry, having that vent meant that frustrations and anger were not internalized or directed at the staff. Several patients called up an image of the patients organizing against the staff—doubtless a pleasant fantasy at times. One man, for example, said that staggering admissions was a good idea because if patients all came at the same time they would be rebelling and ganging up on the doctors.

Many were proud of playing a helping role. A psychologically sophisticated woman said she had helped others a lot; she found it easy to solve other people's problems and it was a great distraction from her own. Not all offers of help succeeded, however: "We've tried, but what she wants is something that's up there in the past that's never going to come" was the comment about a young woman with migraines and epilepsy following brain surgery, and a sad family situation.

Some patients drew on their own experiences to encourage new arrivals. One woman told a new patient to go out to a restaurant on the Wednesday outing, saying she had done it a few weeks earlier and that, although the first time she went out she had been a "basket case," the next time she had been only half a basket case. The patient took the advice and, although she was indeed a basket case the next morning, she was glad she had gone out.

Patients were also aware of imitating the staff. Fred said he had learned to inject a little tough love into his offers of help: "I'd start to behave like the staff: 'Ah, shut up, if you're hurting, you're hurting. You have to mellow out, crying makes it hurt worse.'" Indeed, it was striking to see how some of those patients who most resisted staff members' definitions of their problems were such excellent salespeople of the CPC approach to fellow patients. For example, Fred reported that Davie told him that if he didn't give 100 percent, the only one he would "be screwing" would be himself. "So I started giving all. 'If it helps, fine, if it doesn't, it doesn't,' I said." Yet the staff found Davie so disruptive that, during a special meeting involving both the staff and the patients, Dr. B told Davie he was being discharged that day (this was probably a manipulation). Davie resisted, calling his lawyer and complaining to the hospital administration, and was allowed to stay. Davie continued to resist much of the CPC's approach throughout his stay, but many patients told me how tough he had been with them and how he had encouraged them to "get into the program, give it 110 percent."

This mixture of attraction and avoidance in some patients may have been a stage in their coming to accept at least part of CPC's position on chronic pain. Denying and resisting staff messages, yet giving the same advice to fellow patients, might indicate that they were not quite ready to accept their pain as less "real" than they had thought, but *had* come to see that some of their fellow patients' pain problem might respond to some of the nonphysical therapies offered. Staff members probably saw Davie as a "patient therapist"—someone who hid behind others' problems.[16]

Community Compared to the Staff

Most patients at one time or another compared the community to the staff. Many maintained that the common experience of chronic pain meant patients could offer more help and understanding than the staff could.[17] Some comparisons were more critical. A nurse who clearly had a crush on Dr. B said she was disappointed that he did not interact more with patients—he seemed to be looking down his nose at them. She ended up feeling the community had helped her more than he had.

Yet other patients found the staff more helpful than the patient community. One woman said that "you have to listen to your staff," because they knew what they were doing and, after all, her insurance company was paying a lot of money. Some patients who affirmed that the community had been supportive did not see this as having contributed to their improvement, and credited any progress to staff members' efforts. Certainly many patients said they had discovered it was better to listen to the staff than to negative patients.

Many patients felt that the amount of opposition that appeared between the patient community and the staff was inappropriate; there was a possible need for separation, but it was overdone: "A line has to be drawn, but not a wall built." But a few commented that, while they resented the division, they had come to understand that it was therapeutic.

Division could become quite overt. Several spoke of how the community helped with problems caused by inappropriate behavior by staff members. Davie, the exceptionally angry patient threatened with discharge for being so negative, defended himself, saying that, although Dr. B found him disruptive, the community had unanimously voted him back in as president of the patient community, taking his side.

Finally, some patients saw a sort of synthesis: one woman said that the staff knew the techniques that were likely to work to help get the pain under control, whereas the community had a much better feeling of what a lot of the ramifications of patients' pain issues were. In a way, she said, the staff worked at an intellectual level and patients worked at a gut level; together they made a very effective combination.

Patients speculated about the degree to which community dynamics, in particular the features that built patient solidarity, were a planned feature of the program. Several felt that the community grew stronger in reaction to "attacks" from the staff but did not see this as built into the program's design. Barry doubted that Dr. B and his staff were fully aware of the group dynamic, which probably had not been a part of the program's original design but over time had evolved into the most motivating force in the program. Thus, while some patients saw the patient community as strong and united because of its need to oppose the staff and their tough love harshness, none saw the division as a planned feature to the degree it was.

But we have seen that patient solidarity was vulnerable to many divisive forces—for example, patients complaining about other patients "faking it," pretending to feel better than they actually did to get staff approval.[18] This kind of hypocrisy was mentioned by many, especially with respect to the good-bye speeches departing patients read on Fridays, which contained no mention of the problems they had complained about during their stay. The good-bye speeches—and patients' gripes about how hypocritical some of them were—illustrate some of the tensions in the milieu therapy arrangement at places like CPC. As we have seen, patients complained about negativity in other patients, in particular about its effect on new patients. Certainly, there was pressure to be upbeat, to "get into the program," to "not go on and on," to not compete by saying "my pain is the worst," and so forth. Good-bye speeches were intended to provide a forum for patients to tell their story and evaluate their own progress, thank staff members who had been helpful, and offer constructive criticism of the program. They were also intended to encourage patients who were not ready to leave and, occasionally, to justify the CPC program to outside evaluators (the written-out speeches were kept on file). As a goodly number of patients ready for discharge were disappointed with their continuing levels of pain or other problems, it is understandable that many felt in a bind about this speech.

This conflict—between what one owes to the community in terms of being honest and what one owes to it in terms of not being negative—is very similar to the quandaries many patients reported experiencing on the outside prior to admission: the recurring question of how much to disclose. So the question of whether to "tell it like it really is" or to avoid appearing like a "loser" was a lightning rod for many of the tensions the community dealt with as a whole.

Pain Behavior and the Dilemma of "Real Pain"

As we have seen, patients often mentioned that part of the support they experienced was feeling believed. Most were interested in having their pain seen in medical terms by both members and fellow patients. This was also a goal of the patient community as a whole when it attempted to construct "real pain" as a shared symbol. The struggle to have "real pain" affirmed affected the formation and functioning of the patient community in two important respects: first, much of the opposition between staff and patients revolved around this issue; second, questions about fellow patients' pain as "real" or not profoundly affected the sources and limits of patient solidarity.

Initially patients viewed other patients as having a legitimate organic complaint and as sources of support for their own claims to having "real pain." Teresa, recently admitted, said everyone she'd seen was in pain, physical pain—not an emotional, or psychosomatic, or attention-getting kind of thing. Being believed or not was a problem, of course, because of pain's invisibility. Such problems helped forge the bonds to fellow patients. And we have seen that many recently admitted patients noted that at CPC "it's Ok to show your pain."

But pain behavior and the community's reaction to it were not so simple a matter. Many patients who initially reported feeling accepted and believed soon found themselves struggling in some way for credibility with *both* patients and the staff. Ethan remarked early in his stay that CPC was a place where, when you hurt, you could simply stand up in the middle of a conversation and say, "Excuse me," and walk away and go lie down and nobody would stop you. But he was apparently beginning to feel pressure from other patients to sit or stand rather than lie down, as he added that he sometimes was teased a little harder than he liked.

Issues involving visibility and pain behavior were a concern to all. Some felt that all bad pain was apparent even in those patients who worked hard not to show it. But many patients felt that such visual cues were not always present.

Since a great deal of pain behavior is consciously willed to some degree,[19] it is not surprising that patients said conflicting things about the acceptability of expressing pain on the unit. We have seen that, for all their talk of support, patients did not always believe their fellows. One woman remarked that a recent arrival who said she could not move managed to get to the solarium when she wanted to smoke, and that she would walk easily until she noticed people were watching her and then would start grabbing for the bar on the corridor wall. A man commented that Marvin, who had improved so much some people called it a "miracle," was "bullshitting" as far as he was concerned. Marvin had been through several surgical procedures on his back and entered CPC almost incapacitated. He left walking normally and reporting himself 95 percent pain free. While on the unit, he criticized other patients for getting angry at the program, and wondered aloud whether they didn't want to face the fact that they could do it. His nurse had told him he was an example for the others, because he had had extensive surgery, and that, unlike him, others put up shields. He thought he was the star graduate of CPC, but several patients sourly concluded that his pain had not been "real."

In general, then, the community, like all communities, was a double-edged sword for many patients, simultaneously offering support and producing stress. Many of the troubling conflicts about pain, with physicians, friends, families, and compensation boards, continued after admission. Recently admitted patients hoped their pain would be acknowledged and legitimated and often gushed about feeling accepted; nevertheless, interactions with fellow patients were sometimes a minefield.

For the most part, patients came to admire a stoic attitude. Fred said he did not want anyone to say he was a whiner; whining and crying could be infectious and would not stop the pain. Another patient, seen by everyone as a whiner, finally got the message and said he was learning not to talk about his pain so much because "it brings everybody else down and gets everybody upset, it's just not worth it." If seen as totally involuntary, pain behavior was more accepted. One man, who exhibited no pain behavior himself and was told he didn't look as though he had any pain at all, said he felt less supported than a fellow patient whose pained face and walk elicited a lot of sympathy.

New arrivals exhibited far more verbal and nonverbal pain behavior than their more seasoned fellows. A patient who was also a psychotherapist saw a covert taboo in operation: "It's funny—when you've been here a while, you notice the new people will show those behaviors, but they slowly get extinguished, because no one responds, and I guess maybe you feel embarrassed or something." He added that the mannerisms people in pain have—putting their hand on their hair—are not going to change their headache, they are a behavioral habit developed in response to the pain. Often, he added, they were an indirect request for sympathy or help.

Thus, while patients were not directly forbidden to exhibit pain behavior, the social control *did* exist and was very effective; patients learned by seeing how their fellows were being observed and judged. Hence, despite the fact that virtually all patients said the therapeutic community supported and encouraged them, patients did not support one another's struggles to establish that they had "real" pain in this fashion. Indeed, a great deal of mind- and soul-searching about one's pain problem was prompted by words and actions—sometimes rather tough love in nature—of fellow patients.

These anecdotes are supported by patient responses to questions posed during both intake and discharge interviews about why there was such a range of outcomes at CPC. With remarkably few exceptions, patients accounted for this difference in terms of attitude, motivation, and similar qualities. And even most of those whose replies explained the range in terms of people having "different pain" or "different physical problems" would add that attitude, commitment, and the like were also important.

CPC Compared to Other Intentional Communities

As a community, CPC was distinctly odd. Yet patients and staff members believed it to be a community, most of them also feeling it contributed to patient progress in a major way. If we compare the CPC community to intentional communities of all kinds—communities formed by people who have chosen to live together and work toward a common goal—we can better understand how even the unusually fragile CPC community successfully conveyed an impression of substantiality and efficacy.

First, deciding to join any intentional community, CPC included, is a serious decision; individuals who make this decision are usually very invested, sometimes desperately so, in making the experience work.[20] Those who enter intentional communities have often undergone a major life crisis and feel disengaged from their previous lives and communities (some believe that succeeding in such a small-scale venture will help convince the world at large to adopt their utopian vision on a grand scale). Becoming a member of the CPC community did not require a great deal of knowledge; many patients were admitted who knew next to nothing about the program. But they were powerfully motivated to try *something*, as shown by phrases like "I am desperate," "this is the last resort," "this is the end of the road for me." Of course this is not the entire picture; some may join intentional communities to be disruptive and negative, and undoubtedly some pain sufferers who came to CPC wanted to prove it could not work and that they had little in common with their fellow patients. Still, decisions to enter residential communities are not undertaken lightly.

In addition, all such endeavors require members to focus inward and to loosen and diminish ties to home community, family, and daily routines. For example, promotional literature on even so temporary an intentional community as that formed during Outward Bound courses stresses the need to forge strong community bonds and break loose from daily routines and responsibilities if one is to accomplish "self-revitalization." Primary family bonds compete with the community's claims on members' time, commitments, and affections, a tension revealed by the ways communities legislate and indoctrinate about appropriate and inappropriate family relationships. Some intentional communities require members to radically change the nature of these other relationships; examples are the nineteenth-century Shakers and the Oneida Community.

At CPC, though participation lasted only a month to five weeks, patients were encouraged, in a variety of ways, to pay less attention to the concerns of their ordinary lives. As an exchange, investing a great deal of time and energy in CPC's program presumably would pay off in the form of new tools for coping with pain, new understandings and skills for interacting with friends and family, and greater mastery of one's environment. Ethan's level of investment was extreme: he would tell his friends not to come and tell his close friends and family that, although he really wanted to see them and really appreciated the food they brought, the visit needed to be limited to fifteen or twenty minutes. He felt so totally emotionally involved in what he was doing that visitors were an unwanted distraction. When his friends would become upset at being told not to come, he would tell them, "Look, I hope you understand, but if you don't understand, you can't come anyway." But another patient found the inward-focusing disturbing: "You get absorbed in this, it's so intense, a little community—people here become your friends because the outside ones fall off."

Some analyses of intentional communities argue that they develop loyalty and commitment in their members precisely by replacing families and taking over family functions, including emotional expression, ritual and celebration, space and territory, social and organizational ties, sociability, and requirements concerned with appearance and demeanor.[21] The CPC community at times did indeed perform all these functions, and many patients used familial metaphors to describe their feelings about it. Emotional expression was certainly present around the clock in myriad forms. There were many rituals, from standing in line to get meds four times a day to the cakes and good-bye cards on Friday nights. Space and territory were clearly demarcated; patients had to sign out to leave the unit and could not leave the hospital grounds. The community had social and organizational ties and sociability almost in excess, or so many complained. Finally, appearance and demeanor were big issues, as the discussion of pain behavior (and occasional criticism of a fellow patient's grooming or eating habits) amply demonstrates.

The requirement to participate intensively is found in all intentional communities.[22] At CPC what patients had in common, and what was focused on, was their pain; participating in a program which claimed to

ease their suffering, which required them to accept the communal orientation and goals, fostered what Victor Turner refers to as a condition
of *communitas*, in which members feel an intense comradeship and egalitarianism and where secular distinctions of rank and status disappear or
are homogenized.[23]

Yet regardless how much comradeship, egalitarianism, and self-gov-
ernance are stressed, in therapeutic communities the staff, not residents,
are ultimately in charge. CPC staff members did try to jolt patients out
of passivity and depression, which could involve giving them permission to challenge hierarchy. Yet despite CPC's anti-medical stance and
goals of fostering independence and a strong community, patient self-
governance was minimal. This occurred largely because the patient community was embedded in the larger community formed by both patients
and staff members, which was in turn embedded in the hospital whose
structure and policies greatly curtailed any tendencies toward patient
autonomy or community-building in any real sense.[24] To a greater extent than in many other therapeutic communities, CPC staff members'
attempts to encourage collective decision-making always concerned trivial matters, such as how to spend funds from dues each patient paid
into a common kitty. For example, when at one point the patient community demanded that dining services "give us a treat" to make up for
a foul-up during a Wednesday night outing, Naomi objected, saying she
disapproved of "pampering," but agreed when it became clear the community was not going to back down. This incident generated a great deal
of discussion among patients about just how sincere CPC staff members
were about promoting assertiveness.

The staff definitely bucked collective, independent effort by the patient community when individual patients were deciding whether to
drop out. This prospect would provoke a community-wide struggle, with
staff members almost always contending the patient was resisting treatment and the implications of getting better, and dissatisfied patients
countering with gripes about the program they saw as reasonable and
verifiable. Ethan noted that, since he and other patients had an intense
need to feel the CPC program was good, they were dismayed when one
of their number decided to leave early: "The message is that this program is not working for that someone; is that because there's something
missing in the program? I don't want to have to deal with that one—
I want this to be something that I know is going to get me 100 percent back on the track." But, he continued, it was hard to say simply
that the program was great and anybody who left was clearly missing
the boat once one had become attached to the person and started to
identify with his problems. What followed pitted therapeutic discourse
("these are excuses, the real reason you are leaving is your resistance")

against everyday-logical discourse ("the program is poorly run; it does not address my needs").[25] To patients, if the staff won, a fellow-patient who left early was mistaken and self-destructive; if the patient's view prevailed staff members' arguments seemed defensive and self-serving. Quite often it was a draw. Faced with a potential early departure, staff members would lean on patients to try to convince the person not to leave. Most patients felt inclined to encourage the patient to stay (otherwise it might seem as though they were being rejecting or indifferent), but those patients with similar gripes felt conflicted. The dynamic of the patient community and how staff members tried to use that dynamic to meet its own agenda (albeit an agenda it saw as in the patients' interests) were clearly revealed in these cases.[26]

Hence, although residents in therapeutic communities engage in collective therapy, it is the staff that has final authority to interpret behavior. The staff defines when a behavior is a symptom of an underlying pathology (as with a complaint about the weather causing pain interpreted as a sign of anxiety about upcoming discharge) or an example of resistance. Despite therapeutic communities' intent to eliminate the transformation of patients into passive objects on which treatment is performed, as happens in conventional medical settings, patients in these settings find that here as well, to some extent, their condition has become an instrument with which to dominate them, and thus provides instances of Foucault's notion of clinical gaze, or, as Bloor and his co-authors put it, therapeutic gaze.[27]

Similar instances appear in accounts of intentional communities in situations where communal, egalitarian ideology and policy run counter to the *realpolitik* of everyday community life. The difference between therapeutic communities and other kinds of intentional communities is that the former contain a built-in division between residents and staff. Nonetheless, the Foucauldian notion of "techniques of power and resistance" are present in all intentional communities, and involve surveillance, concealment, domination, and the like.

Given that all kinds of intentional communities, regardless of their purpose and ideology, exhibit tension between authoritarian and egalitarian tendencies, it is not surprising that challenges to authority often focus on leaders. The history of communal movements in the United States reveals many examples of strong, charismatic leaders who also drew harsh criticism and apostasy: John Humphrey Noyes of Oneida, Father Rapp of New Harmony, and Hugh Romney of Hog Farm are some examples.[28] As the amount of talk about him testifies, Dr. B, an extremely energetic, dedicated, and compassionate man, provoked powerful reactions in patients. Some clearly had to do with his personal style, but a great deal had to do with his role as director of a unit where tough love and manipulation were part of the therapy. Admired and fawned over or loathed and challenged, he was a lightning rod attracting many of the tensions over authority that surfaced in the unit.

All intentional communities claim to be therapeutic in a broad sense. Living in a nurturing community will not only heal present wounds and prevent future problems, it will allow residents' true potential to emerge. Therapeutic communities not only reject the biomedical model of therapy but, like communitarian movements in general (many of which, in this century and previous ones, were proponents of radical health reform), they reject certain aspects of mainstream society.[29] We have seen that CPC criticized certain American values, beliefs, and practices such as loyalty to a dysfunctional family system, overdependence on drugs, the championing of invasive pain treatments like multiple surgeries. It also criticized a system seen as "paying people to be in pain."

Changes in thinking are supposed to occur in all intentional communities. If a community is religious, like the Hutterites, members are supposed to grow in grace, becoming more enlightened through religious practice and living the good communal life. In therapeutic communities, residents grow in their ability to "confront reality"—the process of reflecting back to individuals others' views of their behavior, by so doing facilitating their ability to gain insight and change behavior. In secular communes, self-awareness and self-knowledge are often values in themselves.[30]

All intentional communities offer a new world view and provide opportunities for trying out new responses to feelings and constructing new identities, to memorize scripts and rehearse new roles for interacting with the outside world. CPC most definitely saw itself as providing these opportunities; its message resonated with rebirth imagery (an image also used by some patients ready for discharge). Patients negotiated this passage by emulating (or repudiating) models offered by other patients who were farther along in the process. High affect, a marked feature of CPC's emotional climate, was crucial in producing the changes experienced by some patients; when the process worked, the heightened emotion not only increased motivation but helped solidify the process of recoding the meaning of their experiences. Although these new meanings varied from individual to individual, the recoding itself was to some degree a collective process. CPC ideology shared many of the utopians' other criteria for establishing the good community: a constellation involving brotherhood, sharing, and intimacy; the fusion of body and mind; and the general underlying theme of wholeness or integration.

An accompanying idea is that to succeed (in the case of therapeutic communities, with therapy) one has to believe, one has to "give it 110 percent." Even when an intentional community is utterly secular, a kind of religious fervor can always be discerned. Just such a fervor was apparent when gung-ho patients or staff members at the totally secular CPC tried to persuade doubting Thomases to stay, or talked about the program to visitors. Indeed, another link between CPC and communitarian experiments is a tendency to proselytize, as happened when former patients tried to convince friends and family members experiencing chronic pain to consider being admitted.

Initiation Rituals

A final point to be made about how even a community like CPC can produce a sense of community in its members has to do with how their emotions are manipulated. Living for a month or five weeks on a unit like CPC can be likened to rituals of initiation—a topic extensively studied in the anthropological literature and elsewhere. Arnold van Gennep classified initiation rituals as one kind of "rite of passage," the rituals that accompany changes of place, state, social position, and age.[31] Examples of rites of passage include baptisms, coronations, ordinations, weddings, and funerals. In initiation, from an individual's point of view, a change is effected in his or her status; from the community's point of view, a new member has been recruited and received.

Initiation rites impart a new body of knowledge to the initiate,[32] transfer a person from one social status to another, and are characterized by high levels of both arousal and catharsis. The more recent literature on rites of passage pays special attention to the role of emotion, and parallels can be found between these rites' high level of affect and the intense emotions experienced by CPC patients. (For example, despite being "your typical all-American boy" who did not break into tears easily, Ethan's heightened emotions led to crying on various occasions.) Inducing a high negative affect in initiates at the beginning is a frequent feature of such rituals—but what is initially annoying, disturbing, or disgusting becomes over time acceptable, even calming. Gilbert Herdt argues that this is an important part of the process of cathecting to the new world view and its proponents.[33] Neophytes are often subject to debasement as part of ritual induction into communitarian societies, and the mild punishing of patients who exhibited pain behaviors or were otherwise recalcitrant at CPC seemed to echo this—certainly many patients saw it this way.[34] At CPC, patients oftentimes were admitted in defensive and self-loathing frames of mind—bringing their own debasement rituals with them, as it were.

Initiation rituals commonly consist of a set of stages during which individuals or, often, groups of individuals, are processed from rank beginner/outsider to something like probationer (the "plebes" of military schools) to full-fledged member in good standing. Often, initiates are encouraged to identify themselves with people farther along in the process and to learn how to talk and think about the shifts in meaning and affect that will occur if their journey is successful. Very few patients, on entering CPC, agreed with or wanted to accept what they were coming to understand as the CPC message, but when they heard it from former "successful" patients they could not offer these "people in the same boat" some of the arguments used against staff members (e.g., that they did not have pain). Some former patients played a therapeutic role as well, returning to CPC from time to time to chat with current residents in the solarium, or at the monthly family night session in which a panel of former patients talked about their experiences on the unit. Their messages tended to stress the following themes: I was depressed, I am far less depressed now; I still have pain, I now "control my pain." These seemed to be very effective. One man described one such session:

"If after two days I had any doubts about the program, it sure as hell had a change last Thursday night. The second girl that spoke was unreal, absolutely phenomenal, she totally changed my outlook. She [had been a patient] here twice. The first time she just came in and did her thing, she was nice and she went along, 'How is everything?' 'Oh, fine.' She did it to please everybody else, it seemed. Yeah, and yet the second time she came she wasn't going to do that, she was here for herself, she didn't care about anybody else. And this time she worked hard and she got a lot out of it, and even though she had a lot of fights with [Dr. B], she feels that he did his thing and a lot of it is trial and error with him, too. He's not God."

This former patient can be seen as playing the role of guide in an initiation ritual. She was very much a spokesperson for CPC, but since patients knew she was "in the same boat" she came across very differently from staff members. Indeed, part of her message was that she got better *in spite of* Dr. B. The theme of getting better "to spite" Dr. B came up several times. Here is Fred:

"Plus, I've shown up [Dr. B]. He said when he met me he would send me to a shrink ward. He's sort of glad I came in here and it worked well. I am sort of, too. Another thing is if I can keep it up and not be coming crawling back to him in six months saying, 'Lock me up'—eating the narcotics, running around and screaming, cowering in the corners. [Dr. B] could say, 'Ha! I told you so!' I'll literally feel like shit and he'd be right. I'm going to show him up, take the chapter he's got on me in the book and erase it."

Analyses of initiation rituals have shown that, while they do pass on knowledge (for example, boys might spend several years in "bush school" learning tribal lore and skills such as hunting or singing) and do move initiates from one social status to another, giving them a new identity in the process, they accomplish much more as well. These rites also process other members of the community (e.g., a parent adds the role of parent-in-law at a wedding), and perform collective functions, for instance, affirming the society's values and practices.

Patients' efforts to learn a considerable amount of material can be seen as the "bush school" component of the CPC program. There was also an attempt to construct, with the help of the patient community, a change in each patient's identity. The patient might not become "pain-free" but should become a person who can "live with pain," and be far less depressed.

Of particular interest are initiation rituals' liminal features—their "betwixt-and-between," "neither fish nor fowl" elements.[35] Liminal states are states of transition; they were first comprehensively analyzed by van Gennep as the middle stage of a three-stage schema (separation, liminality, aggregation) that characterizes all rites of passage. Turner elaborated van Gennep's analysis, stressing the key feature of ambiguity in the liminal phase. Turner also examined liminality as characterizing certain entities continually, thus applying the attributes of people in ritualized transition more generally. He describes these entities as eluding or slipping

through the network of classifications that normally locate states and positions in cultural space. Liminal entities are neither here nor there; they are betwixt and between the positions assigned and arrayed by law, custom, convention, and ceremonial.[36]

Quite often metaphors are employed to characterize betwixt-and-between initiates as neither living nor dead.

It is possible to think of patients as being in a liminal state during their stay at CPC. People admitted to any hospital move into a liminal state. A great deal of their identity is rendered irrelevant; they are called by their first name unless they request otherwise or are extremely elderly, and wear the ubiquitous hospital "johnnies" and an identifying bracelet. Going through the metaphorical door of the admissions procedure is similar to other ritualized crossings of thresholds into liminal states, which unite people with a new world and often involve purification rites. CPC downplayed some of this stripping of identity because it was engaged in rehabilitation rather than treatment of an acute condition, and also trying to wean patients from overuse of the medical system. Yet CPC patients *were* uprooted from their homes and communities when they came off the elevator and joined the unit.[37] True, their stay was temporary. But, similar to many passage rituals that involve permanent changes in status, a successful outcome meant returning to their families, communities, and workplaces as different beings. CPC, unlike most hospitals, did not speak of cures, but successful patients were definitely seen as having changed significantly. These patients were required to do more than simply learn new material; they had to make a strong and definitive break with the past—with old status, old habits, old assumptions. The patient who was so impressed with a former patient's pep talk had been at CPC five days and showed many signs of being in a liminal state—excited, open, eager, resistant, and confused. Speaking approvingly of Dr. B, he was also furious at him for taking him off injectable morphine "cold turkey."

That much of what went on at CPC, particularly during the first week, was confusing and mysterious is also a very common characteristic of liminal conditions: it facilitates the breakdown needed before profound change can occur. Finally, we have seen that another feature found in liminal situations, a high level of affect, often present in the entire community involved in the ritual, was also characteristic of CPC.

An example of employing heightened emotions to achieve the appearance of a ritual accomplishment can be found in Edward Schieffelin's description of how the Kaluli of highland New Guinea orchestrate a sequenced pattern of emotions to produce a heightened tension, followed by catharsis and at least the appearance of resolution. Jane Atkinson discusses how the Wana shamans of Sulawesi create a similar sequence in their curing ceremonies.[38] In both these examples, even when a given problem may not be solved, the structure of the action lends a sense of emotional closure and other emotions take over. CPC attempted to orchestrate collective emotions, principally in group settings such as rounds, psychomotor, focus group, and doctor's group. Note that consensus is not necessary for the appearance of resolution. Individual Kaluli may not participate fully in a given ritual, just as individual Americans might not actually feel sad at a particular wake. But if the community participating in the ritual in general grants it and its practitioners authority, the ritual will be effective in an overall sense.

Liminal states also almost always contain leveling mechanisms; just as medieval pilgrims donned simple, unmarked clothing and played down other emblems of wealth or high social status, so did CPC patients discard many such signs. Many patients commented on another leveling mechanism: pain itself, which was hailed repeatedly as creating the bonds that formed patients into a community. "It was fascinating to discover what an equalizer pain is, because everyone experiences the same type of emotions."[39] Another patient said that patients' shared sense of loss resulted in their feeling comfortable and safe enough to let both inhibitions and pretensions fall by the wayside, eliminating the "bullshit."

Note that Turner argues that the processes of leveling and stripping often appear to flood their subjects with affect.[40]

In part because of the stripping-down procedures that occur in initiation rites, neophytes tend to develop an intense comradeship and egalitarianism. As noted, Turner refers to this as *communitas*, the feeling of lowliness, homogeneity, and comradeship shared by a group of initiates.[41] This is precisely what happened among CPC patients. Unlike situations in which people are informed about the initiation ritual they are participating in, almost all of them were surprised at this feeling, yet they overwhelmingly affirmed it.

Initiates, in order to experience deeply the changes they are undergoing and come to believe themselves to be truly changed, are often made to feel new emotions, or at least higher levels of emotion. This is one reason why pain is so frequently a part of initiation rituals, as when circumcision, whipping, or tattooing is involved. Society is saying "We have power to produce great pain and to inscribe on your body in permanent fashion a visible sign of this power," as well as sending the message that one's body, particularly one's genitals, is not private property, but must be used and regarded in accordance with cultural rules and regulations. According to Turner, the ordeals and humiliations undergone by neophytes represent partly a destruction of the previous status and partly a tempering of the initiates' essence in order to prepare them to cope with their new responsibilities and restrain them in advance from abusing their new privileges.[42] High affect—produced by fear, pain, and so forth—serves to heighten the event and impress its significance on the minds of the participants.

Some of the difficulties with the CPC program, reported by almost all patients, clearly served this same purpose. For some patients, the first scary and painful physical therapy sessions had this effect, even though the therapists saw themselves as simply getting unused bodies into reasonable shape and injecting tough love messages when appropriate. Thus, when patients who were considering dropping out made statements like "this place would make me crazier than I already am," they were to some extent correctly perceiving a feature of the program, albeit one not discussed in the brochure. According to this line of reasoning, the confusion and disorientation made patients more receptive to the CPC message.

In sum, so many patients found themselves deeply confused, and then changed, as a result of participating in the program that it was impossible not to conclude that the program contained elements very similar to initiation rituals. I am not saying staff members were aware of these aspects of the program; participants need not be aware of all features of a ritual to produce them successfully every time it is performed.

Rituals can be effective only if the participants grant authority to those in charge. Turner describes neophytes in initiation rites as

liminal beings [having] no status, property, insignia, secular clothing indicating rank or role, position in a kinship system. Their behavior is normally passive or humble; they must obey their instructors implicitly, and accept arbitrary punishment without complaint. It is as though they are being reduced or ground down to a uniform condition to be fashioned anew and endowed with additional powers to enable them to cope with their new station in life.[43]

Comments about the rigidity of the program and metaphors about prisons and torture chambers suggest a similarity here as well. The "boot camp" label conjures up images of grunts and drill sergeants, "do it because I say so" justifications for rituals neophytes are undergoing. The CPC staff used confrontational interventions to negatively reinforce maladaptive and self-defeating behavior, but these interventions can also be seen as an illustration of how neophytes are treated in intentional communities in general and as a kind of degradation ritual so often reported in the literature. One must learn to accept arbitrariness, even arbitrary punishment, from the elders. We have heard patients commenting on how staff members punished them—for example, responding to uppity behavior by increasing their doxepin; in some instances this seemed a reasonable conclusion, although Dr. B said he did not increase dosage punitively. In sum, a number of CPC activities had a lot in common with the debasement rituals undergone by those who join small, face-to-face communities. While it is abundantly clear that most CPC patients, even those most happy with their experience, did not learn to accept arbitrariness nor to grant the staff absolute authority, parallels were there.

Finally, Turner notes that sexual continence characterizes neophytes in a liminal state. Ethan made a comment about the striking asexuality of his fellow patients[44] that testifies to this at CPC, although I would guess that pain and lack of privacy were the main reason for diminished libidos. (Interaction among patients did often involve flirting and sexualized horseplay. Two romances developed on the unit during the research period: one involved a man and an unhappily married woman, but did not go very far, and the other was consummated, or so I was told by both parties. The man, Harry, referred to it as "dating"; the woman was more explicit. When and where, I did not ask.)

Likening the CPC experience to an initiation rite characterized by liminality, heightened emotion, and so forth clarifies and explains some of what took place there. Certain features of liminal states, in particular an association with the sacred and with danger, often a polluting danger, did not appear on the unit, though a sense of danger attaches to chronic pain sufferers in general.[45]

In sum, initiation rituals very often involve a dissolution of many categories and classifications, a suspension of numerous rules and establishment of new ones, periods of seclusion for the initiates, a requirement to learn new knowledge, and a stress on the absolute authority of the elders. These features also characterized the CPC experience for some patients: in the midst of a great deal of confusion people bonded and experienced powerful emotions, helping establish a changed identity.

Conclusions

Many staff members and patients felt that the therapeutic community component of CPC's program was its most important feature. However, while patients' sense of belonging to a community was very real, what they in fact belonged to, if we employ conventional sociological definitions, was a very curious sort of community indeed, perhaps best seen in metaphorical terms.

Community processes helped patients learn from their fellows, bond with them, and forge a collective self-image, facilitated to some degree by a division between staff and patients. These processes can be better understood by comparing CPC not only to other therapeutic communities but to all kinds of intentional communities. Patients choosing to be admitted to CPC were making a serious decision: many were at their wits' end and extremely dissatisfied with their lives. Also like these other communities, the one at CPC was intense, inward-focused, and demanding. The CPC community, like other intentional communities, offered benefits of membership such as comradeship, nurturance, acceptance, and the opportunity to achieve insight. No intentional community, regardless of how effectively it presents itself (as democratic, egalitarian, etc.), is able totally to practice what it preaches; all exhibit tensions between authority and participation, and rely on informal means of social control (e.g., gossip) that give the lie to communal ideologies claiming impartiality, equality, or respect for individual rights. Hence members of such communities, including CPC, both sustain and resist the image they collectively construct. Also similar was the fact that some CPC patients became so enthusiastic about the program that they proselytized about it with a kind of religious fervor. As in all intentional communities, CPC patients were supposed to experience significant change, to learn how to live a more integrated, functional, and satisfying life. They would learn not only useful lessons and skills, but also how to recode the meanings of their experiences, past and present—for example, their pain and other bodily feelings. Finally, as in other intentional communities, at CPC all this happened *if* one made a break with the past and got the message. At CPC, such individuals were sometimes called "winners."

Patients also experienced CPC as a kind of initiation rite, occupying a liminal position during their stay. CPC patients certainly differed from the standard image of initiates going through such a ritual, but the comparison helps us understand better why many patients reported such powerful feelings of cathexis, strong attachment, bewilderment, disorientation, and the like.

CPC patient discourse about their community reveals the contradictory nature of what was "good" and "bad" about it. For example, a "positive," strong community was seen as an aid to therapy; yet the processes maintaining it at times involved hypocrisy and "kissing up" to the staff, reminding patients of the game-playing they had experienced on the outside. Building solidarity was also seen as a good thing, even therapeutic; yet if "negative" patients were "pulling the rest of us down," then ostracism was in order, perhaps to the extent of subtly encouraging them to leave and "let in someone who's motivated." The support so many patients raved about was also a double-edged sword, for only the right behaviors merited such support—some offers of support were seen by staff members as buttressing a patient's resistance to CPC's program. A really *responsible* person, patients were told, would confront a friend when it was warranted. And although patients supported one another in their pain and suffering, the degree to which a given pain's cause was "real" or the appropriateness of its expression—pain behavior—was sometimes questioned.

Patients also reported enjoying the intimacy and camaraderie they encountered; some spoke of experiencing warm, authentic relationships and getting past the "bullshit" they had endured on the outside. Yet unfortunate consequences sometimes resulted from self-disclosure and getting close to others, such as being criticized, or even being "betrayed"—by roommates when they discovered concealed caches of drugs, for instance. And while patients welcomed the opportunity to forge strong bonds with their fellow sufferers, they fretted that focusing in on the community meant a loosening of ties to family and friends on the outside.

But CPC's message was promulgated within institutional structures that posed such severe restrictions on community-building, especially in terms of self-determination, that at times patients' collective attempts to act autonomously seemed farcical. Such restrictions, despite the abundant evidence that patients and staff members felt that the community was real and therapeutically effective, are a main reason why so many patients failed to get the message and, consequently, fell far short of being "winners." They left early, they lied during their good-bye speeches, they were discharged with predictions they would return to the "drug-seeking behaviors" and "doctor-shopping" they had been admitted with. In short, neither CPC staff members nor "winner" patients trying to convince their fellows were nearly as successful as the elders who figure in Turner's analyses of initiation rites, for in such rites virtually all initiates make it through successfully.

Chapter 6
"Winners": CPC Converts

"Why it didn't work for me, I'm not sure. Maybe because I didn't have the epiphany."

"I've often thought that maybe we're some sort of sanctioned bizarre cult. We do exactly the same things that cults do."
— Kenneth

Some patients seemed to buy the CPC message so wholeheartedly that I refer to them as "converts." I argue here that the literature on religious conversion can help us understand what produced the changes these CPC "winners" experienced. The discussion that follows is suggestive rather than definitive. First, I did not talk to staff members about the progress of individual patients during their stay, nor see their medical records; my evaluations derived from what I observed and what patients chose to tell me about themselves and their fellow patients. Second, while most patients going through the CPC program changed visibly, it was not always easy to ascertain the nature of these changes. True, some changes were fairly easy to explain: relaxation training reduced muscle tension; ice massages or transcutaneous electrical nerve stimulation devices produced peripheral changes in blood circulation or nerve impulses. But explaining other changes is more difficult, and the caution one must exercise in interpreting what people report to be changes in their mind—attitudes, beliefs, and feelings—is especially applicable to a chronic pain center setting. Other reasons why measuring success— or failure—presented a formidable challenge derive from the nature of the treatment. Any research concerned with the efficacy of a therapeutic community is necessarily complex since the organization itself is part of the treatment.[1]

Although by the end of a patient's stay staff members would have indicated to the community fairly openly their assessment of his or her progress, one cannot, when studying an institution, accept one sector's assessment of the situation as the truth, even if that sector consists of experts.[2] I take no stand on which, if any, unconscious factors contribute to chronic pain. Not only am I not a clinician, but this is a field replete with unanswered questions; nor, for the same reasons, do I attempt to provide a definitive explanation of why certain patients responded to the CPC message in the extremely positive way I call conversion.[3]

Am I Feeling Better Yet?[4]

What constitutes improvement in severe chronic pain, while seemingly straightforward—the pain is reduced or disappears—is not at all simple. Because pain is a multifaceted problem, improvement will be multifaceted as well. Goals apart from pain reduction include lessening the problematic effects of medications (what these might be is currently *very* contested), improving the patient's ability to function, reducing the patient's use of health care facilities, and reducing depression and anxiety.[5] Also, as Dr. B pithily put it, "people will tell you *anything*, it's what they do that counts."[6] Yet many of the data on improvement are necessarily based on what the patient tells us. Furthermore, no consensus exists among pain specialists regarding the criteria for measuring improvement: the goals of staff members in a given pain center are not quite the same as those at institutions dealing with conventional medical problems. As we have seen, a pain sufferer may have excruciating chronic pain but not chronic pain *syndrome*, what Dr. B called "complicated pain." The distinction is based on the presence of behavior not directly connected to the site of pain and inferences about its causes. This difference, in the abstract quite significant, is dealt with poorly in clinical practice and in the literature, for people with such "complicated" pain are a very heterogeneous population.[7] Some of the stigma associated with severe chronic pain occurs simply because sufferers inhabit such poorly defined terrain.

When pain specialists evaluate pain center results and suggest ways to improve success rates, much of their argument rests on a critique of conventional medical approaches and assumptions and, often, on legislation pertinent to chronic pain treatment and disability funding. The consensus is that pain centers *can* produce improvement at rates higher than other approaches in patients who have not had success with other forms of intervention.[8] However, precisely specifying what constitutes improvement or scientifically acceptable ways to measure it is elusive. Certainly, it is difficult to predict success in individual cases, though the literature amply discusses such efforts.

Analyses of performance at pain centers oscillate between upbeat claims of efficacy and warnings about unrealistic expectations. For example, one center director describes a program that stresses educating patients about psychological causes of their pain. He maintains: "Often the apparent acceptance of the diagnosis at five, six, or seven weeks post-admission coincided with a dramatic reduction in pain."[9] But other authors are not so sanguine, especially when discussing chronic pain syndrome in general as opposed to their own centers' results.

We have seen that pain specialists distinguish between improvement and an actual lessening of pain, some even challenging pain relief as a goal; better functioning is what specialists should aim for.[10] But, as another specialist points out, few patients say "I want you to treat me so that I can take care of my responsibilities."[11]

I asked CPC staff members two questions: percentage of patients experiencing significant improvement, and percentage experiencing significant reduction in pain. Table 1 shows their answers. Staff members concurred that measuring improvement was at best imprecise. In fact, they were very forthcoming about just how tricky evaluation and prognosis were for them. Predicting who would do well was even more difficult. Thomas, a psychologist, commented that some patients left pain-free, some experienced a reduction in their pain, some had no reduction in pain and had to learn how to live with it, and he knew of no way to predict who was going to be in which category. Beverly, a PRA, concurred: how patients did after leaving CPC was "totally individual." Vera, a physical therapist, added that sometimes you felt you had not helped a certain patient at all, yet at some point after being discharged something clicked with her and the lessons of the program would kick in. In fact, a person like this might do much better than someone who had been constantly talking about how well he was doing while at CPC, but who after leaving the support of the clinic found he'd lost everything.

Naomi admitted predicting was a mystery. She had known people who staff members felt were not going to make it. She recalled one patient she had found to be so totally disruptive that she did not think he belonged in the program. But he did improve and continued to progress following discharge. With this type of "extremely difficult" patient, she said, you could almost see some staff members sitting back, waiting for the person to fall on his face so they could say, "Uh-huh, I knew it!" Naomi laughed, "That's terrible, but it's true!" In this particular case, other staff members told her to back off—no surprise, because during the fourteen years she had been at CPC at least one or two staff members would fight for any given patient.

The CPC staff certainly felt that improvement was not the same thing as a decrease in pain. Matthew said that although people came to CPC

TABLE 1. Percentage of Patients Experiencing Significant Improvement and Significant Reduction in Pain, Staff Estimates

Staff member	Percent
Significant Improvement?	
Beverly	90
Donna	100
Dr. B	33
Evelyn	50 or less
Georgia	50–60
Karen	70
Linda	less than 33
Naomi	60
Neil	50
Nicole	30
Nina	50
Polly	60
Rhonda	66–75
Sonia	33
Tracy	60–70
Significant Reduction in Pain?	
Beverly	50
Donna	75
Evelyn	50
Georgia	25
Karen	70
Kenneth	5
*Linda	10
Naomi	40
Nina	60
Polly	40
Rhonda	50–60
Tracy	50

*Linda disagreed with Dr. B's estimate because the numbers of people leaving CPC who achieved significant pain relief were clearly getting smaller.

wanting to be pain-free, he was not sure to what degree that happened or to what degree that was even important. What was important was alleviating the suffering: "Pain doesn't have to be suffering—the sensory input and how it's perceived and interpreted and how it gets translated to pain." Linda was adamant that significant reduction in pain was not how she judged the program.

Although my two questions about estimated improvement explicitly asked for percentages, staff members qualified their answers in such different ways that comparing their responses is difficult. For example,

several who gave high estimates for "significant reduction in pain" included patients who reported that their pain level was about the same
but it did not bother them as it had before. Donna said she estimated
almost 100 percent were significantly improved, because, although they
themselves might not think so—they might continue to gripe about the
pain and other problems—"the fact that they have got enough energy
to be doing that as far as I'm concerned, instead of being so dead, that's
a step in the right direction, that's 'significantly improved.'"

In general, staff members said the idea of leaving pain-free was a fantasy. Kenneth said that none left pain-free, and his answer to a follow-up
question about Marvin, who had been admitted severely incapacitated
and had left claiming he was pain-free, was, "Yes, I wonder what that is
all about." Other staff members refused to estimate levels of improvement, saying that what counted was long-term improvement, and the
only information they had consisted of anecdotal examples.[12]

The only conclusions we can draw from these estimates is that individual staff members varied widely in their estimates—in part because
they defined "significant improvement" differently—and that the variation did not correlate with discipline. Patients offered lower estimates
for both measures.

In a nutshell, requests for estimates of patient improvement revealed
considerable disagreement among staff members (and between staff and
patients): staff members' estimates of the proportion of patients who
"significantly improved" ranged from less than a third to 100 percent;
estimates of "significant reduction in pain" ranged from 5 percent to 75
percent.

Conversion

The term *conversion* (referring to religious conversion, not the psychological meaning of the word) is used as a heuristic device; I am not
arguing that those patients who came to accept CPC philosophy wholeheartedly were in fact converts to a new belief system, but will use the
concept as a metaphor, somewhat like Weber's concept of ideal type, because I believe it helps us understand what happened at CPC for many
of the patients reporting significant improvement. This means that I will
not try to count how many patients during the period of study were
"converts." Because this notion is only a heuristic device, a conceptual
aid rather than a term designating a kind of empirical reality, such an
endeavor would be misleading and unproductive. If we were to devise
a "conversion" scale, at one end would be patients who were disgusted
with the CPC approach, many of whom left early,[13] and at the other
end would be someone like Marvin, the "miracle" who entered on a

stretcher severely incapacitated and who left walking, riding a stationary bike, and singing the praises of the entire CPC staff. But any attempt to locate individual patients on such a scale would be open to challenge. My information was far from complete, and such decisions would be extremely impressionistic. Furthermore, specifying the criteria and how they should be weighted would be useful only to illustrate how ill-advised such an exercise would be. In the pages that follow I speak of CPC "converts" as if this were an empirical category; the reader must keep in mind that it is not.

Needless to say, a highly successful experience at CPC did not resemble religious conversion in several respects. To begin with, people joined CPC for a specified period of time. The changes successful patients experienced were supposed to be permanent, but I do not know how long after discharge patients continued to believe in and practice what they had learned at CPC. Also, the profound experiences of fellowship reported by so many patients were limited to the month or so of residence at CPC (although some friendships lasted, and two reunions were held during the year of study). Furthermore, CPC patients were not motivated to go through the program by a desire to explore a new belief system (in fact, many were extremely resistant to the idea), but to get help with a pain problem. In addition, because CPC was an utterly secular institution that stressed empowerment and self-actualization, converts did not report feeling as though they were surrendering to a higher power, or feeling themselves to be passive spectators of a process being performed on them, as often happens in religious conversion. Finally, CPC patients' lives did not change as radically as our stereotypical convert's, and it seems unlikely that any patients experienced a fundamental change in their "sense of ultimate grounding" or "root reality" (terms used to describe religious conversion).[14]

Despite these differences, comparing CPC converts to religious converts is useful because for some patients the CPC experience involved processes that cannot be explained simply in terms of learning new information during workshops, classes, and informal conversations, or in terms of the effects of psychotherapy. This is not to downplay the effectiveness of education and counseling—both certainly played a major part in producing change in converts and other patients who improved. Yet there were other important ingredients in the stew CPC patients simmered in that greatly affected outcome, often remarked on by patients themselves.[15]

The literature on conversion does not agree on how to conceptualize it or how to identify the convert. However, authors do seem to agree that conversion involves radical personal change (the speed and precise nature of the change are also debated). Yet, even using the term metaphorically, we still need specific criteria to distinguish CPC converts. The simple act of becoming a member of an organization identifies neither the CPC convert nor, according to most researchers, the religious convert. Nor does participation in "demonstration events," like baptisms or testimonial ceremonies, a measure sometimes used to identify religious converts. This is because such events are characterized by an emotionally charged atmosphere involving considerable pressure to demonstrate the strength of one's convictions,[16] so participation may reveal yielding to intense normative pressure more than the radical inner change associated with conversion.

The one feature of the CPC program that resembled "demonstration events," the good-bye speeches, illustrates their inadequacy as a measure. We have seen that at CPC there was pressure to avoid being "negative," and extremely negative patients were isolated and ostracized. The uniformly positive good-bye speeches, which might easily be seen as a kind of testimonial ceremony, actually provided little information about which patients so thoroughly bought CPC ideology that they would be classified as converts in my scheme.

One model of conversion posits four rhetorical indicators: biographical reconstruction, adoption of a master attribution scheme, suspension of analogical reasoning, and adoption of the convert role.[17] CPC converts engaged in significant biographical reconstruction in the sense that, prior to admission, pain had dominated their lives, but on discharge they had a new explanation for their pain and accompanying problems such as depression or medication dependency, exhibited physical changes and reported a decreased level of suffering (some, not all, reported a decreased level of pain), and testified to a fundamental change in the degree to which pain dominated their lives. Other kinds of biographical reconstruction—about other problems patients were struggling with upon admission—also occurred.[18]

The model's "master attribution scheme" adopted by the convert "authoritatively informs all causal attributions about self, others, and events in the world." While this is too totalizing to apply to CPC converts, a major shift in thinking about the causes of pain is characteristic: acceptance of internal factors (although perhaps not as initial cause) always increased, and, concomitantly, accepting that one was responsible for how one experienced the pain to some degree also occurred.

CPC converts did provide examples of the model's third criterion—suspension of analogical reasoning—but not in a very significant way. Analogical reasoning involves thinking about resemblance and leads to the use of metaphors and similar rhetorical devices, as in "the pain is like a hot poker on my tooth." Some statements by converts were not like this, and were puzzling; they seemed to be bald assertions with little attempt to be logical or persuasive, almost challenging the listener to accept them. The model labels assertions that do not involve analogical reasoning (an example is "God is love") "iconic," because they "picture what things are, rather than how things are alike." [19] Indeed one heard phrases at CPC like "before, pain controlled me; now I control my pain," which, while sometimes connected to a logical explanation, often were simply statements about the new state, not seen to need further explanation. An example is the comment that "after one week I have 50 percent pain reduction and it's largely due to the support of the community." This might sound like an explanation, but when questioned, the speaker supplied no causal link—he was making a statement, period. (Note that religious converts typically use iconic assertions much more than CPC patients, and I do not want to overemphasize their importance.)

The fourth rhetorical device of the model, adoption of the convert role, does characterize CPC converts—although not as much as it does newly converted Moonies who exhibit their new identity in every situation. Although almost all patients were resistant at some time during their stay, at leavetaking CPC converts were testifying and witnessing, offering a plethora of reasons, including their own and others' stories, to show why CPC's approach was correct.

The model asserts that converts adopt group-specific guidelines for interpreting and recounting certain experiences; for example, one who becomes a Zen practitioner learns not only how to practice Zen but also how to think and talk about that practice. [20] CPC converts adopted CPC guidelines for reinterpreting their, and other patients', personal pain history.

We can argue, then, that CPC converts should be identified through their discourse. But why did only some CPC patients embrace CPC ideology so passionately while others did not, even though they had been helped? [21]

Some hypotheses about conversion focus on predisposing personality traits and cognitive orientations, sometimes termed "susceptibility," often seen as deriving from having been socialized into absolutist or fundamentalist beliefs and values. [22] These do not go very far in explaining conversion at CPC. However, the hypothesis which holds that "seekers" are more likely to undergo conversion precisely because they are in active pursuit of just such a self-transformation does seem to describe many CPC converts, as does the picture of converts as people who have had to confront a whole host of intellectual problems for which the old cosmology is no longer sufficient. [23]

A number of studies indicate that tension-producing situations—marital strain, loss of a family member, and so forth—increase the likelihood of conversion. Some scholars question these findings as susceptible to the failings of biographical reconstruction and because many people under great stress do not undergo conversion, but it does seem that the high stress levels in CPC converts' lives prior to admission made them particularly receptive to the CPC message. This is speculation, however, and I do not believe that CPC converts necessarily experienced more stress than nonconverts, at least certain ones. Conversion, actual or metaphorical, is clearly not the result of any discrete single cause.

Finally, the model sees two kinds of social influence playing a significant role in conversion: first, affective and intensive interaction; second, role learning. Illustrations of both processes at CPC fill these pages; for example, Chapter 5 stressed the strength of interpersonal ties, and evidence of patients being bombarded with messages about adopting new attitudes and behaviors appears throughout the book.

Some studies attribute the conversion experience to a psychophysiological response to coercion and induced stress—"brainwashing." Analyses of groups like the Unification Church often point out how potential converts are deprived of food and subjected to stimuli calculated to make them unusually receptive to what they are hearing. The model we are using disputes this conclusion, pointing out that most conversions are completely voluntary and that the incidence of defection among cult members is high. Clearly some of the intense, confusing, and high-affect-producing stimuli to which CPC patients were subjected following admission did disorient them, produce feelings of vulnerability, and elicit strong defense mechanisms. Those reactions at times seemed exceptionally rigid and irrational, which perhaps increased the likelihood of challenge or open confrontation from staff and fellow patients—a significant feature of the CPC approach (and, I might add, the recruitment techniques of various organizations, religious and secular, that seek converts).[24]

Most situations involving conversion share some features, such as stress, a sense of desperation that can make people more receptive to change, and so forth. CPC converts were on a quest for a kind of meaning that was absent in a very significant part of their lives, an absence that troubled them greatly, and they found meaning, at least for a time, in the CPC program. Hence, while those I call converts did not change as radically as our credulous stereotype who sells everything and joins a cult, they did report experiencing a profound change, and those around them remarked on it as well. To some extent, then, CPC converts did undergo a change in values, beliefs, and identity features significant enough to change some features of their universe of discourse—to become in some ways "true believers."

Three Examples of CPC Conversion

Rebecca

Rebecca, a very attractive and lively African-American woman in her late forties, was admitted to CPC with a complicated neck, back, and arm problem that began two years earlier when the car she was driving was hit from the rear and the side by another car. In the initial interview she reported constant pain and numbness from nerve damage, which had been treated "by a score of doctors" in different hospitals since the accident. She had undergone a variety of diagnostic tests including X-rays, myelograms (an X-ray of the spinal cord that involves injection of a special contrast medium), and a range of treatments including chiropractic, medication, and physical therapy (heat, ultrasound, and massage).

Despite all this, the pain persisted, resulting in problems at work, both in terms of getting her job done and in relationships with coworkers. Rebecca said she resented their "nosiness" and their expressions of sympathy ("I would think, 'goddamn it, you never asked about me before, so why are you asking about me now?'") She also complained about the "bullshit" she heard because she was in litigation: "'Oh, you're going to go out and buy yourself another diamond now.'" In the process, she felt she finally found out exactly who her good friends were; everyone else, she said, dropped right by the wayside thinking she was pretending to be hurt in order to get money.

When a myelogram revealed a ruptured disk, she agreed to surgery—her fourth operation in four years (including an appendectomy, hysterectomy with removal of one ovary, and surgery to remove the second ovary). She went back to work, but this proved difficult when the pain returned and, she reported, fellow workers made comments like, "You had an operation, what do you mean, you don't feel good?" She then started seeing a neurologist, who scheduled another myelogram, following which she became violently ill and experienced something resembling convulsions. She was hospitalized, but specialists in several fields were unable to ascertain what had gone wrong, though they eliminated various possibilities. Psychiatrists were then brought in, she recounted, and began examining her, asking her to sing, and asking questions like, "How was your childhood?" She was then given the option of being discharged or going onto the psychiatric ward of the hospital; she chose the latter because she felt too sick to leave. Residence on that ward involved several extremely unpleasant experiences and she left, but not before demanding and getting (with the help of both her attorney and her boyfriend) a very dramatic meeting with the staff.

Following discharge, she became seriously depressed. Several months later she had a third myelogram which revealed nothing that could account for her symptoms. Her most recent doctor had referred Rebecca to CPC because both she and he "were really frustrated." She summed up her situation in these words: "Something happened to you; someone did something to you, but you're the one who's going to suffer for it. And I'm thinking, you know, they put men on the moon, but you cannot help me—why? I want some answers. I want some answers!"

Initially, her interest in CPC involved physical therapy for her neck, arm, and back. She was on the lookout for staff who might try to "bullshit" her—having raised her own child, taken in two others, and had grandchildren, she said, "I can see a snow job coming." She had reservations about the psychological component and wasn't sure whether she was going to open up in groups or not.

However, she had nothing but praise for the community even at her first interview: although after discharge her fellow patients might never see one another again, these were people you could sit down and talk to, or cry with and not feel any humiliation whatsoever for doing it. Actually, talking wasn't even necessary, "we can look at each other, and we just know."

A few days later, she found herself feeling extremely anxious. When she mentioned this during group rounds, she reported, Dr. B had said she should think about the reasons she was feeling anxious. She took a walk to calm herself. But the next day, again at rounds, he referred again to her anxiety, and suddenly, "something in the back of my mind was, like—it was more of a challenge than anything, because I thought, 'He's trying to tell you something deeper than the way you would like it to be.' So I started thinking about it and it hit me right in the back of my head like a cast iron skillet: 'you know what it is, you know what it is!'"

Rebecca had had a breakthrough. She did not tell me what "it" was, nor did I ask, although it seemed likely, as we talked, that she was referring to some kind of childhood abuse, probably sexual, by a man. Rebecca began to make connections and to talk with her social worker and Neil, the psychologist. She was very upset, "but you have to go through these stages in going through a painful recollection of things."

Although at the beginning of the final interview Rebecca summarized her CPC experience by saying, "I came in on a stretcher and went out on a stretcher—I was better off the way I was," this was not true; Rebecca was a convert. She continued:

"I came in with a very open mind, with a resolution to do everything I possibly could to work with the program, because any support I got here was certainly not going to go with me when I leave. So it was incumbent upon me totally to give it my all—and I did that except for one thing, and that one thing was a problem that, subconsciously, I simply did not acknowledge, never thought of it in the context of it having anything to do with my pain; it was totally disassociated from that in my way of thinking, so I really didn't have to deal with it in here.

"My major accomplishment here has been to acknowledge the problem that—oh, gosh, for unpleasant reasons—I didn't really want to face up to it because, being human, you don't want to tackle a problem in any way that would put mental strain on you if you were already under the tremendous stress of physical pain. I mean, it's like *this* [physical pain] is really what's hurting me, *this* is preventing me from doing anything, *this* is preventing me from doing anything else, so this other thing isn't that important. I want to be able to do things again—physical things. So that's one way I looked at it."

Why, then, did she say she was "going out on a stretcher" in her final interview?

"Ultimately, the real reason why I didn't want to acknowledge it was because it was unpleasant and it was going to bring up a lot of bad memories. Acknowledging it also means that I am going to have to really work at it; just saying it is not enough, I'm going to have to dig kind of deep inside of myself to get rid of it, and the problem is hostility and anger and the feeling of having been abandoned. So, it's something I have to work at, but the hardest part is done." The hardest part was admitting it to herself, extremely important because no one else—even though "others might be trained, and might *think* there was something else going on," did not really know; all they could do was speculate; "there's something going on, there's something making you . . ."

Rebecca's hatred of "bullshit" applied to herself as well. "So the most important aspect of my admitting this anger and hostility and the feeling of being abandoned was admitting it to myself." And she knew that she would have to try to resolve it, at least to the point of not letting it affect her life as much as it had: "If this is contributing to my pain in any way, even in the most minute sense, then I am doing myself an injustice by not confronting it and dealing with it." She said she knew she was not going to get rid of the pain, but perhaps there was a way for her to get rid of the anger, the hostility, and the feeling of abandonment, which would give her a greater chance at being able to cope with the pain.

She said she was proud of herself for opening up. Talking about what happened in the past was a real milestone, because basically she was a very private person who only let people in as far as she wanted them to come. She was not about to let somebody sit and "pick my brain." When a staff member suggested it would be very helpful for her to talk about this in group she refused, saying she was not ready to admit any weaknesses she had to anyone.

Rebecca said her pain was like a heavy weight, an anvil, and that after her flash of insight she had a sense of "taking the anvil and not even lifting up, but, it's like when you sit for a long time and you just kind of shift—you still can't get up and walk around, but you can kind of shift the weight and it gives you a little bit of comfort." The anvil was still there, but "getting it off of one shoulder will do me good."

She was not expecting any miracles, she said, though she thought it was something of a miracle for her that she was not bitter about getting such severe pain; she still wanted to help people. The feelings of being abandoned and hostility and anger did not totally destroy her willingness to try and trust. Yes those feelings bounced her ability to trust around a lot, and for a while "I set [the ability to trust] on the back burner, but I did not turn off the fire. I just left it there until I was ready to go and deal with it again, and I'm thankful for that."

Rebecca was sure other patients had not seen her deep anger and hostility, "but we are not always what we seem; in fact, most of the time we're not. So, at least that's out, they all know there's deep anger and hostility." In fact, it seemed to me that her intense anger and hostility were apparent to all—although clearly not directed at them. An extremely warm, likable woman from the very beginning, during her stay she became much more mellow, often treating us to her lively and witty comments on the world around us.

When she was ready to leave, Rebecca reported that her level of pain had not changed but that her ability to recognize it and accept it and live in spite of it had greatly changed. Moreover, she could describe her pain: "Since the accident I always felt there was a tall, dark figure behind me, always. I could look over and it was there, kind of looming. And that was the pain and my fear of it." It had come to dominate her life. "I was extremely accommodating to this tall, dark figure, but since coming into this program, I have taken the cloak away and have invited him to stop hanging over my shoulder and have a seat right here beside me."

"You invited him to sit down beside you?"

"I made him. Just walked up one day and pulled the cloak off. That was quite an experience. 'Now, we're going to have to live together and I'm not going to do so much compromising, you're going to have to do some for me, now. We're going to have to get along.' "

The figure had no face and no color. She had made "a certain kind of peace with this presence. Before, I always had to ask permission from it: 'Oh, please, I want to put on a nice pair of high heels today. I want to look pretty. I want to be sexy with my boyfriend and enjoy it. Please, can I do that?' And the answer was always, 'No. If you want to do it, go ahead and try it, but you're not going to have any fun at it because I'm not going to let you.'

"And now, I said, 'stop leaning over my shoulder. Come, have a seat and let's just work this out. It's going to have to be equal now, because you're going to do as much giving as I am; I'm not going to give in to you any more. And, really, if you don't like it, you can leave—which is what I wish you would do anyway—but if you're going to stay, there will be compromise on both of our parts. I won't take advantage of you, and you're not going to take advantage of me, we're going to coexist here.' "

I asked whether the presence was completely separate, or somehow a part of her. She said no, the figure was a separate entity. "I think that if I felt it was something inward, it would have been much harder for me, because I would have had to exorcise it."

So, she said, recognizing and accepting the pain as part of herself was one profound change. Another was admitting her "deep hatred and hostility and anger—all the bad adjectives that can make a person very, very bitter, and start to not be able to recall the good times, and just be overly consumed with hate—it eats you and it ages you inside as well as outside. I never would have thought that my recognizing the anger and hostility would have had anything to do with my pain. But mental pain can be just as debilitating as physical pain. You know, you can become crippled mentally, just like you can physically. If you have a physical ailment, it is going to do something to your mind—if nothing else, it alters your lifestyle. So the two of them have to be together when you're dealing with pain."

In fact, she said, her anger had been the anvil that was weighing her down. "It's one thing to talk about anger or hatred for another person, but when you know in your heart without a doubt, and don't have to go back and deal with that anymore, it's just like saying to someone, 'you've done this to me, but I am wiping the slate clean, and all those feelings I had about you are gone.' Because this is all excess baggage—I don't need this, it's too heavy for me to have to drag around everywhere I go."

Later in this final interview she said, "I won all the way around because I have been able to get significant information and make significant gains from each part of the program. And still not have it diminish the pain, but I'm still a winner." Those who had not been winners, she concluded, had held back in some way; they simply had not given it their best. She added: "They aren't ready. When you're tired—when you've reached your level, you're going to do something about it . . . you're going to do it with your last dying breath, you're going to fight it. And until you've reached that point, then it's not so bad."

Several themes from Rebecca's narrative suggest that she had become a CPC convert. She began her interview (as many patients did) with a history of her difficulties, which had many typical elements: a complicated problem that did not get better, a great deal of interaction with the medical system, disillusionment and then anger with doctors and hospitals, a representation of her problem as basically physical (although she acknowledged a need for help with depression), and fury at suggestions that "it's all in your head." She was in litigation. (She did not, so far as I knew, ever have a medication problem.)

Her images of pain included a tall, dark male figure, and anvils: the connection between her neck and arm pain and the symbolic and psychological aspects of her pain is apparent from her request to the looming figure to "stop hanging over my shoulder" and sit down beside her. Another theme is weight that causes pain: here an anvil on her shoulders and talk of excess baggage that drags and is too heavy. Although Rebecca removed the hood of the presence, she indicated that learning his identity was not as important as gaining control over him—she just walked up one day and pulled the cloak off and made him sit down beside her. Her discussion of the negotiation with the figure also contained a great deal of control imagery. The figure seems to resemble a parent who has authority and who denies permission (perhaps significantly, to enjoy sexual behavior). Rebecca's achievement was renegotiating the terms of their relationship.

Rebecca believed in fighting and in not being weak or passive. Her remark about the person whose car hit hers also describes the person who gave her bad memories: "something happened to you, someone did something to you, but you're the one who's going to suffer." There is anger—at the driver who hit her, at her coworkers, at doctors and hospitals, at the person who produced the bad memories, at the pain—and there is fear of the cloaked pain figure and of being seen as weak by her coworkers, her fellow patients, or CPC staff.

Another theme is honesty. She was angry with her coworkers for expressing sympathy although they didn't really care, and for suspecting *her* of pretending pain in order to receive money; she was suspicious of "bullshitting" and "snow jobs" from CPC staff. But she also said of herself "we are not always what we seem; in fact, most of the time we're not" and talked at length about why she had not lived up to her own standards of truth. She was defensive about this because her stated goals had been to work, to keep an open mind, to "get the most out of the program." In short, to be a winner.

At first Rebecca had not wanted to speak of her pain as part of her; both physical and emotional pain were seen as coming from outside sources. During her stay, physical pain remained separate; the emotional pain had become more difficult to deal with because it was a feeling inside of her. For some patients, coming to see their pain as a part of themselves lessened its horror; they found they were more accepting of it and felt a greater sense of control. But for Rebecca visualizing the pain as a separate being was better—if it had been internal, like her feelings of anger, she would have had to exorcise it. Exorcism is intended to rid a

person of an alien and harmful other. Rebecca's visualization was not unlike the hurt inflicted on her earlier in her life—she saw her pain as external, a harmful presence, a figure—but it had human characteristics;
it was a he, and he talked—he said "no." Rebecca's work involved both
standing up to this powerful, harmful being and getting close enough to
yank his cloak off. She invited him to sit beside her. She talked to him,
negotiated with him, and, although always firm (and at one point threatening—saying she would like it if he left), she struck an agreement with
him which, interestingly, included her promise not to take advantage of
him. Reciprocity is the hallmark of dealings with, if not peers, then at
least beings seen to participate in one's own moral universe. In some
way, then, this figure was seen as meriting decent treatment—if he kept
his part of the agreement. Although she never accepts the figure as a
part of her, Rebecca does get closer to him, thereby increasing her control of him, in a fashion similar to those patients who came to see their
pain as part of themselves. Forgiveness—"all those feelings I had about
you are gone" eases the need for distance.

Rebecca's remarkable statement that she was a winner because she
had gotten something out of every part of the program ended our final
interview. Her remark about the level of pain being the same slipped
in almost as an afterthought; she spoke very little of her neck, arm,
and back.

What, in fact, *did* Rebecca get out of the program? She said the pain
was the same, although her ability to "recognize it and accept it and
live in spite of it has greatly changed." She still had no clear diagnosis or explanation of why the pain persisted: she saw a connection with
the bad memories but did not tell me exactly what the connection was,
nor how those events contributed to the pain. She had had an epiphany
when she saw the connection, experienced relief and a sense of forgiveness toward the person who had hurt her, but this experience was not
followed by any reduction in pain. She spoke of physical and emotional
pain interacting, but nonetheless saw them as separate. In short, many
of Rebecca's questions were still unanswered. But she saw herself as a
success, and so did her fellow patients and CPC staff members.

Rebecca illustrates a CPC success story in many ways. She showed
progress while on the unit, and potential for more progress after discharge. She was a lot less angry and depressed; she left excited, full of
energy, and full of plans. She felt better physically (the anvil on her
shoulder had shifted, giving some relief). Physical therapy had helped,
although, interestingly (as it was her main reason for coming to CPC)
she did not mention it in the discharge interview. She had loved being
with fellow patients. Other characteristics of the generic CPC success
story also applied: she accepted that she would not get rid of pain, and

planned to continue dealing with the underlying emotional problems contributing to her pain. She was leaving with higher self-esteem—at one point she said "I'm proud of myself"—and felt she would be able to cope. She spoke of achieving a more integrated self, and she spoke approvingly of CPC patients who integrated all parts of the program. She was also proud that she had opened up, because, while basically gregarious, she was nonetheless a very private person. Rather than constantly complaining about her pain, she said she had come to focus on it in a healthy way, imaging pain and interacting with it. When she was not explicitly dealing with her pain, it would take a back seat, as happened at the end of the interview—during her comments about how she was a winner, she slipped in that her level of pain was the same almost as an afterthought. Although she attacked the pain figure (yanking off its cloak), she subsequently invited it to sit with her and negotiate peace terms. The new agreement indicated a forgiveness and acceptance of the pain, just as she forgave the person who hurt her earlier in her life: "wiped the slate clean."

Mary

Mary was a nurse and ardent athlete who had had two automobile accidents. These, and the horrible pain that followed, had greatly changed her life: "Everything that I loved about myself, I lost. I lost my pride in myself—I had such self-esteem and such confidence and such love for myself and all those things got flushed down the toilet. My job got flushed down the toilet, my relationship with my husband—he's a triathlete and an exercise physiologist-nutritionist, so that makes it even harder. I would say I was killed in that car accident."

Plans to have a baby had become impossible. She described how she took out her pain and frustration on her husband, and how, at the same time, she hid a great deal of her suffering from her large Irish-American family. She resented both their pity and their ignorance—they thought pain centers were a type of "insurance scam that dwells on people's misery," or a drug detoxification facility, and were surprised when she announced she was being admitted to one. "Hiding pain is a full-time job," she commented.

Mary was particularly eloquent about depression and the changes in her self-esteem; we saw in Chapter 3 how she would spit at herself in the mirror, calling herself names like "bastard," "cockroach," and "leech."

Her stay at CPC began with some difficult moments. "There's lots of things I can't give up yet. I don't want to say I can't be like I was before. In this place, what they're talking about is you've got to forget what you were like and take on a whole new—I just don't want to do that because

I liked what I was, it took me a long time in my life to get the things that I got." But the stressed-out life she lived, pretending the changes had not occurred, did not work any more; she could no longer control it; she was a hypocrite, she was "sick."

Mary's initial struggles at CPC included a big blowup with Dr. B over doxepin. During group rounds, when several visiting physicians were present, she complained about the medication's side effects. "He more or less shuffled through his papers and said 'Nah, it's nothing, you've only been on that a couple of days.' So, I said, 'it's something to me, it's very important to me.' And then he just started calling the next patient's name—didn't even answer me." She began to cry and walked out, embarrassed. Dr. B called after her, "And *that's* why I have you on an antidepressant." Furious, she went to see him that afternoon:

"I said, 'you are the most arrogant son-of-a bitch that I have ever met in my life' and I told him that if he ever dared speak to me like that again I would spit in his face. 'I don't know who the hell you think you are that you can talk to people like that. You told me to tell you how I felt. I did, and not only didn't you respond but you treated me like some sort of dirtball. If you went home tonight and looked in the mirror and looked deep down inside of yourself, I'm sure that you would find just as many insecurities as the people in this program have.' "

She accused him of not caring about the patients. "He asked me, 'What do you want me to do, apologize to you? I do apologize if what I said upset you.' I said, 'don't turn it around and put the burden on me. You're the one with the problem.' "

In our talk, Mary rather deftly pulled out several contradictions of the CPC program: "they teach you to express yourself, to talk about how you're feeling" and then "dump on you" when you do. Her account of her encounter with Dr. B circulated among the patients, who claimed that he softened and became more involved in patient life for a few days.

Despite these contretemps, by the end of her stay Mary was a convert, although she, like Rebecca, reported that her pain was the same. Mary had reasons for added disappointment because her problem proved even more complicated than she had thought (muscle tissue, scarred during a bone graft, had tightened up). However, she had been given new exercises and said the clinicians were hopeful, but not sure, that with long-term physical therapy it might get better. Nonetheless Mary spoke of her CPC experience with great enthusiasm: "I'm able to talk about how I feel, you know, recognize that I have definite limits that I have to stick to or I'll never be able to do anything, basically, mechanically." Prior to admission, she said, she had always gone past her limits. Now, "It's funny, you can still have the physical pain, but as long as your head is clear, you're able to refocus, and more or less direct your talent in another direction rather than putting all of my energy into trying to be my old self."

Being more at peace with herself meant "you can really deal with anything and you'll get on with your life instead of fighting yourself all the time, which leads you to nowheresland." She had also come to believe that people would accept her in a different way, which was scary—she would have to reeducate everyone close to her. Another issue for this self-described hyper-nurturant nurse was telling them, "I can't be there for them all the time like I was before; I have to keep myself as my number-one priority, setting limits all the time." She had needed to learn that "it's good to be selfish."

Like many patients she spoke of control, saying one could definitely "control the pain from getting to a further point than it should." This "should" is telling: a few moments later she confessed that the "terrible situations with pain" in which she had found herself were "strictly my own doing." Now far less depressed, she found she could read again, whereas before "I couldn't even get through three lines and remember what the first line said." She had learned relaxation and had learned to separate the pain stresses from regular stresses. She was apprehensive about going home because "life isn't set up like this place," but planned to continue individual and group psychotherapy and try working in her husband's fitness business for two hours a day.

Echoing other converts, Mary mentioned the theme of a silver lining in every cloud. Thus the CPC program brought "tremendous things I probably never would have gained if I had never injured myself." In particular, for her, this meant she could talk about "deficiencies in my own personality that I was always aware of that caused me terrible stress, but I was always able to squeeze by without letting anybody know what they were, more or less thinking that it didn't make any difference." It became impossible to hide these imperfections after her accidents, so she had to learn to talk about them, and this brought great relief, even calm: "It's the weirdest thing to feel calm. I've never felt calm a day in my life. Now I truly believe in the powers of the mind. Before I always looked at it from a physical sense: if I felt stronger, I would feel better. But it doesn't work that way at all. I think it was just that everything about the strength of the mind was just so alien to me."

She said that the power of the mind was obvious, because before being admitted "I could never believe what I could do physically, being in the worse, most severe pain possible. So I saw that if I had my head and body working together instead of against each other, I could definitely make gains in both directions. I just never incorporated the strength of the two together." She had realized that tension exacerbated the pain, but had not known how to stop it; now, "I know I don't have to react like that." She said that attitude was "as big as 80 percent of it"—because there was no way you could go into a program like CPC's and get that much better physically in a month. The gains were a different mental and emotional attitude: she had become "a totally different person; I know how I was—I was a crazy person when I walked in here. I couldn't even think straight; my mind was filled with hate and every other terrible feeling."

Mary's enlightenment was more diffuse than Rebecca's, in that she made no specific connection between her past and her pain, but very similar themes emerged: of self-transformation and radical change, of answers to questions (some of which predated the injury that marked the onset of pain), of gaining control. Both exhibited what we can call "convert" language—talk of excitement, newfound energy, new plans, but also of peace, calm, and forgiveness. Neither reported a reduction in pain, both said the diagnosis of what was wrong was still not entirely clear, and both faced uncertain futures with respect to their pain problem. But both said they were happier, more integrated people, with far less self-hatred and free-floating hostility.

Edward

Edward, in his early forties, had been injured on his job as a mechanic for a town. A myelogram resulted in a grand mal seizure; he then underwent surgery for a ruptured disk, followed by a second operation which, if anything, made him worse. The town's retirement board forced him to retire, "sent me down the tubes," which infuriated him. Financial problems resulting from all this were a severe blow to his self-image as provider for his family, and he entered a job retraining program and began physical therapy. Then he was blown through a door when a building he was in caught fire and exploded. This seriously aggravated his back problem, but he found doctors unwilling to treat "a chronic back," as he put it, except with drugs. He became dependent on pain medications and tranquilizers, despite facing a "lot of grief about that" at home. He complained of trouble with doctors, claiming that one neurologist was brought in only because he was good friends with his own doctor, and that another doctor he had seen later lost his license because of drug abuse. His current physician had taken him off pain medications, resulting in serious withdrawal symptoms, including depression and insomnia; this led him to agree, very reluctantly, to try a pain center.

In many ways, Edward's was the classic story of the worker hurt on the job—resentful of what he considered a runaround from workers compensation boards and physicians, and angry with people who suggested his pain was not "real" because he was suing his former employer. Abuse of alcohol and medications had led to serious marital problems. He acknowledged that he had amplified his pain behavior at home when it had been convenient, reporting that sometimes when his wife suggested going out he would agree, then "hobble" until she said that he looked in too much pain, whereupon he would "reluctantly" agree not to go, even though he hadn't wanted to go in the first place. And he "always told the doctor I was lousy so he would give me the prescriptions. It was fun being a legal junkie, it's the answer. All the rationality goes down the drain when you're in serious pain." But he had lost a year of his life and almost lost his family, experienced a severe lowering of self-esteem, and acquired a "to hell with all of them" attitude.

He had hated being in a hospital because the longer he was there, the more it reinforced the idea he was disabled. He hadn't liked living with the idea and hadn't liked living with himself. It was easier to retreat and say "the hell with it." And he had lost his ability to reach out.

When he came to CPC, "I understood almost nothing. I was looking for [physical therapy] routines. I didn't think there would be so much emphasis on the psychological, because I've got a real thing. I'm trying to get insurance and I've heard it said, 'You're in this for the money, it's all in your mind.' If they get that idea, I'm going to have to pay $28,000 worth of medical bills. It's scary the power a doctor has over you when it comes to something like that. When I was first disabled I had the idea I was worthless, but at least I had the retirement coming in, and a doctor could wipe that away with a little scratch of his pen."

But from the first Edward was open to change, especially to learning things from fellow patients: "What I trust here is not the doctors as such but what the other patients have gotten out of it. Now I'm starting to believe in myself again. You can't separate the head stuff in the program and the community. In here you take a long view, you take a step back and you see yourself in other patients."

During this interview, after a week at the center, Edward grudgingly acknowledged CPC's explanation of chronic pain syndrome: "I can see how much of it is in your mind, but here they almost goad you with this." Asked why some patients did not improve at all, he said, "I honestly feel they don't put enough into it. Maybe they don't give it a chance." He himself felt sorry for the people who were in horrible pain, but "some need the good boot in the ass. The day before there was a patient who couldn't move and I think just needed a good boot. I try not to get high and mighty because I've been on both sides of the coin." He sometimes even sympathized with staff. Commenting on a physical therapist refusing to help an elderly woman get up from a mat, he said that their job "has to take a great mental toll on all the people who work on the unit if they're going to help people in pain."

Edward also quickly began to feel better physically: "Yesterday I went for an hour and a half without pain, without medication; just relaxation and an oil massage. Everything clicked and went right and I felt super. It's attitude. I feel better about myself, I'm taking control of what's going to happen to me."

Twenty days later, at the end of his stay, Edward said it had taken two weeks for him to "acclimate" himself to the program's focus, but once he figured out what was going on it was easy. He became a lot more open and receptive to some of what was being said. At first he had not had much faith in CPC, nor had he been "exactly happy about being here," but that when he "made up my mind to put some effort into it and see what I could get out of the program, things turned around."

However, in contrast to his optimistic statement after a week at CPC about pain-free periods, he reported that his pain was always there, with the same intensity, though now he "broke it up" with relaxation, ice massage, and using a transcutaneous electrical nerve stimulation unit. He emphasized the idea of doing something about the pain before it became overwhelming; prior to admission, he would postpone taking medications during the day and then "overtake real heavy" at night. His attitude had changed as well; whereas before he had "dwelled on" the pain, now, he said, he "focused on" it: "It used to eat at me, now I look at it a little more realistically, almost like from an analytical standpoint. I try to remove myself from it and look at it and say, 'Ok, what has caused it to flare up?'" In this way, he had discovered that tension made his back particularly unbearable at times. He had not recognized what a strong connection there was between stress and additional pain, or stress and more "noticed pain." He talked of "noticed pain," he explained, because "the pain is always there but sometimes it seems to block every-thing else out." Before, when this happened, "if there hadn't been any drugs around I would have gotten half in the bag and just started drink-ing." But he had learned not to let it get to the point where it blocked everything else out completely.

He had hoped to leave with a decrease in pain and was disappointed that this had not happened. However, because of what he had learned about himself, he was experiencing less "felt pain," adding that he won-dered if this distinction made any sense. "Pain is there and I know it is there, but I don't dwell on it."

"Before, the only thing I was looking for was mechanical change. Now that just isn't as relevant as the change I have made inside me—the idea that it's just not something that is going to rule me, control how I live my life. I could go on with the attitude that someday something physical is going to be done, but I think that would alter what I can do on a day-to-day basis." (Note that Edward mixes control language with acceptance language in a way similar to that of Rebecca and Mary.)

In fact, physical therapy did play an important role for Edward. He had been very happy at one point in his life about the way he looked; he had enjoyed working out, had not had a gut, and had always been proud of his arms. He had got that feeling back again, of starting to care, "not so much about my appearance, but about how I feel. And I feel good. When I can get ahold of something and do something physical, I derive a lot of pleasure from that. For a long time I didn't care to do that anymore—you know, I felt I couldn't do it."

An interesting aspect of Edward's conversion involved his relationship with his roommate Kurt. They became close buddies (they were roughly the same age, and both were manual laborers who had been hurt on the job). But Kurt was the opposite of a convert, and Edward felt torn about the difference between their experiences. His attempts to work out some of this confusion show in his answer to a question about how things could be improved at CPC; he offered a list of complaints, but ended by saying that whatever elements he objected to had been good for some patients. For example, he complained about the rigidity of the program, but added, "I needed the rigid structure; it's one of the things that made the program work for me. They don't cut anybody any slack; they are forcing you to think, forcing you to look at yourself, to push yourself. Some people see that as a threat, or get hung up on the fact that they are being told they have to do something, and they rebel. It took me a few days of saying 'this is ridiculous,' and refusing to look at some of the stuff before I started saying, 'wait a minute, it's not such a bad idea.'

"It sounds easy to tell somebody 'try looking at something from a different point of view—try changing the way you perceive something or an event. Instead of making it a negative thing, make it a neutral thing, and by changing how you perceive your feelings on the opposite end, [you can] change quite a bit.' And at first that sounded ridiculous to me, and then once I started trying it, it works real good."

But, he noted, for some people (in particular, his roommate) this approach "just made them more belligerent, and flat out refusing to go along with any part of it. And that is sad, because you know, they were the losers. But I don't know if the program, even if it was changed, would help that person anyway. How do you know if this person can be pushed a little bit more? Maybe there isn't any way around it. There could be a little more human side to it, yet I can see there would be people who would simply take advantage of that, if they knew they could get away with one thing, they would try something else, trying to push it a little bit further."

Edward was a convert who seemed to understand every aspect of the CPC approach, including confrontation and manipulation. For example, the more he understood that doctor's group involved "set-ups" designed to provoke a response, the easier it was to "roll with the punches."

He also understood and accepted that staff used physical therapy and anti-depressant medication for manipulating patients "like a cattle prod," as he put it, and deemphasized physical problems, because of the risk of returning to thinking that "if there was something they could see, then there was something they could do," which usually was not the case. For example, he admitted he would have liked more instruction on what specifically was happening and why his body was reacting the way it was, but followed this comment by acknowledging that such instruction was a double-edged sword because of the danger of overfocusing on the body.

And he understood why the community was so necessary: without everybody "being in the same boat" he would have withdrawn more. When the community worked, he added, patients did much better.

Like many other converts, Edward reported no significant reduction in pain and faced an uncertain future with respect to his pain problem. He remained confused about some aspects of pain. Like Rebecca and Mary, he spoke of self-transformation, had reworked important parts of his narrative about his problem, accepted that internal factors (e.g., personality) had contributed to the problem, and spoke of control, responsibility, and acceptance.

Discussion

Patients who improved at CPC to the extent of self-reporting a radical change in certain crucial areas of their lives (not necessarily a decrease in pain) offered several kinds of explanations for their own and fellow patients' improvement (or failure to improve). Insofar as these concern better physical conditioning, the effects of medication, improved mood from socializing, and benefits of learning useful information, they are fairly self-evident. But neither converts nor the fellow patients observing them attributed improvement exclusively to these factors. Marvin, for example, reporting remarkable improvement with his back problem, said: "I don't know why. [Dr. B] said it was probably motivation. Other people have shields, I don't, because I want to get on with my life." (But we saw that several of his contemporaries cynically suggested that he had initially exaggerated his pain as he could not have improved so much in only a month.) It is not always easy to discern other helpful factors—partly because, as noted, "improvement" was a contentious issue at CPC: Marvin's case—"miracle" or "bullshit" (as one patient termed it)—was an example.

CPC selected patients who were deemed to be in need of change— change in their coping mechanisms, their relationships, their understanding of earlier periods in their lives, or their attitudes toward their pain. Once admitted, patients understood these goals imperfectly at best. By the end of their stay, converts had not only come to understand this basic goal, but reported actually making many of the needed changes and considered themselves successes—"winners"—despite, often, experiencing the same level of pain. Staff members and fellow patients concurred with this assessment. Converts' narratives of what was wrong with them had altered greatly during their month as residents.

Certainly converting to CPC ideology could be difficult. Rebecca had to face guilt at not being entirely up front about certain events in her life; Mary had to admit "horrible deficiencies" in her personality; Edward had had to confront his medication and alcohol dependency and the fact that at times he had misrepresented his pain to his family and physicians. Many patients struggled with the idea that their attitude and beliefs had exacerbated the pain to some degree—and, after admission, had facilitated improvement. One convert, a month after being admitted on a stretcher, was climbing five flights of stairs at a time. She, too, faced other patients' skepticism, but was anything but embarrassed: "Some patients are more strong-minded. I'm pigheaded, I said, 'I'm going for it.' So they can't believe I walked a mile." She was comfortable with the idea that her previously intractable "real" problem had been so responsive to therapy because of her personality and attitude.

Converts spoke of a crucial change in their attitude toward themselves. Franklin, who had also come in on a stretcher, said that seeing other patients struggle encouraged him to find the answer within himself; it was like being given a mirror and seeing himself in it. Ready to leave, he reported a 15–20 percent decrease in pain, an encouraging improvement in range of motion and muscle tone, and a significant change in his mood and outlook on the future. Before, he said, he had come to think of himself as "bad." Although he had learned a lot from classes and from observing other patients, "you basically found most of the answers in yourself." Any more medical intervention, he said, would have greatly increased the psychological component of the pain, leaving him feeling trapped like an invalid.

Like many patients, Franklin struggled with issues of conscious versus unconscious processes and the degree of one's responsibility for one's pain. For example, some of his attitudes probably helped cause

the injury and increase the damage subsequently, he said, — "like ignorance" — treating his body like a normal body and trying to do athletics
at a normal rate after injuring himself many times.

A young woman had concluded that the patients who were stuck on
being disabled, for whatever reason — this was an unconscious process —
could find themselves grabbing the ball and starting to run once it was
brought to consciousness. But they also could choose not to. She did
not think they consciously thought "I don't want to change" when they
came in — "I think it is totally unconscious. But the program helps bring
all that stuff to the surface. I mean, they look for that, they dig for that.
And you have a choice."

This issue of choice was addressed by Linda, a staff nurse, who offered
the CPC perspective: one of the hardest things about learning about the
kinds of things you were doing in life that were not in your best interest is that then you had to take the responsibility to decide whether you
were going to continue along this path or work at changing. But this
kind of work is extremely difficult, she said, and so people sometimes
decided to continue what they were doing. Changing may seem so devastating and so hard to do, that they choose to continue with that pain;
suffering the pain is not as difficult as changing.

"I think that once a person makes that decision, they have the right
to live with it if they want, that's their choice, and I have to respect their
choice. There are people who have chronic pain who choose to keep
it rather than — say they're in a bad situation with a spouse that beats
them, they may choose to stay in that situation, and that may seem horrible to other people who can't imagine that, but it's their choice, and
they have the right to make that decision. It's not what I would do, but
that's their choice."

Choice entails responsibility for the outcome. In this respect, CPC's
approach was similar to the approach taken by Alcoholics Anonymous.
Although not an inpatient program, AA, founded in 1935, originated
some of the treatment models used in many therapeutic community
programs today. AA helps alcoholics stay sober through mutual support,
self-examination, and "spiritual guidance." Because alcoholism is seen
as a disease, to some extent the alcoholic is viewed as not responsible up
to the point of joining AA. At that point, however, he or she *is* responsible for controlling alcoholism by not drinking.

Both alcoholism and chronic pain syndrome can be seen originally as
not the fault of the individual (e.g., the alcoholic grew up in an alcoholic household; the pain sufferer was rear-ended by another driver);
treatment, however, involves learning about one's true condition and
choosing to behave, feel, and think differently. This acceptance was an
important sign of conversion to CPC ideology and resonates with the

theme of correct thinking and practice found in much convert discourse in general.

Unlike coping with alcoholism, however, the path to chronic pain management is not clearly marked; indeed, different paths are appropriate for different people. Not drinking is an easier—albeit often resisted—concept to grasp than becoming more responsible for your pain. It is easier to see that certain behavior exacerbates the urge to drink or take drugs. Another important distinction is that no one except a masochist consciously (unconsciously is another matter) wants to feel severe pain, an experience quite different from the "highs" addicts seek from alcohol or cocaine.

The Mystery of Pain

Significant improvement at CPC clearly was not solely a straightforward matter of ending medication dependency, getting into better physical shape, or acquiring helpful information. I have tried to convey the nature of the unstraightforward aspects of this change by comparing them to initiation rites and religious conversion, for both involve intense, rather totalizing communal experiences—unlike what happens in a classroom or during a psychotherapeutic interaction, or results from physical exercise or meditation.

Converts said these parts of the program were important, but they had changed in other more profound ways. Several spoke of the change as ultimately mysterious, inexplicable. I am not including here those like Marvin who were content to describe their improvement as "a miracle," but patients who were puzzled and tried to analyze what had happened to them. Edward, an extremely intelligent man, said that without the patients the program just wouldn't work. How did this happen? He did not know, and felt that no one knew why it worked, adding that no one even knows why most chemicals work on your body. They know what these chemicals do more or less, but they do not know why, and he thought it was the same kind of thing with community feeling: when people get together and jell, and everything goes off right, it produces a reaction whose precise mechanism would probably never be known. It was just that when things work, they work.

Some comments had a religious or spiritual tinge (not including remarks by those few who explained their problem and whatever help they found at CPC in fairly conventional religious terms). In his discharge interview, Franklin conceded that his attempts to explain fell short, because you could not really explain a lot of the process. Some of what had happened to him was a mystery: it all came from within and much was unknown. "I gave it a chance and it helped. The doctors do not know the answer, they cannot see inside your body." Furthermore, he continued, most of life is unknown; despite the communication revolution of this century, most of the unknowns have not changed.

There was a similarity—*not* identity—between CPC converts and religious converts. Those CPC patients who fit into that category underwent a major change, one they initially mistrusted and resisted despite being desperate and very open to *some* kind of change. Converts spoke of "hitting bottom"; we saw that Rebecca said that "until you've reached that point, then it's not so bad."[25] The nature of the change, despite a plethora of descriptions, was never entirely agreed on: it was not clear *how* things such as attitude and unconscious processes had contributed to, and, at CPC altered, their experience of their pain.

While CPC staff members sounded authoritative at any one time, myriad ambiguities and outright contradictions emerge when one examines the total corpus of therapeutic information in texts distributed as handouts or delivered in lectures and informal comments. For example, patients heard of the dangers of being dependent, of being spoiled by one's caretakers, but also heard that chronic pain sufferers were more than usually likely to be hyper-nurturant types who consistently put others' needs ahead of their own. They heard the value of "going for it," of "giving 110 percent," but also of not "setting yourself up to fail" by ignoring limitations. They saw that CPC, despite its claim to espouse policies and procedures contrary to standard medical practice, nonetheless still concerned itself with determining to what extent a patient's condition was "real" as it made recommendations regarding a patient's status in civil and criminal suits and in workers' compensation and other disability decisions, which most often rested on determining to what extent a patient's pain was the result of physical processes. Hence even those patients most satisfied with their experience left CPC with a significant number of unanswered questions and confusion about what went on there.

Although it would be extremely hard to document, the gaps in knowledge, ambiguities, and contradictions that were constantly apparent in CPC discourse—both patients' and staff members'—contributed significantly to the profound experience reported by converts, paradoxically facilitating the process. This confusion was built into the CPC program, although staff would probably deny its existence. It served to disorient patients, a consequence of the amplified stress and heightened affect they felt while simmering in the emotional stew of the CPC atmosphere, particularly during the first week. Being offered no consistent, easily discernible, systematized, structured, well-worked-out explanation of chronic pain may have permitted individual patients to feel more comfortable in their initial, often ambivalent and tentative explorations of what CPC offered. People are often quite adept at "hearing what they want to hear"—selecting just those elements of a message they feel apply to them. The sometimes chaotic messages CPC patients received—from a heterogeneous staff, from fellow patients, and from their own thoughts and feelings—made it easier to receive those parts of the message they were capable of receiving at a given time, because different parts of these disjointed messages appealed to (and applied to) different patients and to the same patients at different times during their stay.

The heterogeneity of disciplines represented by CPC staff also contributed to patient confusion. Some staff members were extremely conventional in their medical outlook, while others ran workshops on reflexology and "love medicine." In addition, some (albeit a small part) of the confusion was due to simple misunderstandings of the accepted distinctions in the medical vocabulary about such terms as chronic pain, disability, psychogenic, somatization, malingering, and psychosomatic.[26]

The full CPC message about causes and treatment of pain was thus so varied, in both content and form, that it can be likened to a smorgasbord. One is not supposed to eat every dish available at a smorgasbord table, but to choose among individual dishes in a given course according to one's appetite, tastes, and so forth. Similarly, some stop-smoking programs present a long list of techniques that have worked for other smokers, and individuals are supposed to respond to these different options, saying, "that one just might work for me!" Something like this often occurred at CPC. To be sure, CPC was vastly different from a smorgasbord or a varied set of aids for quitting smoking. Diners presumably approach a smorgasbord table anticipating an enjoyable experience; whatever problems they might have with overeating or eating unhealthy items, this activity is fairly straightforward—as is signing up for a class to quit smoking, whatever issues, denial mechanisms, resistances, and so forth, people may have. But patients choosing to enter CPC did not face such a straightforward situation. Like eaters or smokers, CPC patients wanted something—but what they wanted was to get rid of, or at least reduce, their pain.

Those who did come to agree wholeheartedly with what they understood to be the CPC perspective faced the difficult task of discarding their initial objections. They were in a bind: insofar as treatment did not involve procedures that could be explained in conventional biomedical terms, any improvement was a sign that at least some of the pain had been, in a sense, "all in your head." Accepting that improvement was partly due to motivation meant grappling with far-reaching implications, for they had basically seen pain as an organic problem that needed medical attention. Patients who converted did not say that the pain had been "in their heads," and I do not think they saw it this way.

But they did negotiate with themselves and others over the elements to include in a narrative about the changes they had undergone that featured many elements of CPC ideology. One important element involved responsibility: to some degree converts came to accept the notion that "while you were not responsible for your pain until now, from now on you are." In addition, CPC converts accepted the notion that personal history could sometimes help explain the persistence of pain, even pain initially produced by an injury or malfunctioning body part.

These are very complicated issues, and patients dealt with them in different ways. Some of those who improved accepted no responsibility for their pain or its persistence, but did accept responsibility for "getting on with their lives" and finding ways to control, if not the pain, then their responses to the pain. Other patients accepted some responsibility for pain or its persistence as well as for how they would handle the pain in the future. Those who reported an overwhelming decrease in pain, it was clear, had radically altered their notion of pain, either believing that relaxation (in its role of reducing muscle tension) and physical therapy were the main reason behind the decrease (in cases of musculo-skeletal types of pain), or believing that changed cognitions and emotions were the main reason.

Of the various factors that contributed to the overall confusion about pain at CPC, two played a leading role. The first has to do with the confusions patients brought to CPC. That they were admitted in a confused state was not in doubt. They were confused about their bodies' responses—most chronic pain sufferers had suffered some initial injury, yet had been told their pain was no longer entirely due to that. They were confused about their current identity as a pain sufferer: Am I normal? Surely not. Sick? Not in certain crucial respects. Should I be a patient in a regular hospital? Usually not. In a rehabilitation hospital? No—chronic pain, unlike chronic conditions such as stroke or multiple sclerosis, is *not* characterized by periodic acute episodes requiring hospitalization. Am I disabled? Many CPC patients were on disability, but many reported their claims had been challenged, more or less openly, and we have seen that chronic pain sufferers have difficulty legitimizing their status as "ill" or "disabled" especially if they are mobile and have no visible infirmity. They were also confused about identity on a more fundamental level—who am I, now that I cannot engage in many of the activities that actualized who I was? Other confusions involved the duration of the condition (temporary or permanent?), managing a pain problem (disclose or dissemble?), about mental stability (tell me, doctor, am I crazy?), and about moral responsibility (I think I deserve what I'm receiving for my pain problem—workers' compensation, narcotics, etc.—but maybe I'm actually a deadbeat / drug addict).

The second source of confusion has to do with CPC's treatment program: the bombardment of patients with information and challenges, especially during the first week; the vague, profuse, and contradictory explanations of why pain persists; the confrontations and duplicitous psychological interventions. Of course these last two factors are connected. Staff members had to present the CPC message in a roundabout way to prevent patients from becoming so angry or withdrawn they would not respond, and patients became angry or demoralized in part because of the status of psychogenic explanations of pain and disability in mainstream American culture. As staff members had to gain patients' cooperation and try and keep them from leaving early, they had to rely on hints and suggestions, although no-holds-barred statements were issued when staff decided to openly and collectively confront a patient.

The very issue of improvement—what it was and how to measure it reliably—was also a source of confusion. While some improvements made by patients during their stay were observable and empirically verifiable (e.g., range of motion, stamina), for the most part indices of improvement took the form of verbal and written reports from patients and staff. Marvin, the young man who considered himself a CPC success story because he had improved so much, elicited doubts in his fellow patients as to just how extensive his physical problem had "really" been on admission. Both staff members and patients made comments about "snow jobs" and false improvement. One young woman, for example, told me her good-bye speech had been almost all lies (no one was fooled, however). Hence, subjective measures were potentially inaccurate, especially if we are concerned with predicting long-term outcomes.

The aggregate staff estimates of degree of improvement sketched above show a significant range, and I have noted an overall discrepancy between staff and patient estimates. So many unknown or only partially known factors influenced these evaluations they did not warrant exploring in more detail.

This account of confusion, contradiction, and negative patient evaluations is not meant to categorically imply that CPC was not doing its job. Rather, one must avoid overly simplistic notions about the value of well-worked-out, crystal-clear instructions for changing the way people think, at least when there are excellent reasons to hold on to one's beliefs and reject the offered paradigms. Edward compared what happened at CPC to the difficulty some people have giving up smoking, even though they know the dangers: " 'Quit smoking!' You know, 'smoking's bad for you, why don't you quit smoking?' It's very easy for me to say it: 'I did it—see?' Doesn't always work that way."

It is possible that the enormous confusion reported by virtually all CPC patients was an extremely important ingredient of the program and facilitated a shift in the meaning of pain for a substantial number of patients—if we accept suggestions made by Arthur Kleinman and Leston Havens on paradox.[27] An analogy would be the "brainwashing" used in certain intensive language-teaching methods because of the need to break down assumptions derived from one's native language before being able to introduce the phonology, grammar, and semantic structures of the language to be learned. Our model of conversion argues that profound religious conversion cannot be explained by a brainwashing model. However, psychophysiological reactions to the high levels of stress at CPC, especially during the first week, did probably contribute to some of the shifts made by those patients who experienced profound change during their sojourn. Jerome Frank, in a study of the similarities among psychotherapy, primitive healing, religious conversion, and thought reform (brainwashing) notes that methods of thought reform involve harassment and strong group pressure in an attempt to produce an intense, disorganizing emotional state. He cites experimental evidence that suggests an optimal level of central nervous system excitation to facilitate learning, but goes on to suggest that various psychiatric treatment methods, like other forms of persuasion (such as thought reform), produce much higher levels of arousal, to the point of extreme unpleasantness or exhaustion. The value of inducing such a state may lie in a state of excitement so intense as to be disorganizing, thereby paving the way for a new reorganization of attitudes.[28]

In short, the abundant confusions and contradictions found at CPC constitute a systematic mystification of pain. Parallels can be found in the theory behind paradoxical therapy, the practices of various human potential organizations during the 1970s, and a great deal of ritual practice.[29] Staff members would almost certainly disagree. They saw themselves running a difficult but internally coherent (with respect to the ideology behind it) program. And, to be sure, some of what they were trying to do was indeed clear, consistent, and agreed-on by all. Staff members did agree that parts of the CPC program were very confusing to patients, at times to the point of chaos, but explained it as resulting from the program's problems rather than something systemic. But surely some of the confusion was indeed an implicit part of its structure, sometimes facilitating what CPC tried to accomplish. Because institutions reproduce the ideology of the social system they are embedded in, to some extent the CPC's program would be expected to derive from and reflect the mystery and mystification of pain in the larger society.

Conclusions

Determining precisely what produced improvement at CPC and measuring it are extremely difficult tasks. A minority of patients accepted CPC ideology so passionately that they can usefully be compared to religious converts. CPC converts exhibited several characteristics. For one, they came to accept a mind/body connection in chronic pain. As one convert said, "If you have stress for twenty years, when the human mind can't take it anymore, then the mind lashes out against the body." Sometimes the idea of "useful" pain accompanied patient talk about such connections—as happens when, for instance, patients spoke of pain as a warning to be heeded rather than something to be dreaded. This discourse speaks of pain as the body's forceful way of showing people they are under stress, an index of their mental state, and a symbol of the possibility of preventing problems from getting out of hand. In addition, converts also accepted that some part of their continuing pain had to do with ineffective coping mechanisms, as illustrated by Mary's and Edward's accounts. Also, they accepted that past experiences can contribute to pain, as Rebecca's story illustrated. Furthermore, they came to agree that the pain sufferer has a considerable amount of responsibility for improvement. In addition, converts came to understand how support—or the lack of it—can influence the pain experience, as this quote from a migraine sufferer illustrates: "It's so clear . . . within a focus [group psychotherapy] session I can see the headache disappear; the support comes, and I've worked it away, like I can get rid of it." Finally, some of the more mysterious aspects behind patient improvement were examined, and a suggestion was made that high levels of confusion might, paradoxically, have helped patients examine CPC messages that they initially resisted.

Of course, while the metaphor of conversion is a useful device, what took place was more complex, which is why the notion is useful only as a heuristic device. For one thing, improvement is hardly identical to becoming a CPC "true believer." Some of the patients who improved had wholeheartedly joined the *patient* community but had opposed the official CPC position, or at least significant parts of it. It is possible to argue that their improvement was facilitated *because* of such opposition. Using this model, let us assume that a given patient needed to oppose something oppressive and unhealthy, and that CPC represented the totalitarian, self-serving medical establishment. After it was symbolically vanquished, this hypothetical patient could improve. This may seem far-fetched, but we have seen that some patients did improve while fulminating against the staff. Patient conjectures about staff using "reverse psychology"—daring the patient, as Naomi put it, to "prove us wrong—we think you *can't* do it," build on this dynamic.

In sum, what made CPC work, when it did, was that people confronted their pain (what this meant differed for each patient). Those who improved significantly were able, somehow, to turn an anomaly into something normal, or at least significantly more normal, and feel more in control of their situation. Patients spoke of making pain more familiar, of "owning" pain in the sense of accepting they would always have it. And, using a variety of images, they also spoke of accepting it either in terms of its being a part of themselves, or in terms of having a relationship with it.

Chapter 7
Me/Not-Me: Self, Language, and Pain

"The pain is me"

"No, I am not going to accept myself the way it is. I am going to will myself better"

—Teresa

Self, Body, and Pain

At CPC, pain-sufferers, their families, and staff members provided fascinating reflections on the relationship of body, self, and pain, how self-concept changed after the onset of pain, and what happened to self-concept as a result of therapy. I call the constellation of issues around pain, body, and self the problem of "me/not-me" because patients struggled so much with questions of how much pain was a part of their selves, and whether one should see pain as the enemy, or try to make friends with it—should it be "owned" or "disowned"?

This is a complicated topic for a number of reasons. First, the variety of cases and the ways patients and staff members talked about such abstract issues make generalizing difficult. Second, since patient and staff discourse was for the most part concerned with getting better and only rarely became philosophical or cultural-analytical, I often had to infer the underlying concerns. Patient talk most often was about a specific example of suffering or confusion about the best attitude to take toward one's pain. Also, because of stigma and other culturally ascribed attributes of chronic pain (and resentment at CPC's heavy-hitting tactics), patients were sometimes reluctant to discuss any issue connecting pain to mental processes.

Mind/Body Dualism and the Definition of Pain

One of the many fascinating aspects of pain is its ambiguous status between body and mind. Pain is seen as involving both a physical sensation ("real" stimuli producing "real" electrical signals) and an aversive feeling; however, one can argue that to separate the pain experience into two different feelings seriously distorts its nature. The definition of pain given in Chapter 1 provided by the International Association for the Study of Pain requires that we think of pain as an emotional experience rather than a sensation that has an overlay of emotion. Pain without aversive emotion would simply not be pain. If we imagine someone feeling pleasure from a nociceptive input we know usually produces pain, we have to conclude the person is not feeling pain; pain is a concept, not a thing. Where pain is deliberately sought—as in "no pain, no gain" exercise or as a path to sexual or religious ecstasy—it can be called desirable because of a learned association; however, in these cases, pain is welcomed as a means to an end *in spite of* its aversive qualities. True, pain is sometimes sought for itself, but usually humans and other animals try to avoid it. In general, whether we are speaking of clinical practice, biologic function, zoological evolution, or simple experience, a core, necessary feature of pain is its aversiveness.

A model that postulates a linear, chronological process involving origin in either body (e.g., pain resulting from a burn) or mind (e.g., psychological origin with subsequent peripheral physiological changes) does not account for pain; it is too simple. Memory, culture, previous experiences, speculation about the future are all part of any kind of pain, most especially chronic pain. The phenomenologist Alfred Schutz compares pain to an eye blink, but this is not correct: eyes blink whether or not we are aware of it, and this is not true of pain.[1] Eye blinks that are not perceived have no meaning, but pain always has meaning; even the oft-remarked meaninglessness of chronic pain is meaningful. It is true that the proximate causes of pain can be very similar to the proximate causes of eye blinks—electrical impulses in the nervous system—but what produces the onset of a pain experience (nociception) is not the same thing as pain itself (the experience of pain), just as what makes pain disappear is not the same thing as the absence of pain.[2] This statement seems quite obvious, yet when we distinguish, as we often do, "emotional pain" from "physical pain" either we mean by "emotional pain" pain with no embodiment or we are indeed differentiating the two in terms of cause. Of course, a significant amount of emotional pain (defined in terms of cause) is in fact embodied pain. The important point is that any pain experienced in the body is experienced in the body, period, and will be experienced as physical pain, regardless of the cause.

Of course, knowing the cause of a pain is often important. For one thing, such knowledge is a factor in decisions about what to do. Also, since Western culture places such emphasis on the mind/body distinction, someone who believes her pain is due to a physical cause (e.g., angina produced by hardened arteries) will probably experience a pain in the region of the heart differently from a pain she believes to be emotional in origin (e.g., heartache caused by unrequited love). This is of particular concern to many pain sufferers because of the stigma that accompanies pain that is seen to be emotionally caused and does not go away. A lover's heartache draws disapproval (romantic literature and Celtic ballads notwithstanding) if it does not diminish in time: the sufferer should "get over it" after a while. A clinician's diagnosis of such a pain would probably seem stigmatizing to the sufferer. Hence, although cause and experience are related in that the sufferer's belief about the cause of the pain will almost always have an effect on the experience, cause must be kept conceptually distinct from the embodied experience of pain.

We have seen that the fact that one usually must choose to communicate the presence of pain, to exhibit pain behavior, carries the possibility that one is actually communicating about other things instead of, or in addition to, pain. This creates a problem for a self grappling with enormous amounts of pain, for the more the pain is communicated, the greater the risk of the self becoming illegitimate because it is that much more likely to be seen as inappropriately using the body to accomplish goals of the mind.

In addition, this pain-full self must grapple with our culture's construction of the healthy self—and of the "stiff upper lip" approach to pain and suffering—as morally superior (although this attitude has been accused of actually producing ill health[3]). Part of the discourse on pain in America concerns "pain threshold." While this concept is sometimes couched in neutral terms, having a "low threshold of pain" often means that one is less than mature, strong, and, in some contexts, manly.[4]

Subject, Object, Self, and Pain: Me/Not-Me

An important component of pain is its ontological status vis à vis the sufferer's core self. Since CPC patients were desperately searching for ways to cope with their problem, most were highly motivated to think (and if necessary rethink) about ways in which pain was and was not an integral part of their selves. Pain was a part of their selves because it was a feeling, it was inside their bodies, and it dominated their lives; pain was not a part of their selves because it was usually seen as due to an exogenous cause, temporary, and at a specifiable location (limb or organ) rather than deep within (a character trait would perhaps be seen as closer to the core self). The fact that chronic pain was considered bad played a part as well. Scarry says, "even though it [pain] occurs within oneself, it is at once identified as 'not oneself,' 'not me,' as something so alien that it must right now be gotten rid of."[5] While patients sometimes spoke of "good pain," in the conventional sense of warning, or as a sign of muscles being "whipped into shape," clearly, in general, patients saw pain as the enemy, making it more "not-me" than if it were a friend. Although staff members hinted about secondary gain, where pain is an ally (helping to obtain benefits like money or attention), for the most part, patients, when talking about themselves at least, resisted this notion.

Chronic pain challenges the notion of the body as object and the self as subject. While the subject can be the conscious mind "having" an objective body and an objective pain, it is also true that the subject can identify with, and combine with pain and become the "pain-full me"—perhaps contemplating a past or future "pain-free me." Byron Good asks, "Is the pain an essential part of the self, or is it 'merely' a part of the body? Can the pain be separated as object from the self as subject, thus differentiating the subject from the world which acts upon it, or must he 'passively endure' the pain?"[6]

Objectification

According to phenomenology, in the everyday lifeworld we do not normally experience our bodies, nor our pain, as objects.[7] When fully experiencing severe pain, we simply are "in pain," we are "pain-full."[8] It is when we pay attention to pain, talk about it, try to make sense of it, that we objectify it. Good interviews Brian, who attempts to objectify his severe pain and his body but is not wholly successful. He is frustrated because pain resists the kind of objectification provided by standard medical testing. Although diagnosed as a temporo mandibular joint disorder sufferer, this label does not suffice—Brian wants more of the information a name should provide. At CPC, Edward said he had hoped to leave with a decrease in pain. Although this had not happened, because of what he had learned about himself there was less "felt pain"—although he wondered whether such a distinction made sense. This notion, while at first sight contradictory, can be made consistent if we accept that in daily life we seldom become objects to ourselves.[9] In talking, Edward begins with a pre-objective and pre-reflective experience of his body and finds less "felt pain." Yet when he objectifies himself and his body he finds in fact no decrease in pain.

Although patients found it difficult to express this idea, I recorded many similar remarks—for instance, "less noticed pain," or, "you don't dwell on it"; Fred said "the pain's the same severity, but it doesn't hurt as much." These statements illustrate the need to see the core meaning of pain in terms of the experience, not in terms of a sensation.[10] We resist this because to say that a decrease in the negative impact of the pain experience—in the feeling of helplessness, the obsessive focusing on pain—alters the pain itself postulates a merged body and mind that is very difficult for many Westerners to contemplate. Intention and control of consciousness are involved here, but so is a preliminary understanding of the difference between pre-objective and objective. One often finds one cannot eliminate pain—at least very few CPC graduates found they could—but some of them reported achieving "less felt pain." Examples of similar statements can be found in the pain literature. Reynolds Price, in a Public Radio International broadcast, states, "it just absolutely doesn't concern me anymore." He clarifies what he means: although the level of pain has remained the same, in a kind of "oriental, mystical" way his mind has ceased worrying about it. What was once a huge bonfire had turned into "a small campfire about a hundred yards away."[11]

The usual response to pain involves attempts to objectify it, to separate it from the self. If we experience a mildly pleasant trance state, as in daydreaming, we might not attempt to find its cause or control it, but we do try to objectify pain in order to understand and control the difference between painful and painless states. The vast majority of CPC patients saw themselves as subjects and their pain as an object in the sense of being "out there"—physical, bodily, "real" pain. The body, another object, "has" pain. Patients spoke of, and presumably experienced, their pain in terms of an identification of self apart from pain.

We are also likely to think of severe pain as an object because it is so powerful and produces such grave and aversive effects. Something that can virtually obliterate consciousness of anything but itself, that can, as Scarry says, "destroy the world," is clearly an "it," existing apart from the self in some fashion.[12] In this model pain is an alien, an intruder invading the self. Good's interviewee Brian describes his body as being taken over by pain. For him, "the pain has agency. It is a demon, a monster—Pain is an 'it.'"[13] Pain threatens the objective structure of the everyday world in which pain sufferers live. Good comments on Brian: "We act in the world *through* our bodies; our bodies are the subject of our actions, that through which we experience, comprehend and act upon the world. In contrast, Brian described his body as having become an object, distinct from the experiencing and acting self."[14]

We also objectify pain by thinking of it as physical; since pain is of the body and we see our bodies as physical objects, so do we see pain. The conventional model of pain is physically based: touching fire with a finger initiates chemical and electrical processes that result in pain. In addition, pain is sometimes conceptualized in terms of the presence of a physical object inside oneself. I collected many statements from both patients and staff members characterizing "real" pain in this way—real because one can see it in an X-ray, CT scan, or blood test. Again, the cause of a pain (a ruptured disk, arthritis) is conflated with the experience of it. An example of the distinction between cause and experience does occur in the inverse case: when an X-ray suggests there should be massive pain and yet no pain is reported.

Finally, in a clinical setting pain will be thought of as physical because nonphysical pain is suspect. CPC patients, in their search for validation of their pain, tended to rely on any available objective measure that made their pain as "real" as possible. At times they competed with one another over this. A young man who bitterly complained that ten doctors had all told him it was in the mind described why his pain was more serious than many other CPC patients':

"My surgery was five and a half hours. I had three discs let go and that was from the fall, and it wasn't bruised or something like that, or herniated or degenerated disc or something. Mine was smashed from the fall. And when I saw the X-rays it looked just like an octopus, fluid leaking out from the disc and stuff. It was horrible. And you thought I was in pain now? Two years ago I was 90 percent worse."

Although CPC patients struggled to maintain dualisms that separated mind and body, and subject ("me") and object (pain/body), many also struggled to rethink these two dualisms, in hopes that their lived painful bodies and selves would be reconciled in some fashion. Ethan said that, prior to being admitted, his mental response to try to resolve the pain had been simply to "go away"—he had tried to find distractions, like books, that would take his mind out of himself.[15] This separation of part of the self from the rest did not work for him, yet some patients said they had learned to use something very similar, if not identical, which they tended to call distraction, as a way to cope with pain. The difference was the meaning such an exercise held for the person in pain.

Subjectification

Pain straddles the object/subject boundary. CPC patients talked of trying to distance the self from pain by objectifying it, but in some instances, they identified the self with pain, and spoke of pain experienced as coterminous with the body—of pain-full bodies that were at least at times coterminous with the self. In extreme cases, at times phenomenologically one *is* pain; one's selfhood and one's pain-full body combine. When it claims so much attention from the self that it is experienced as within the self, the "me," pain is subjectified. In a sense, the self finds itself subject to the rule of pain, and this subjectification can increase as pain progressively destroys the world. Unlike, for instance, a fervently sought merging with the Holy Spirit, merging with pain is unwelcome. This process can be terrifying: Teresa, the young woman with severe back pain we met in Chapter 1, spoke of becoming "psychotic with pain."[16]

One part of this process has to do with the individual pain sufferer's personal history, when her or his self was greatly changed because of pain. An individual with a pain-full body finds that, to a great extent, this body has determined the self he or she has acquired. Although unwanted and rejected, this new self is, like the new body that accompanies it, still one's self. Some CPC patients had subjectified their pain prior to being admitted in less consuming ways, and spoke somewhat unselfconsciously of an identification with pain of one sort of another. A recovering alcoholic at CPC said he could identify with his pain more than he identified with alcoholism. An elderly woman spoke ironically of her shingles "liking" her. And a machinist who had loved his job and had became very bitter following a needless work-related accident that forced him into retirement, commented, "If this is retirement, you can have it. I guess the only thing keeping me alive is the pain." But few entering patients spoke in terms of accepting their pain or identifying with it, or of seeing it as a friend or ally.

Pain, then, is both subject and object, both "me" and "not-me." It is not unique in this respect: people speak of many kinds of feelings as being both "me" and "not-me." In love poetry, it is the poet's own heart that is pierced, the poet's soul that has found bliss, the poet's self that has become all it could be—a "truer self." Yet there are many descriptions of feeling "possessed" by love, or of merging with the beloved. All powerful, overwhelming feelings have this property: being profoundly in love, like being in severe pain, requires leaving the everyday lifeworld and thereby transforming the experience of self so the "me" and "not-me" converge in some ways—or at least have different boundaries. The difference is that one usually journeys to the province of passionate love willingly whereas pain animates the sufferer to return to the everyday painless world.

Changing the Relationship Between Self and Pain

For pain sufferers, the important consideration with respect to the issue of pain as "me" versus "not-me" is its implications for how one copes. People clearly have different styles of coping.[17] The idea of fighting pain, seeing it as an enemy to be conquered and destroyed, figured in a great deal of patients' talk early in their stay. Control is the major trope; a migraine sufferer said that if she ever were to completely give in to her headaches, she would be an invalid. Would she win, or her head? Another woman said that her pain might win for one day, but the following day, after regrouping and coming up with a different strategy, she could attack the enemy again. A man spoke about losing: "I was thinking about this the other night, I just don't have the heart to lose any more fights. I mean, I've got to win this time."

"Who's your competitor?"

"Me."

"You?"

"What I'm saying is, if I lose this time, I really believe I won't make it at all. If I give in to it, it will kill me." In his case, the enemy is a part of himself.

Prior to admission a few patients had thought in terms of separating mind and body in order to bring about a reduction in pain. Davie, who had practiced TM (transcendental meditation), explained that it helped with pain by letting you separate your mind from your body. It works then, and you're free from pain, but when you combine them again the pain comes back. Although most patients had tried to separate themselves from their pain and their bodies, many felt this had not been a good idea. Mary said her attempts to separate the pain from the rest of her had not been healthy.

Entering patients, for the most part, saw their problem as one of "matter over mind." Intractable pain had made them feel that their bodies were powerfully influencing their minds. Some went so far as to use an idiom of possession, saying their bodies were taking over, driving them crazy. Once admitted to CPC, they immediately began hearing messages about "mind over matter": that one could use the mind through biofeedback training, relaxation, or imaging exercises—not, probably, to eliminate pain but to cope, to control, to push pain aside, to go beyond it. "Get on with your life," and, "before, pain controlled me; now, I control my pain" were CPC rallying cries in the fight to harness will and knowledge (and, according to some staff members, love) to reverse pain's dominance. This changed relationship, according to the CPC philosophy and the patients who converted to it, affected the perception of pain, making it less horrible, sometimes to the point of almost neutralizing it.

The stark contrast of "matter over mind" and "mind over matter" illustrates our legacy of Cartesian dualism. Neither adequately describes the lived experience of people in severe constant pain, nor CPC converts' accounts of their success.

Staff members offered many reasons to explain why patients resisted the "mind over matter" message. An important one concerns the change in self-concept that was sometimes required. Rhonda, Dr. B's clinical assistant, said that such a change "goes to the core of the person." Bad relationships, for example, being abused by a spouse, living with an alcoholic, or taking "crap" from somebody and meeting others' needs at one's own expense, were basic, long-term, ingrained behaviors that had a lot to do with how the person felt about herself or himself. To really face and confront that fact, and admit that it contributed to a pain syndrome, would have been "real scary" because to do something about the pain would require "total self-upheaval. It means breaking marriages or relationships they've been in years and years."

Patients sometimes resisted "core of the person" change not only because it meant "total upheaval" but because of the unavoidable implications: once you accept greater responsibility for your condition, if you fail at improving it, you will feel worse—more guilty, more resentful, more misunderstood.

Staff members seemed to feel that patients' resistance resulted simply from a fear of change or of losing the benefits of pain. But perhaps part of the resistance could be part of a more or less rational adaptation to a threatening situation: an already-battered self becoming quite conservative, especially given that the kind of aid offered to pain sufferers often seems dubious at best: it comes with no guarantees, and some of it requires taking risks that will leave one worse off if the risk-taking does not produce results.

Imaging Pain; Shifts in Me/Not-Me

One way CPC tried to promote changes in attitude was by encouraging patients to image consciously their pain during individual relaxation training sessions. This produced some extremely interesting accounts of how patients saw their pain vis à vis their selves. Some visualized inanimate objects. One woman reported to Georgia that her pain was gray, and like a medieval instrument of torture with spokes. Davie in a session with Georgia visualized his migraine as an ivory oval-shaped image inside his head, which, when touched, was so excruciatingly painful he let it go. But when he grabbed it, it started pulsating but diminished with every beat as he held on, finally going away. Unlike some other images, this one is vague; we do not know whether it is a part of Davie (e.g., an organ) or not, nor whether it is sentient or not.

Most often, patients would imagine a living being, which Georgia referred to as a "pain creature." The patient would then draw associations between this pain creature and ideas or memories that popped up. For example, Helen said after three weeks at CPC she found herself having terrible pain one evening and Nina, a nurse, came to help. Nina asked her to visualize her pain, and she saw a white crab, waving its claws. Then she found herself thinking about her father for the first time in years.

"[Nina] asked 'What is he doing?' 'He's very strict, he's telling me I was a tramp.' I'd taken the dog and let the dog go for a swim, and he called me a tramp for walking the streets. I was 18. I thought [the memory and hurt] had gone, but it never had. I saw them thinking about me in seventh grade. I was kept behind for three years, I hadn't learned anything. The nurse wrote a letter to my mother saying I couldn't learn because I had water on the brain. I found the letter later, she never told me. My mother took me out of school."

These examples of pain images reveal several processes. During the imaging session, the pain image usually came to be seen as having humanlike qualities. The interaction between the pain image and the narrator frequently involved confrontation and struggle, requiring the pain sufferer to move from passivity to activity—even at times to risk danger and perhaps even more pain. Although negotiation with the image was not the rule, there was almost always recognition and acceptance that the pain was not as alien as had been previously thought; by the end of the session the pain was seen as closer in some way to the self. The realization that one's pain was connected to oneself however remotely (e.g., although Helen connected an image of a white crab with memories of her father, she did not say the crab *was* her father), was often accompanied by a realization that one could control the pain to some degree. Sometimes simple talk was involved; one patient said that if he lay down twice a day for about forty-five minutes and talked to his pain, it decreased.

In many cases, realizing that one had this power resulted in coming to see that one was not a total enemy of the pain, engaged in a life-and-death struggle. Rebecca's reassuring the brooding pain image that she would not take advantage of him illustrates this, as well as one man's realization that after he came to associate the ugly black monster on the sea floor with his father, he did not want to kill it, but simply wanted it to leave him alone.

A young woman who reported that the surgeon who had operated on her back had been drunk and had severed a nerve said she envisioned her pain as "of course—a long snake with scales and fangs and breathing fire."

"Is the snake you or not you?"

"I believe the snake is me. I believe that we really have the ability in our brain or our mind to deal with pain if we are taught somehow to deal with it. I think we all have the ability to handle things like that, but I think that we need help. I really have always thought that anyway, but it wasn't until [Georgia] had talked to me about it and we went through this imagery session that I realized, 'my God, I can talk to it.' I was afraid of it. And, plus, I have these two Knott-rods in my back, and to me it was something foreign in there, so it was very easy for me to [see the pain as foreign]. But the pain is me."

The object of rethinking one's conceptualizations about pain and self, so as to see the pain more as a part of oneself, was to gain more control over the pain. An elderly woman commented that Georgia's guided imagery therapy had helped her see the connection between her "obvious need to control" and the exhaustion she felt trying to deal with her thalamic syndrome pain. She went on to say it had become clear that she did not see the pain as part of her, which was unfortunate, because she probably would be more able to manage it if it were.

Acceptance—of pain, of body, of self—was an underlying theme in the CPC program. Several patients felt that simply accepting that one was always going to have pain was a major achievement. Edward said that accepting that he would never get to a point in the future when he would have no pain also meant accepting that he had to deal with it. He described his previous attitude as *thinking* he had accepted it, "but always in the back of my mind, there was maybe one of these days I'm going to go to a doctor and they're going to do some X-rays, they're going to do a test, and they're going to say, 'Ah-hah! Here it is, here's a bone chip.' It's kind of a fairy tale of mine that some day, wave a magic wand and make it all better." That day was not going to come, he said, and now he really did not care.

This kind of acceptance was often accompanied by other kinds. Some spoke of incorporating pain, or reincorporating the painful body part, in a process of resubjectification. Stavros Cademenos describes this process as a movement from a person thinking of his body as an "alien and onerous entity" to relaxing the distinctions between "I" and "my body" and between "I" and "my pain."[18] CPC converts tried to decrease the distance between pain, self, and body by increasing their subjectification of pain in a healthy, beneficial way. Mary had come to see her pain as a part of her; it did not have to be as bad, if one worked with it instead of against it, and worked at integrating it into one's life.[19] Those who moved in this direction reported that the power their pain had over them was lessened. Some were not able to achieve such subjectification but saw the advantages of doing so. The crucial element seemed to be how pain sufferers connected pain to their bodies and to their identity. To claim, accept, and identify with it—paradoxically, just as martial arts tells of incorporating the enemy—was to control the pain better than if one were to construct barricades against it. Rebecca draws physically closer to the pain creature and emotionally closer to the individual who hurt her earlier in life; she forgives him, "wipes the slate clean." The man who connected a sea monster with his father discovered that he did not want to kill it after all.

Another way to draw closer was coming to accept that some of the cause lay within the self. Although Rebecca, while drawing closer to the pain, did not use images of incorporation into body or self, she did report achieving insight into how various internal states such as anger, hate, and hostility had contributed to her pain.

My discharge interview with Mary took place in her room, with her new roommate, the recently admitted Teresa, lying on the bed. Mary said that before coming to CPC she had been a "totally different person" because of fighting pain, which only produced worse pain. Fighting pain was fighting yourself, but the goal was to be at peace with yourself: "self-acceptance, I think, is the big thing."

To which Teresa responded: "How do you get on that side of the pain, kiddo? How do you get there? Because I'll tell you what, they say, 'love your self, love your body.' If one more person tells me to love this fucked-up spine, I'm going to put my fist right down their throat. I don't love this fucked-up spine, I just don't." The next day, Teresa commented that she was going to "fight this damn thing" and that she had not come to terms with Mary's recommendation to "be on the side of the pain."

We saw that after being discharged from CPC, Teresa, while in an acute care hospital, took the elevator to the roof and jumped off. She both lost and won the fight—she lost her life, but by dying she got rid of both her pain and her "fucked-up spine." She had finally gained control. Having said she was not going to accept herself the way she was but was going to will herself better, and having failed, she at least had the last word, so to speak. Her tragedy illustrates some of the dilemmas posed by intractable, unending pain. Given that her bodily pain made her self unacceptable, if her pain was both an unbearable, monstrous "it" and an unwelcome but inescapable "me," one solution was to eliminate both the "not-me" and the "me."

Edward's reconceptualization of pain involved changes in his sense of control over self. Pain, he said, was not going to rule the rest of his life. He had gained an incredible feeling of power over his body, over his self. "And that power is a rather nice blanket, you know, to be wrapped in. I enjoy that feeling, of having power over myself, being able to control how much the pain is going to be able to limit me."

His new approach was complex. "I'm not going to give it an inch, I'm going to keep pushing it, and who knows? Maybe in a year, maybe in ten years, maybe never, but maybe someday I'll have pushed it back to the point where I don't feel it, where it is all not felt."

Notice that he did not say the pain would disappear; he no longer trusted in magic wands. Pressed on this, he replied, "It's how you perceive the pain—how I perceive the pain. When I came in, the pain controlled what I did, it stopped me from doing some of the things I enjoy doing; the simple enjoyment I derive from working was taken away from me. Now there has been a turnaround in how I perceive the pain, where I look at it in an analytical manner and say, 'hmm,' instead of just saying 'my back hurts,' locating the specific spot where it hurts, and exactly how the pain radiates—almost being sadistic about it, watching it travel, and feeling it and saying, 'OK, yup. That's the way it is.' And then standing back from it a little further and saying, 'OK, now it is time to do my exercises.' "

Edward's talk is full of mental control images. The experience of pain is influenced by how one thinks of it, how one perceives it: if you looked at the pain as being a horrible, terrible thing, then it was indeed going to do horrible, terrible things to you. But if you looked at it as being a neutral thing—as just *there*—it lost a lot of its power.

Images of fighting, enemies, conquering, and the like remained in many converts' discourse about pain. Edward's remarks provide such images, but I think this does not present a contradiction with his accepting the pain. As Edward's talk illustrates, these are slippery issues. Although he talks about "less felt pain" his fight is actually with himself—over changing his conceptualizations of his pain. "Pushing it" here refers to gaining control, with relaxation and other approaches, of his experience of pain. In other words, the battle is just as much with himself as it is with the pain, and the fight is to acquire self-discipline. In a sense, his remarks also contain the notion of pain coming to be seen more as a part of oneself. Clearly, the me/not-me division is elusive because of the slippery boundaries between pain, body, and "me." This slipperiness explains some of the more noticeable contradictions patients heard at CPC.

Thus a woman reported gaining more control of herself by discovering how to "forget" herself: she spoke of the community in terms of distancing—not from pain, but from herself. The community's expectation of automatically supporting one's fellows gave one permission to forget oneself and try to understand somebody else's feelings, she said. Being able to forget one's own problems at least for the moment was important in itself, and doing it often enough turned it into an exercise in distancing oneself from one's own case.

Mary said that fighting was the wrong approach because it splintered her self: fighting the pain, she said, was actually a fight with her self. Such battles had resulted in ever-growing self-hate because she had been separating herself into so many people. At the beginning of her stay at CPC, she said, she had fought to retain her old self but, by the end she was seeing this as denial and claiming to have achieved an "incredible integration." Part of this integration was accepting her body: accepting that although she was "out of shape" (something utterly invisible to anyone else), this was no longer "traumatic." And part involved integrating the pain: if you were in tune to the pain, on the side of the pain rather than hating the pain, she said, you would actually feel better.

Language and Pain

We have seen that chronic pain sufferers have trouble conceptualizing and communicating about their pain. David Morris points out that, whereas acute pain elicits eminently social cries, the natural language of chronic pain is silence; after a while, chronic pain constitutes a radical assault on language: "There is simply nothing that can be said."[20] One difficulty of writing about CPC patients' experience of pain was this: although I was determined to avoid "pigeonholing" them into standard diagnostic categories, to enter their "lived world of perceptual phenomena"[21]—a world in which neither our bodies nor our pain are objects—I had to depend on their talk about their experience of pain, and this talk used everyday-world language.

Recording the language of pain itself without objectifying it is virtually impossible. Even tape recordings of "pre-linguistic cries and shrieks"[22] would involve some objectification, and an instrument like the McGill Pain Questionnaire, used in evaluating pain,[23] requires much more. Furthermore, many words and phrases in the pain treatment lexicon are ambiguous and polysemic, like "psychosomatic," "chronic pain," "real pain." While pain, acute or chronic, has as a core meaning an aversive feeling associated with tissue pathology, quite often it denotes and connotes a vast range of other meanings. The pain literature reveals that even clinicians who specialize in pain treatment display a variability and ambiguity with respect to these issues. This is currently a highly contested domain; the variety of staff responses to my requests for definitions parallels the disagreements in the literature.[24]

Of course, despite their complaints, pain sufferers do manage to say something about what their pain is like, some of them becoming "a pain" themselves because they talk too much. But despite successful attempts to talk about their pain using everyday language, a great deal of their thoughts and feelings about pain did not seem to find satisfactory expression, either in the form of concepts for their own thinking or when talking with others.

Sometimes pain sufferers' accounts are confusing simply because they have difficulty articulating what they are experiencing; this can occur when a person is not very "psychologically aware," as staff members put it. At other times, the difficulty derives from inadequacies in the language available to them, as opposed to what is available in specialized fields (the distinction between nociception and pain, for example, is useful). Thus Edward said that, although the level of pain was the same, there was "less felt pain"—but finding himself speaking of pain that was somehow both "there just as much" and "not there as much" led him to wonder whether he was making sense. Yet another difficulty lies in the fact that Western culture hampers acknowledging certain characteristics of a pain, for example, when a more comprehensive understanding would threaten self-esteem and so is resisted. In this instance the pain sufferer's inarticulateness eloquently communicates something important about the experience.

The Body as Pre-Linguistic

The mind/body division in Western culture sees language as belonging to the mind, not the body. It is significant that we use the term "body-language" to describe communication by using the body. True, we speak and think from an embodied perspective, with some aspects of this embodiment favored over others: for example, visual perception is semantically encoded, at least in English, far more than aural or olfactory perception.[25] Patients' images of pain were visual ones, despite the fact that pain is not a visual experience. However, bodily communications, whether within the body (the body's reactions to external stimuli such as odors or music, or inner states such as hunger or sexual arousal) or using the body to send a message, are seen as "primitive" or "pre-linguistic."

In what follows, I revisit the issues of invisibility and subject/object to examine how language is used to describe pain and reconceptualize it. I will consider the notion that a pain sufferer is, in a sense, speaking the language of a world, the pain-full world, different from the everyday lifeworld, and that helps explain why people with chronic pain report feeling so profoundly understood by fellow sufferers and so profoundly misunderstood by nonsufferers. Then a discussion of how CPC patients decide whether to talk or keep silent about their pain teaches us something about the adequacy of language for dealing with lived experience.

The invisibility of pain creates difficulties for people attempting to conceptualize or communicate about it. Pain announces itself only to the person experiencing it unless that person announces its presence to others. There are, to be sure, physiological indicators of the probable presence of pain, but these are inferential, based on either physiological responses to pain or, in tandem with pain, the presence of nociceptive stimuli.[26] Their absence can help validate the absence of pain, as when a man undergoing a religious ordeal, who looks as though he ought to be experiencing pain (he is chewing glass or sticking a sword through his side), says he is not, and his claim is supported by a remarkably small amount of bleeding.[27] But the bottom line is that, since pain is an experience, people must use some kind of language—speech or gesture—to communicate that they are feeling pain.

In other words, pain, that quintessentially private experience, depends on social action to make it "real." In general, a chronic pain sufferer who communicates about pain intends to do so; the vast majority of those who do not can hide it quite successfully. With the possible exceptions of extreme pain and borderline consciousness and pediatric pain, the body does not communicate chronic pain without some degree of conscious intention. Cries and screams under properly administered anesthesia are not examples of pain being communicated.[28]

The example of people reporting they feel no pain when observation indicates they should is illustrative. How do we ascertain the presence of pain? Are flagellants in religious ordeals experiencing pain? We can ask, but the answer will depend in part on the meaning for them of what they are doing. Some might say they are experiencing pain and thereby atoning for their sins; others that they feel no pain because God, or Allah, is in them. From a biomedical perspective, we do not know whether they are "really" in pain: it is known that some individuals so control their bodies in an altered state of consciousness that the painful stimulus in fact causes very little tissue damage: they can pierce their eyeball, hang from hooks, or drink strychnine with minimal physical consequences, including nociceptive messages. In other cases, damage is apparent, and the usual messages are going from the periphery to the central nervous system receptors but the practitioners are in so altered a state of consciousness that they do not consciously experience pain—a situation analogous to what occurs in surgery under anesthesia. Another class consists of individuals who intentionally injure themselves while undergoing religious ordeals and experience excruciating pain. In all these situations we must accept the experiencer's account: we can measure the amount of trauma and determine the extent of tissue damage, and so estimate the degree of pain felt, but there is no independent method of finding out about the experience of pain itself. Clearly language, both verbal and nonverbal, is crucial for ascertaining pain.[29]

Since most measurements of pain depend on what pain sufferers tell us, we need to make sure we understand what they are saying, to speak the language they speak and to understand what pain *means* to them. For instance, the fact that some of the people undergoing painful religious ordeals welcome trauma and pain is extremely significant.

The issue of conscious versus unconscious is relevant here—and complicates things a great deal. For example, clinicians sometimes attribute unconscious masochistic impulses to flagellants and chronic pain sufferers—a "meaning" they are not aware of. Most chronic pain sufferers would probably reject this interpretation of their own situation; CPC patients certainly did. One man said, "[Dr. B] in that meeting said all the patients are masochistic. I couldn't believe it, but I heard it." A serious methodological issue in much social science research concerns "outsiders" interpreting an activity in a way "insiders" contest.[30] Patients contested CPC authority to determine meaning many times a day. As noted, chronic pain "insiders" claim authority about their own subculture because they know so much of the pain-full world. And "outsiders"—social scientists or clinicians who do not experience chronic pain—claim an authority due to the expert, who interprets meanings underlying a behavior pattern in light of extensive knowledge about other cases. These debates about authoritative interpretation are ultimately unresolvable; in the end the authority is whoever is most authoritative—that is, the most convincing. Finding an authoritative position from which to make comparisons is difficult with pain or any other kind of experience.

In short, pain cannot be measured or ascertained apart from the sufferer's affirmation of its presence. Pain is seen as pre-linguistic, as "resisting language," in part because it is invisible. Infants and animals illustrate this, for we can determine very little about a pain (absent any other signs) when the affected individual can make only non-verbal responses. With information about the cause of a pain—a proximate mechanical or chemical cause, say, or a more removed cause (such as food poisoning), we can begin to treat it linguistically: give it a name, describe its characteristics. And with information about the body's and mind's reactions to a pain, we can handle it linguistically in a much more expanded fashion. But without such information, pain—and other bodily-based feelings—resist verbal description.

Pain as Linguistic Object and Subject

Much of the time CPC patients were trying to objectify their pain, to speak of it always as something "real," with a "real" cause, as something physical, and, often, something seen and measured.[31] And they often complained about the way pain resists objectification; describing experiencing a pain that was always there was extremely difficult. Talking about the connections between pain and consciousness was unfamiliar—and risky, since any mention of emotional or cognitive solutions diminishes the pain's physical quality and so threatens its legitimacy.

CPC patients did try to speak of pain in nonobjectifying ways, although trying to speak of a pain that permeated, infused, dominated, merged with their lives and consciousness—possessed them—was extremely difficult, since they had to talk in ordinary language (that is, language in which one must objectify one's body and one's pain). Sometimes they spoke of the opposite of "real" or "object" pain and tried to deal with what we might call "subject" pain, which was "all in your head" pain. Since it is a figment of the imagination, "all in your head" pain cannot be an object "out there" (note that "out there" can refer to inside the body). Patients sometimes said, almost always in jest, that they would welcome this because, even though it is stigmatized, a pain that "doesn't exist" would be less threatening, less horrible. Good's interviewee Brian, for example, wants to "explain it away . . . say that it's all just imaginary, it's a figment, it really doesn't exist." [32] A CPC patient felt the same way: "I tried willing it away. 'Well,' I figured, 'if I did it to myself, I can get rid of it.' And I kept telling myself, 'I don't want you, get out of here.' Didn't work." To be sure, she is speaking of the pain as "it" and so objectifying; however, the distance from the subject, the self, is far less when pain is seen as imaginary. Mary illustrates both the hope and the guilt that can accompany this kind of reasoning; she would look in the mirror and say, "You are sick!" and argue with herself: "This can't be as bad as I think it is," followed by, "You're imagining it, it's really not as bad."

Of course, to some extent there is no such stark division between "real" and "imaginary" pain. CPC staff members had a more sophisticated and variable model of "all in your head" pain, and many patients, particularly the converts, succeeded somewhat in reconceptualizing how mind and body interacting produced the bodily pain they experienced. But the potential hazards of seeing one's pain as a part of the self, as being caused by self in any way—were apparent to all.[33]

Though patients occasionally welcomed the opportunity to deobjectify their pain by boldly labeling it imaginary, such an exercise did not bring peace of mind. For one thing, they were confused about what, then, to do with the continuing pain experience. We saw that Franklin said he thought that some of his pain was in the mind, but—where do you draw the line? Do you pretend it is not there? He also said you had to learn to listen to your body, but you should not let your body dictate everything to you, there was a fine line. He saw a struggle between the self telling the body the truth versus listening to the body tell the truth, and he offered no resolution. Most patients found that such reasoning simply did not succeed: their attempts at linguistic (de)representation, deobjectification—whatever its effects on how one thought about one's pain—"didn't work." Finally, if something so horrible is imaginary, then one must be seriously delusional.

When pain sufferers like Good's interviewee Brian and CPC patients like Mary and Franklin try to say "the pain doesn't exist" they are trying to use language to escape from their current experience of pain; they are trying to change its meaning (and therefore their experience) by attributing it to a different cause. CPC maintained that gaining insight into the "real" causes of one's pain often brought a change in the experience of pain and sometimes a reduction in pain, and other pain centers make the same claim. The strictures and ambiguities of our language make it difficult to analyze just what happens: again, Edward's statement about pain that is unchanged but "less felt" illustrates the difficulty of talking about perception without metaphors.

Scarry maintains that physical pain cannot be easily talked about, is pre-linguistic, whereas emotional pain has meaning and can be discussed. It is not clear whether she is drawing a distinction between felt pain in terms of physical versus emotional cause, or between embodied pain, regardless of cause, and pain felt only in the mind.[34] As she bases her discussion on physical torture, it would seem that "physical pain" denotes physical causes; if so, her dichotomy is not useful for an analysis dealing with the lived reality of pain; for, phenomenologically speaking, emotionally caused pain, if it is experienced physically, *is* physical pain. This is another example of the confusion that derives from a tendency to conflate cause and experience when speaking about pain.

How does embodied emotionally-caused pain differ from purely emotional, unembodied pain? Because our culture sees mind and body as significantly different, it is likely that a person would experience the two types of pain differently, despite semantic overlap (for example, severely depressed people speak of the "pain of depression"). Thus the two should be kept conceptually distinct, even though some clinicians suggest that all kinds of chronic pain involve, at least in part, an emotional pathology (indeed, Swanson wants to define chronic pain as the "third pathologic emotion"[35]), and many scholars maintain that every strongly felt emotion is accompanied by changes in bodily state.

The difficulty of talking about pain derives from the way in which language robs it of some of its pre-objective quality. In the lived world of perceptual phenomena neither our bodies nor our pain are objects. We normally live through our bodies in the "world of everyday life."[36] As phenomenologists of the body maintain, our usual relationship to the body is that of non-experience: "the absent body." Sometimes we are made aware of it—when aroused or, most often, when something is wrong with it.[37] Although Hilbert is correct in saying that the idea of continually experienced pain is culturally meaningless in the everyday world,[38] it has meaning in the pain-full world. Someone totally engrossed in a musical experience cannot use everyday-world language to describe the experience because the act of experiencing music relies on another kind of communication—another language, so to speak. One can report about the experience afterward in everyday-world language, describe, albeit at times awkwardly, some features of the music, but one can speak of the experience only metaphorically. Similarly, everyday-world language must objectify pain, and this distorts the experience, in a sense betraying it.

Phenomenologists want to avoid treating the body as a linguistic object. Merleau-Ponty illustrates how we would talk about the unobjectified body: "I am not in space and time, nor do I conceive space and time; I belong to them, my body combines with them and includes them."[39] To talk about pain, he would have to say something like, "I combine with pain, I include pain"; in fact, he talks about a painful foot as a "pain-infested space."[40] The awkwardness of expression here reveals the difficulty of using everyday-world language to describe the experience of pain, even when we want, with Merleau-Ponty, to analyze the pre-objective act of perceiving pain. When it is talked about, pain automatically acquires some subject-object distinction, and so loses some of its pre-objective, "pure" quality.

CPC patients reported feeling frustrated when trying to talk about their pain on the outside, and feeling understood "for the first time" by their fellow patients. They reported something akin to joy at being in a community of fellow-sufferers, even though some had dreaded the prospect; they talked of a sense of shared experience and shared identity, of feeling comfortable, finding it much easier to talk about many problems connected to chronic pain. Patients did disagree with one another sometimes, but about the cause of one another's pain, necessary pain behavior, and proper treatment; when they were effusive about how well they understood one another, they were talking about the phenomenological experience of pain.[41] They felt that only their CPC fellows really understood their pre-objective, pre-abstracted pain experiences precisely because this understanding did not depend entirely on everyday-world language. In a community of sufferers like CPC, all members met the preconditions for understanding *bodily-lived* meaning.

The World of Pain and Its Language

A pain-full body occupies a world different from the everyday world. Like the ineffable worlds of dreams, daydreams, or deep religious or musical experience, the pain-full world has its own system of meaning, its inhabitants their own forms for communication. But the pain-full world is unique among non-everyday worlds in that pain is aversive, although nightmares or unwelcome compulsive fantasies would also have this quality. When a person has severe chronic pain, we can think of him living in a world with its own language and its own cognitive-affective style. We speak of the body having its own language; we can also speak of the pain-full body learning to speak the language of the pain-full world it inhabits. This helps explain why pain "resists language," as Scarry puts it—it resists everyday-world language. Entering the pain-full world requires, as Schutz puts it, making "a radical modification in the tension of our consciousness, founded in a different *attention à la vie.* [i.e., the kind of attention one pays to one's lived reality]."[42] Just as we can remember having experienced emotions or other feelings, but cannot reexperience the emotions or feelings, so also can we remember having had pain, but not remember the pain itself, in the sense of reexperiencing it—for that would require going back through the looking glass into the pain-full world and again speaking the language of that world. Becoming familiar with that world results in some of the "pain habits" clinicians speak of.

Although everyday-world language has trouble describing the lived experience of non-everyday worlds, it becomes adequate to the task—indeed, often eloquent—if it is allowed metaphor. Here are migraine sufferers: "It feels like a pair of pliers on the optic nerve." "It was like a football helmet seven sizes too small." On post-herpetic neuralgia: "Like a blowtorch—it's as though the devil pulls his pitchfork out only to heat it up to put it back." On thalamic syndrome pain: "Have you ever been burned by dry ice? Have you ever received a very severe electric shock? I feel a severe burning sensation while at the same time a freezing sensation." Mary on musculo-skeletal pain: "I used to call it 'slice pain,' meaning that in order for me to bend or anything, I would have to be sliced in the back, everything was so tight." Another young woman: "The pain in my side feels like I've been kicked with cowboy boots." The metaphor of "seeing stars" when subjected to a sudden, intense pain is an example. The metaphor does not describe the actual experience, for: "What is meant by 'seeing stars' is that the contents of consciousness are, during those moments, obliterated, that the name of one's child, the memory of a friend's face, are all absent."[43]

In such pain the contents of consciousness have been obliterated, but one does not lose consciousness. Communication, embodied communication, is clearly taking place, but it is so different from everyday communication that the two are virtually incommensurable. The experience of "seeing stars," stripped of this metaphor, illustrates what I mean by "the language of pain." We might call it "anti-language," so antithetical is it to ordinary natural language. But it communicates something. In this sense pain is "pre-linguistic" because severe pain curtails the possibility of a fully developed everyday-world language. This is not the same as saying pain obliterates meaning, for pain always has meaning, from the moment it appears, just as the body always has meaning (and its own language). But since these meanings differ from those assigned by everyday-world language, there is a sense in which we can agree with Hilbert that the experience of severe chronic pain is "meaning-less."

Moving from the pain-full world to the everyday lifeworld entails what Schutz refers to as a shock.[44] Yet, to some degree, living in chronic pain requires constant traveling back and forth between these worlds—when, for example, a sufferer becomes so engrossed in some aspect of the everyday world that he or she is momentarily distracted from experiencing the full force of the pain. However, when pain is severe enough, as Scarry so aptly describes, one does not easily cross over to the everyday lifeworld. I emphasize movement because experiencing severe pain is not the same as losing consciousness—something most sufferers long for desperately at times. What one does lose is normal occupancy of everyday reality. Thus, although at any given moment one can be mostly in the everyday world or mostly in the pain-full world, if we think in terms of many of these moments strung together over time, we can see the potentially grave consequences for one's experience of the building blocks of the perceived world—time and space.[45] As we have seen, one's self-concept (and one's concept of others) are also profoundly altered. The phrase CPC staff members used—"major life disruption"—fails to convey how totally shattering these changes can be.

Keyes also discusses the "shock" of the pain experience in the sense that it forces the sufferer to break with a commonsense perspective on the world.[46] This shift in understanding of the world and the self must be maintained so long as a chronic pain condition persists, although the shock will be somewhat modified and routinized over time.

While all other worlds modify the everyday lifeworld that is the basis of our experience of reality, the world of severe constant pain seriously threatens that world. Thus moving between these worlds involves a greater shift than, for instance, moving back and forth from the world of daydreaming or of ephemeral mild pain. This is why so many pain patients feel so profoundly misunderstood; as one man said, his family seeing him as having a sore back, much like their morning backache, could not fathom what he was going through. His difficulty comes in part because according to Schutz, any language pertains to the intersubjective world of everyday life, and hence will obstinately resist serving as a vehicle for meanings which transcend its own presuppositions.[47] Good's interviewee Brian's pain shaped his world to itself, resisting objectification and threatening the objective structure of the everyday world in which he participated.[48] The pain-full world is one others "could not possibly understand," one that cannot be described except with its own language, its own morphology and syntax, and by members of its own speech community. Attempts to translate the language of the pain-full world are understandably never very successful—"traddutore, traditore" (the translator betrays).[49]

Many patients at CPC said they had stopped talking about their pain. Talking was superfluous, for communication had already taken place: "We have something in common, it's sort of a bond between people. No one says anything to complain, not any more."[50] Most patients came to find even non-verbal pain behavior unnecessary.

Chronic pain sufferers learn that normal, everyday-world language can be a serious stumbling block to communication. Many feel that language is not only inadequate, it is also the handmaiden of the medical establishment. Good's interviewee Brian points out that the professionals have their own answers and solutions that do not match his,[51] another illustration of the struggle over who should be the authority about pain. Pain sufferers search for meaning and so try to escape from inauthentic, imposed, inadequate meaning. Thus it is possible that those patients whose pain diagnoses are somehow inadequate, and are so dependent on the medical establishment to provide an explanation, a proper diagnosis, and, hopefully, treatment, have special reason to be suspicious of the available language. CPC staff members engaged in medico-scientific, psychotherapeutic, and, occasionally, holistic-medicine discourse about pain, but although virtually all patients granted at least some authority to these approaches and the languages they used, most had failed them. They were all too aware that they were, as one woman put it: "the failures of the medical community."

A clinician might see the reduction in pain behavior exhibited by many patients during their stay at CPC as evidence of improvement—a sign of less pain, less depression, or greater ability to be distracted—or credit the change to lack of rewards for such behavior from fellow patients and staff members. These factors were no doubt influential. But there may be another reason for the apparent lack of communication about pain after a week or so at CPC: since they had found so much difficulty communicating about pain in ordinary language, and since their principal message ("I am in pain and I realize you are in pain") was sent and received early on, they may have felt little need to talk or otherwise communicate about their pain. They knew from experience of pain's pre-objective and pre-linguistic quality and that attempts to provide more information about it could be frustrating. Many commented on this fact, and, after a time, came to feel it was not necessary for feeling understood: "they know when you don't grimace that you aren't necessarily free of pain."

Pain, in a sense, *is* a language, one that competes in several ways with everyday-world language. Scarry's discussion of language destroyed by severe torture is at one extreme location in the world of pain. For chronic pain sufferers, the messages their pain sends replace and transform everyday-world language, so that messages sent or received in this language are distorted or trivial. Having made the effort temporarily to leave the pain-full world—for example, CPC patients who have, with considerable exertion, listened to a lecture—they return to the world they inhabit so unwillingly feeling exhausted and resentful, even betrayed, for what they have just made a great effort to comprehend now resembles Jabberwocky. And the reverse is also true: when sufferers attempt to translate the language of chronic pain into everyday-world language—using gestures, cries, or words—they say they feel a sense of failure, a sense of speaking a nonsense, so poorly does one map onto the other. Kirmayer questions whether we can ever say the body is a certain way when that knowledge is worked out through a language that imposes its own structure on experience and thought.[52]

Chronic pain sufferers live out the pre-linguistic and pre-abstract meaning of pain, and in this sense they understand its meaning. But since only a very few can accept that meaning, they, like Good's interviewee Brian, search for an everyday-world meaning. Because they so ardently reject the meaning provided by unmediated chronic pain, they search for a name, a prognosis, something from everyday-world language that will provide an exit. They do not long to stay in the province of pain, they do not seek to continue learning its language or its customs. Despite their familiarity with the terrain and their "pain habits" developed over the years, the vast majority of chronic pain sufferers are unwilling residents in that province. Yet it is understandable that, having inhabited the territory by themselves for so long, they are pleased to find fellow sojourners with whom they can commune.

Language can betray. Good's interviewee Brian and many other sufferers have come to suspect language, with good reason. This is why, although CPC patients searched for ways to communicate the meaning of their pain in everyday-world language, to make nonsufferers understand, and to get help from the professionals, their disappointment in this quest meant that they sometimes found comfort in not talking about their pain. While at times certain patients could not seem to focus on anything but their pain, others would report feeling tremendous relief at being accepted by their fellows without having to communicate anything, verbally or nonverbally, much as people at a concert will report feeling a spirit of musical *communitas* with fellow listeners that needs no words, a feeling, moreover, which they feel words would only misrepresent.

This, then, is one of the many ironies about pain. Patients at CPC searched for the meaning of their pain, at many levels. The human response to the search for meaning, "to reverse the deobjectifying work of pain by forcing *pain itself* into avenues of objectification"[53] was very evident in CPC patients. But since patients continued to be unwilling sojourners in the province of pain, they were frustrated in this search for meaning, for language, for names. Despite our perception of language as communicating, clarifying, enhancing, and creating experience (as in the case of performative language[54]), everyday-world language is inadequate for conveying ongoing subjective experience because it objectifies, and so inevitably restricts, distorts, mystifies. This is particularly true for pain, for, as Scarry points out, pain in particular resists objectification: one's extremely real pain remains unreal to others.[55]

Kirmayer correctly opposes the order of the text and the order of the body, questioning how can meaning and value be sustained when consciousness is constricted, degraded, and defiled by pain.[56] As Scarry points out, "making" a world involves destruction: wounding and creating are closely related, and language plays a part in this. Pain, torture, and war destroy; humans collectively create languages that permit one person to destroy another: "The torturer asks the questions."[57] Similarly, language can facilitate domination, as illustrated by the hegemonic discourse of the CPC staff (in which, following Gramsci,[58] we can see patients participating). Language allows distance from experience, and while we may benefit from this when we try to gain control over aversive experiences, language does not reproduce the link between the experience and the "me" undergoing it. We intellectualize with language, we see it as distinct from the body, and we privilege it—often stripped of the emotional[59]—over the body. Since pain is experienced in the body, is an emotion, and contains much that is indeterminate and inchoate, it is often poorly served by everyday-world language.

Thus, paradoxically, patients both pursued language—answers, names,[60] definitions, meanings that promised reassurance and cures— and avoided it. Although they had found that language failed to represent their being-in-the-world, that meanings which held promise turned out to be siren-meanings, had not fulfilled their quest to be understood as pain-full beings, they still wanted to use language to escape that experience, that world. Although they reported feeling profoundly misunderstood and pigeonholed by everyday-world language, this is the language they were compelled to pin their hopes on.

Conclusions

Good's interviewee Brian, talking about experiencing temporo mandibular joint disorder, expresses the difficulty of feeling that his body is a part of him when he describes it as "a decayed mass of tissue that's just not any good." Pain and the body have become aversive agents; he has lost the sense of himself as an integrated person; and at times he feels as if his mind is separated from his self, "outside myself."[61] This chapter has examined what the lived reality of severe chronic pain does to one's sense of self, how one's self-concept changes after years of inhabiting a pain-full body, and how a facility like CPC tries to alter this sense.

Many patients improved by putting the CPC's message of "mind over matter" into practice; others discovered that this strategy "didn't work" for them and felt worse. When they came into CPC, patients were engaged in many battles—with pain, with bodies, with families, with physicians, with selves. Teresa, at war with her body and self, having failed to "will myself better," killed that self. Another patient characterized his struggle as a final battle with himself. A woman understood "love therapy" to mean that one should love one's self so much that it will be reintegrated and one will feel better; she also saw the underside of this philosophy, which was, that if one could will oneself better, one might have to some degree willed oneself sick and she concluded that if the therapy did not work one would not only still have the problem, but have an increased sense of failure and self-blame.

The domain of self, body, and pain is a highly contested one at present, and the terms of debate have shifted considerably since the research described in these pages was completed. The overall theme remains, however: severe chronic pain greatly alters one's sense of self and how the body connects to that self; and alleviating this element of the suffering that accompanies intractable chronic pain is a challenging task, in part because of the way Westerners construct the mind and body, and in part because language does not represent the chronic pain experience very well.

CPC patients not only sought meaning for their pain, they also resisted, as unacceptable, some of the meanings attributed to their condition. What they lived was an abomination, it was hell itself; no one should be in constant, severe pain, and no one should have that pain exacerbated by being subject to doubt or condescension; rejected, laughed at, or blamed. They longed for a different explanation in everyday-world language, for a language that promised distance, control, and abstraction precisely *because* representation is not coterminous with experience itself. Every time they chose to speak, or groan, or remain silent, and were disappointed (at times a disappointment approximating despair) at the results of these choices, they compellingly illustrated the incommensurability between embodiment-as-lived and embodiment-as-represented.

Chapter 8
Conclusions: The Puzzles of Pain

This book has looked at how chronic pain sufferers experience pain and experience themselves as people living pain-full lives. Some of the horror of intractable chronic pain has been portrayed, along with some of the social and cultural factors that contribute to this horror. The viewpoint of pain sufferers themselves has been privileged because their perspective has been underrepresented in the literature.

Interpretations of pain exploring its cause or meaning (diagnostic, prognostic, ontological, existential, etc.) have varied considerably over time and cross-culturally. What went on at CPC illustrates some of the ways we in the West respond to it—study it, treat it, cope with it. Some of these responses conflict with one another: for example, our models of pain stretch from one that sees it as a healthy sign of the need for psycho-physiological communication and discharge all the way to one that says pain can virtually be eliminated by practicing a discipline that distances the perceiver from the perception until it diminishes to the point of becoming inconsequential. One reason for this range of models is that pain is not a "thing" "out there"; it is a concept we apply to some of our experiences and to inferences about others' experiences.

The experiences of patients reported on in these pages were specific to their time and place. Attitudes toward pain have changed, as have attitudes toward pain treatment.[1] The research concerned a single pain center practicing in the mid-1980s, but what happened there can teach us a great deal about chronic pain in the United States and the West in general. CPC patients and their experiences do not supply all the answers to why pain is so puzzling, but they do help sharpen and clarify the nature of these puzzles, which are explored (employing a somewhat arbitrary scheme) below.

Puzzle 1: Mind/Body Interaction

This first puzzle stems from the fact that pain is a psychological experience that is somehow, at times mysteriously, associated with tissue
damage. Pain confounds biomedicine's need to establish a clear connection between a cognitive and emotional experience and physiological
processes, to establish clear-cut means for measuring degree of pain,
and to discriminate between "functional" (neurotic origin) versus "real"
(organic origin) disorders.[2]

The distinction drawn between pain and nociception (the biological
mechanism that produces pain) is useful. Cases in which nociception
is present but pain is apparently absent have been well documented.
The most extreme examples involve people dying seemingly blissful yet
violent deaths: certain Christian martyrs, Buddhist monks immolating
themselves in protest, and some of the South Asian widows burned to
death in the practice of *suti* seem to have died such deaths.[3] Examples
of situations in which nociception and pain are unexpectedly absent include certain religious ordeals and martial arts discipline over the body.[4]
Religious ecstasy, trance, and hypnosis are ways we describe mechanisms
operating on the mind that can alter the normal relationship between
tissue damage and pain.

Pain is always an experience felt by a person with memories (conscious and unconscious) who is located in a social and cultural milieu.
Pain always involves the central nervous system and therefore always
involves cerebral representations. Pain always involves experiencing an
emotion—aversion; this is a core feature of almost all definitions of
pain.[5] Regardless of the type of injury, if pain is not experienced, if aversion is not experienced, there is no pain. A great deal of confusion could
be avoided by observing this simple stipulation. For example, one pair
of authors writes of a man "unaware" of pain.[6] Such usage is confusing,
and another word besides *pain* should be used to describe what he is not
feeling.

This stress on the need for great clarity is based on the extremely
harmful consequences of a lack of clarity. Many analytic schemes oppose
pain-as-sensation to pain-as-subjective-experience. Such opposition is
useful in biomedical research concerned with the "structure of [pain's]
intimate mechanisms,"[7] or with investigating possible biological variation in proximate responses to nociception within the species (there appears to be very little[8]). However, such an opposition is useful only for
these purposes. As it is always an individual, with a personal history, embedded in a social and cultural environment, who feels a given pain and
interprets it, it is not accurate to think of "overlays" of cultural meaning
that somehow follow nociception. While such linear thinking might be

useful in formulating analytic models, it trips us up when we are faced with reality; as one author puts it, "What is given to us first and foremost is not a determinate sensation of pain but a form of life in which pain has a specific place."[9] Meaning, culture, psychosocial input—whatever terminology one wishes to use—is at the core of any pain experience, so much so that in linear models of pain it is these inputs, not nociception, that perhaps should be postulated as occurring first. One pain specialist, J.-P. Natali, recognizes this in his discussion of the consequences of formulating the opposition between nociception and pain:

When this being is reduced to cellular dynamics and molecular exchanges, pain loses its primary meaning [and becomes] a profusion of nervous signals dependent upon the release of neuro-hormones. It is not clear what this will lead to with regard to the affect and rationality of the person who is suffering. Paradoxically, at this point, the object of study gives way to the study of the object.[10]

Similarly, Melzack and Wall, perhaps the best-known experimental researchers, state that pain perception goes beyond the problem of injury and the sensory signals of pain.[11] In sum, pain-as-sensation, when opposed to pain-as-experience, is strictly an analytical construct and does not occur empirically, not even in research laboratories.

We might expect everyone to agree that a sensation is pain only when it is an aversive experience and therefore, automatically, more than "just" a sensation. But, as Melzack notes, Descartes's views continue to permeate our notions of anatomy and physiology.[12] Because of a reluctance to see the mind and emotions as playing a role in bodily health and disease, because of biological hegemony (biomedicine's grounding in organicity), and because so much rests on establishing the legitimacy of a given pain experience, discussions of pain in the literature are still at times confused on this issue. The future is promising. Research has shown that the areas of the brain involved in pain experience and behavior are very extensive; furthermore, the interaction is two-way; the brain not only detects and analyzes inputs, it generates perceptual experience. The best example is phantom sensations—feelings and spasms—generated by the brain responding to the lack of input from dead nerves—a completely normal process. Rather than see memory in terms of a process of "cementing" synapses, Melzack argues that it is a "sculpting" process.[13] The implications of this change of model for understanding pain are significant. Our notions of cause and effect will change: the model of a nociceptive event followed by interpretation will have to be radically modified,[14] as will the medical distinction between mental and physical. Our understanding of the role of emotions as feelings that "cloud" perception, as feelings that distort our ability to understand events will also be revised, as will the entire legacy from the eighteenth century that sees the nonrational aspects of existence as defective or in need of rationalization. And as a consquence, because theory determines how we treat people in pain, treatment will be far better.[15]

While it is quite legitimate to distinguish among causes of pain, a problem arises when potentially ambiguous terms like "physical" or "real" are used and it is not clear whether a distinction is being drawn between types of causes (physical or emotional) or experiential dispositions. Experientially, pain experienced in the body *is* physical, real pain. Hence, although some distinctions, like that between nociception and pain are useful, some others are confusing. Terminology that confounds the cause of a pain with its phenomenality is sloppy terminology.

Not only is the phrase "physical pain" sloppy terminology, it is often packed with judgmental implications. Lurking in the background of many of the distinctions currently used in the literature is a notion of entitled pain—and along with it, of course, of unentitled pain. This notion springs in part from our desperate hope that people should suffer only when it is utterly unavoidable: no one should suffer *needlessly*. The writer Reynolds Price's story of how he conquered his severe pain through biofeedback and hypnosis is truly inspiring.[16] Why, we ask, can't *everyone* get to where he is? Why can't everyone come to find that their pain is no longer an insult to identity, but a source of strength and self-assurance, because of how they have changed their experience of it? CPC staff members often seemed to passionately hope for such changes. But of course concealed on the underside of such a wish is the notion that somehow if you are suffering needlessly, it is your fault . . . you *could* if you only *would* . . . you say you *cannot* but it is really you *will* not. We have seen that this notion has very deep roots. Anyone who has occasion to think or say anything about chronic pain should keep in mind the incredible tenacity of this notion, and its impressive imperviousness to attempts to deny its influence.

When our observations of an individual, accompanied by our expectations about the nature of our bodies, conflict with what we believe to be the subjective reality of that individual, we naturally want to privilege our perceptions and assumptions. Pain is in fact a very complex and at times counter-intuitive phenomenon: since it is unsatisfying to simply conclude that what we observe is a puzzle or mystery, we simplify and suggest subtly (or not so subtly) that the pain sufferer is mistaken in some way. Of course, this is possible—misunderstandings occur, defense mechanisms operate, and so forth. But the point is that our thinking and language often give *us*, the speaker, the benefit of the doubt— often rather automatically authorize our way of seeing things. And there is only a short distance between this and denigrating the pain sufferer being referred to or spoken to. Notice that, more often than not, implications concerning the moral responsibility for an unwanted condition accompany what we are saying, although we periodically try to cover ourselves with statements like, "For those who might mistakenly infer . . . that a number of chronic pain patients are judged pejoratively . . . we are *always* dealing with a desolate, deep distress which underneath everything . . . is experienced as harrowing, existential misery."[17]

In sum, while pain does not occur in mindless bodies, it seems we often like to think it should. This book has tried to explore just why we are so invested in conceptualizing pain as a sensation, and are so uncomfortable with the puzzles and paradoxes that accompany a more accurate and comprehensive conceptualization. Part of the answer is that a more extensive view of pain threatens the boundaries set up between mind and body (see endnote #1). Many challenges to this pervasive and tenacious dualism freely circulate in the Zeitgeist, as illustrated by the ubiquity of sayings like "he's a pain in the neck."[18] There is a fairly widespread understanding of hypnotism as a process that allows a person to produce very real burn symptoms on another person's arm (or, conversely, reduce dental pain) using only symbols (speech), and of fakirs in India who manipulate parasympathetic processes normally far beyond our control—to slow down breathing and heartbeat, for instance. Those who practice biofeedback find they can effect similar, although more modest, changes. Holistic medicine also challenges a too-mechanistic model of the body and mind. Finally, most people are aware of psychoactive drugs. However, the paradigm shift that would fully explain these pieces of evidence and incorporate them into the dominant biomedical model has not occurred yet, so they remain anomalies in the current paradigm.[19]

Puzzle 2: Several Levels of Causality

A multilevel model of causality helps straighten out some of the puzzles about organic and psychogenic inputs to pain. Such a model posits that a given pain experience is produced not by one, but a series of determinants at varying distances from it.

"Voodoo death," in which an individual dies because he has been cursed and believes in the power of such a curse, illustrates the importance of distinguishing levels of causality. The final cause is psychological—a belief—but this belief sets in motion physiological processes that lead to death, and are anything but imaginary.[20] Hence, that some pain's ultimate cause is *sine materia*—lacking an organic cause (psychogenic pain)—does not mean that organic factors do not play a role in its more proximate causes, as demonstrated by much of the research on psychosomatic disease, psychoimmunology, hypnosis, and placebo.[21]

Surely if in some instances the mind can produce astounding responses that effectively protect the body from what would bring certain injury, as can happen in ordeals, the mind can also produce "physical" pain defined however one wishes, but through utterly organic mechanisms: electrical and chemical processes. Therefore, keeping in mind that pain is multiply determined, and that those many determinants stand in varying degrees of proximity to the phenomenon (a given pain experience), will help us cut through some of the confusions in the literature and construct a model of pain that incorporates both psychological and biological inputs.

During a 1994 conference at the Department of Social Medicine at Harvard Medical School on Latino mental health, a spirited discussion broke out about the syndrome known as *ataque de nervios*, which occurs in Latin American populations, in particular among Puerto Ricans. *Ataque de nervios* is an emotional outburst characterized by loss of control which can also involve fainting, heart palpitations, rapid breathing, dissociation, and often an inability to remember the attack. It is frequently precipitated by situations eliciting fear or anger, but can apparently occur spontaneously. An example was given of a woman in a situation involving battering and marital rape who felt a lack of control over her own and her children's lives; upon hearing that her husband was leaving her for his mistress, she had an *ataque* during which she destroyed his car.

This syndrome has been variously interpreted as panic disorder with possible biological inputs (not enough is known about it to be certain); it has also been seen as occurring in people who cannot control their anger and unconsciously select a "safer" response to insurmountable stress. Furthermore, people who have experienced trauma early in life (sexual or physical abuse, for example) are apparently especially susceptible to *ataques*. Hypothesized determinants of *ataques* range from hereditary disposition, personal history (childhood stressors such as abusive or absent parents), and inadequate coping mechanisms (inability to control angry impulses), to patriarchy, oppressive caste and class systems, and culture (*ataques* are part of the Latino cultural repertoire—a kind of "black box" conceptualization of cultural inputs). In short, the debate on *ataques* provides an excellent illustration of this issue of multiple levels of causality. Questions arose at the conference about the appropriate unit of analysis: should it be the individual, the family, the society, the culture?

Such questions appear, for the most part covertly, in the chronic pain literature as well.[22] Some explanations look at the individual, and seek either biological factors, such as genetic predisposition to depression, or personality factors and speak of chronic pain sufferers as rigid, masochistic, or passive, perhaps as a result of a history of abuse or neglect in the individual's childhood. Other psychologically-based explanations refer to precipitating factors in the present, such as high amounts of stress. Symbolic interactionist explanations see chronic pain, like *ataque de nervios*, as indirect communication, perhaps expressing resistance to patriarchy, or an attempt to gain control of a difficult situation, or to use a metaphor for expressing great distress.[23] Still other kinds of explanations look to cultural and social determinants; some of these are surveyed below.

Models that do not clearly incorporate the fact that chronic pain is the result of several causes operating at different degrees of distance contribute to the confusion about even defining chronic pain. Some authors, for example, define it simply in terms of duration, but most think this is not sufficient. Many authors outline the various differences in neurophysiology, neuropsychology, and behavior that justify the distinction between acute and chronic pain, concluding that, regardless of its initial etiology, chronic pain cannot be perceived only as persistent acute pain.[24] That many authors writing about chronic pain have in mind the "worst case" population—those with an "intractable" condition—is pertinent to any discussion of chronic pain. As a consequence, chronic pain tends to become defined in terms of its opposition to "real pain," a definition far from a concern with duration. Again, inattention to multiple levels of causality has produced confusion: everyone knows someone with the kind of chronic pain sometimes called persistent acute pain—as in "uncomplicated" chronic tendinitis, arthritis, and so forth. There is no specific point at which "persistent acute pain" ends and "chronic pain" begins, if the shift is based on psychosocial inputs, because such inputs occur in all kinds of pain. Yet it is also easy to see that some people manage severe arthritis quite well, whereas others are enormously incapacitated by it, and hence health care professionals find this distinction important.[25]

In short, chronic pain is a very complex phenomenon caused by multiple determinants. Puzzles are compounded when researchers champion a particular cause over other seemingly competing causes, whereas in reality these various hypothesized causes occur at different levels and might all contribute to a given instance of pain.

Puzzle 3: Pain Is Subjective and Private

Pain is ubiquitous; no less inevitable than death and taxes, its nature becomes a matter of great significance to all of us at certain points in our lives. Our attempts to avoid pain form the basis of many of our most important ideas about the human condition. However, although we are all knowledgeable about pain, the experience is extremely private. We can only assume that what others feel is somewhat similar to our own pain experience. As Scarry notes, "pain comes unsharably into our midst as at once that which cannot be denied and that which cannot be confirmed."[26] Harry put it this way, "if someone drove a nail in your hand, two hundred people would have two hundred different descriptions of how much it hurt, but only you would know for sure."

A corollary is pain's invisibility, its presence made apparent to others only through pain behavior. Artistic representations of pain all depict its outward manifestations, either by showing damage to the body or by showing pain being expressed in the face or elsewhere in the body. As symbolic representations of pain these examples are excellent. However, as ample testimony from CPC patients shows, when such manifestations are absent, people are often misled into thinking that an individual is not suffering "real," severe pain. But as Roy Porter points out, all illness tends to reduce even the most articulate to states of mute misery, a misery that can be completely invisible.[27] In short, associations we make between bodily suffering—especially suffering that lasts and lasts—and its putative outward signs are often misleading and can lead to even greater suffering and confusion for everyone.

Puzzle 4: Distinctive and Competing Discourses

Patients and staff members at CPC were engaged in constant negotiation about which of two competing notions of authority concerning pain would prevail: the clinical authority of experts who treat pain, or the authority of people who actually live pain. Thus CPC was a setting for a struggle for dominance between two rather fundamentally different discourses. The first discourse, that of Western medicine, is well defined, widely dispersed, and extremely authoritative. The second, best termed a phenomenological or experiential discourse, is not nearly as structured or agreed-upon, for it is concerned with an "insider" reality that is by its very nature difficult to objectify and generalize. It is important to stress that the battle lines drawn up between staff members and patients at CPC were not coterminous with the battle lines of these two discourses. We cannot accurately represent the interaction with a simple equation of staff = biomedical perspective and patient = experiential perspective, for patients championed the biomedical perspective and staff members argued that, in the end, relying on the siren promises of medicine to cure pain was futile, and one needed to accept the reality of the pain and work on changing how one experienced it. Most pain sufferers grant extensive authority to biomedicine (although less to its psychotherapeutic branches), and staff members at centers like CPC need to promote some aspects of the experiential discourse to achieve their programs' therapeutic goals. In sum, CPC clinicians did not always promote biomedicine and patients did not always fight for the supremacy of their lived reality.

The second discourse has several of the features outlined in Gramsci's notion of counter-hegemony[28]—for example, it opposes the dominant biomedical one, throwing into relief some of its unexamined assumptions, internal contradictions, and inadequacies. When engaged in this discourse, patients insisted on the reality and accuracy of their feelings —their gut sense of what was "really" happening in their bodies—despite any misgivings and doubts. Furthermore, we have seen that at certain crucial times patients reinforced one another's claims to this kind of knowledge. When this discourse held sway, it counteracted biomedicine, first, by affirming that patients' feelings played an important part in the transformation that was supposed to happen during treatment. Staff members therefore needed to validate patients' feelings and affirm that they were a legitimate and important source of information—indeed, staff members often insisted that patients needed to work hard to become *more* in touch with their feelings, a message that resonated far more with the human potential movement's insistence on the need to focus on one's own phenomenological reality than with biomedicine. Also, patients were supposed to "take control" of their lives and their pain, to renounce passivity and dependent attitudes, most specifically their dependence on the medical system to solve their problems (or to take the blame if their problems continued). Finally, because of the nature of pain and the various puzzles it poses to the medical system, at times patients' experiences were, in some important senses, accorded a kind of primary truth status, as when, for example, staff members would say things like "pain is what the patient says it is." The information contained in, say, an X-ray, was at these times accorded a kind of secondary truth status because the extent of pain had to be inferred. (However, we have seen that at other times patients were bludgeoned with the *sine materia* nature of their pain, as evidenced by X-rays and similar diagnostic measures.) Hence patients' phenomenological knowledge of their pain was at times a weapon they could use against superior-acting professionals who seemed to question sufferers' motives and intelligence — a kind of "weapon of the weak," perhaps.[29]

Following this interpretation, we can say that patients used this "weapon" on some of the occasions when there was open conflict with staff members. It was also a weapon for a fifth column, penetrating the ranks of the enemy (unbelieving medical authorities) by chipping away at the ideological grounding of the master narrative, biomedicine (in some ways staff members were also part of this fifth column).

It has been difficult to portray this struggle and the nature of this second discourse, because patients differed among themselves with respect to this matter and even held contradictory positions within themselves. An additional source of difficulty is the fact that I, too, accept a great deal of the biomedical model. But if someone were to come across my fieldnotes and interview transcripts in, say, fifty years, I feel sure she or he would nod and say "uh-huh!"—easily seeing the mistakes flowing from erroneous assumptions of both staff members and patients, the politicized decision-making and institutionally-produced distortions characteristic of this branch of medicine as practiced in the mid-1980s. Therefore, although I have my own beliefs about pain and its causes, I am also absolutely sure that much of what I believe is wrong—not because I am not a medical scientist or clinician, but because a significant part of what medicine holds to be true today about pain will prove to be either inaccurate or far too limited to provide an adequate account of the clinical data on hand. The impressive advances in pain research during the past thirty years would seem to buttress this prediction.

We are experiencing a shift in our *doxa* about pain. *Doxa* characterizes situations in which a basic tenet in the culture is so taken for granted that it has never occurred to anyone to examine it.[30] As previously unquestioned assumptions about pain are now being scrutinized and challenged, we are shifting to a situation characterized by a dialectical interaction between *orthodoxy* and *heterodoxy.* The biomedical *doxa* concerning some aspects of chronic pain is being challenged from within the traditional medical system and by other institutions such as holistic medicine.[31] Of course, ideas about mind/body interaction have been around for a long time (e.g., the theories of Mesmer or Reich), but until now they have been marginal.[32]

Dissemination of recent findings in neurophysiology and neuropsychology about changes that can accompany severe chronic pain challenge some aspects of its "in-your-head" (i.e., "imaginary") image. The answer to a pain specialist's question, "Does anyone really believe that a tooth is capable of hurting? Or a back?"[33] is probably still yes. But the broader spread of knowledge that pain does indeed occur "in your head"—and that activity at that location involves "real" physical processes graphically revealed by state-of-the-art, solidly empirical technologies like positive emission tomography (PET scans) and magnetic resonance imaging[34]—will help dispel the too-simple dichotomy between "real" and "imaginary" pain. Functional brain imaging techniques such as PET scans are important because they provide what looks like an objective snapshot that demonstrates that a disorder exists in the brain. Brain imaging allows people who are fighting to have their diseases seen as "real" to succeed: they have pathological *signs*, not vague symptoms they can only claim to experience. If the trend from Alvarez's time is any indication (see Chapter 1), the number of diagnoses based exclusively on imaginary, hysterical pain will probably decrease; as Boureau says, such diagnoses must be based on a positive semiology and not serve as a default category whenever physical findings are absent.[35]

Demonstrating with such "hard" diagnostic technology that these disorders are biomental rather than strictly mental[36] will produce a shift in popular conceptual models that accept that psychological inputs can alter the brain. Ascribed responsibility for severe chronic pain will lessen because, according to one researcher, the diseased brain will become a part of a biological body that is experienced phenomenologically but is not the bearer of personhood: "The patient who looks at his or her PET brain scan is an innocent sufferer rationally seeking help."[37]

However, although lessening the stigma, doubt, and shame chronic pain sufferers report, the shift will not eliminate them, and the condition will remain problematic with respect to the real/unreal and responsibility discourses. If we look at the literature on what Joseph Dumit refers to as "emerging diseases" (or, as he more playfully puts it, "diseases you have to fight to get") such as Attention Deficit Disorder, Chronic Fatigue Syndrome, Gulf War Syndrome, Multiple Chemical Sensitivity, and Post-Traumatic Stress Disorder, we learn about important recent shifts in the way money, explanations, research, and theories become aligned and in opposition to each other. According to Dumit, an anthropologist studying the social movements that have sprung up to fight for the recognition of these disorders, they share the following characteristics: 1) their status as primarily mental, psychiatric, or biological conditions is highly contested; 2) their equally contested etiology is variably attributed to social, genetic, toxic, and personal causes; 3) many of the people with these disorders are organized, coordinated, and feel a kindred spirit with one another; 4) the nature of these disorders is fought over in court battles, administrative categorizing, and legislative maneuvering; 5) how to treat these conditions is also contested, suggested treatments ranging far and wide; and 6) they are cross-linked—each has been linked to the others as subsets, mistaken diagnoses, and comorbid conditions. Such disorders resemble severe chronic pain in some respects; while it is not a single disorder, it is biomental, its nature is highly contested,[38] and the explanations of sufferers of severe chronic pain are often rejected, their disability status challenged.

Dumit's and similar research show that the twenty-first-century body will still be constructed as an object by medical science, a body that will continue to be culturally and historically contingent, the object of a scientific and medical gaze that changes with the times and according to discipline, site, culture, and circumstance.

"Proving" that pain is real—brain-based, neurobiological—will not be the salvation of chronic pain patients, because the very terms of discourse will alter once the idea that symbols can materially impact the brain is fully accepted. Issues of responsibility will remain, as will issues of "entitled" disability, and fights over description and cause, because the economic stakes will be high. Chronic pain will perhaps lose some of its stigma as a purely psychoneurotic disease, but sufferers will find the Brave New World of total mind/body integration no utopia.

Puzzle 5: Culture and Meaning

How are we to analyze a situation in which an individual is suspended by hooks for hours and reports no pain?[39] If he says he feels no pain, and, more strangely, his body shows only minimal damage, we can only conclude that the mind is profoundly controlling the body's reactions to nociceptive stimuli and that culture has played a fundamental role in this process. Abundant evidence can be marshaled which suggests that cultural factors significantly influence perception of, and peripheral response to, nociceptive stimuli.

Discussions of culture in the pain literature tend to focus on ethnic differences in notions about the meaning of pain and how pain is expressed. Mark Zborowski's work on variability in reported response to pain felt by Old American, Irish-American, Jewish-American, and Italian-American veterans is the classic case.[40] This work may be useful insofar as it demonstrates cultural variability in how pain is expressed and what it means, and Zborowski's generalizations may very well continue to be consistent with the anecdotal experience of many nurses and physicians. But the crudity and offensiveness of his ethnic stereotypes remind us that research and commentary on ethnicity are always positioned—the position usually being one of superiority to the research subject—and that at times paternalism enters in. Zborowski's having been an émigré from the Soviet Union notwithstanding, it is clear that we are supposed to identify with the Old Americans in his sample. The recent work by Maryann Bates and her colleagues on ethnicity and pain is far more sophisticated.[41]

Clearly, in an ethnically diverse and highly stratified society[42] varying attitudes and values toward pain will result in variations in pain behavior and, by inference, in the pain experience itself. This applies as well to gender differences.[43] But we also need to look at the role played by values in general. For example, Porter convincingly argues that pain *itself* is seldom the main focus in the West's religious, philosophical, and ethical works, a puzzle he finds so perplexing that he concludes taboos are in effect.[44] These taboos can be partly explained by paying attention to certain Western values, for example, the association between withstanding pain and moral character (an association made in certain other cultures as well). As one scholar points out, we tend to view the stoic as mentally sound and morally upright.[45] Pain sufferers are failures in a system that sees the body as inferior to the mind and spirit, and they will suffer guilt by association with matters physical and carnal.[46] Pain is, along with disability, the most compelling reminder we have that we are, in fact, spatially and temporally limited by our physicality—in a word, mortal—although we might want to see ourselves in mental and spiritual terms. Furthermore, pain sufferers will be devalued in a system that (with some exceptions) sees beauty and health as outward signs of inner worth, a sign of favor from the Deity. The associations we make between pain and disability, ugliness, and falling from grace partly explain the conflict between our impulses to care for those who suffer and our desire to flee from them. In sum, pain is a deeply disturbing subject, in part because it is associated with other deeply disturbing, negatively valued subjects such as disability, ugliness, death, weakness, and failure.

These connections between pain and failure are more strongly linked to masculinity than to femininity. Traditionally it has been far more incumbent on men to resist pain; real men should be so hardened they do not feel pain or at least do not show they do. (In a book entitled *Will*, G. Gordon Liddy reports holding lighted matches to his palm to train himself to resist pain.[47]) Such strength and steadfastness, elevated to the spiritual plane, is a sign of righteousness. Military images abound: one fights, conquers, defeats pain. (The puzzles that result from fighting something that, while disliked, is nonetheless part of one's self were discussed in Chapter 7.) Duby argues that an even closer symbolic connection was made between women and pain during the Middle Ages,[48] and the Sun Dance "self-torture" ritual in certain American Plains Indian societies is often mentioned as an illustration of the association between manliness and the ability to withstand pain.[49]

Certain values deeply held by CPC patients clashed with the program's ideology. For example, in mainstream American society one is supposed to be independent and optimistic, to search actively for solutions to problems, and always to hope a solution can be found. What health care providers at pain centers recommend can appear to require rejecting these values. "Learning to live with your pain" can easily be seen as fatalistic and pessimistic, not only suggesting that one should "give up," but also indicating a copout attitude on the part of health practitioners. America is the land of "can do," and magazine articles and inspirational books telling how people overcame their own or their loved ones' health problems abound. Thus some messages from pain centers can sound as though asking sufferers *not* to be responsible for getting better. A CPC staff member might write that a given patient "resisted treatment"—perhaps, for example, right up to discharge resisting the idea of accepting that he would always have pain, saying instead, "my case is different," or "the doctors haven't found out what is wrong." But these were attitudes patients often saw as admirable, for they indicated that the sufferer was still willing to fight, to hope, not to give up. We want to be in control, and the value we attach to being in control plays an important role in how we deal with pain, our own and others'.

This desire for control explains much about our uneasiness with regard to certain pain puzzles. An illustration comes from Robert Ader, who has carried out numerous research projects exploring the interaction between conditioning and medication. Conditioning can be used to cut down on doses of powerful drugs by first establishing a regimen that administers medication to subjects (animals or people) and then periodically substituting a facsimile pill containing inert ingredients. The body responds as if it had been given a pill with the active ingredient (sometimes subjects even exhibit some of the side effects as well). Conditioning is a fairly well understood phenomenon and does not depend on the influence of something so nebulous as culture, as Pavlov's dogs and countless laboratory rats demonstrate. Yet Ader reports not only that pharmaceutical companies do not support his research (perhaps not totally surprising), but also that many scientists and clinicians researching related topics appear to be very uncomfortable with it.[50] This is because, bluntly put, this research requires that its subjects be deceived.

Daniel Moerman estimates that roughly half the effectiveness of modern internal medicine results from active medication (specific medical treatment), and the remaining from various placebo effects.[51] He finds it curious that, despite such impressive evidence, physicians seem reluctant to prescribe inert drugs. Perhaps not so curious, for such prescriptions would also involve deception. Furthermore, as Moerman points out, the placebo effect works to a large degree because physicians are convinced of the biological effectiveness of a given medication; if physicians knew they were prescribing a dummy drug, the effect would probably greatly diminish. Such variable responses to prescribed medication are evidence of the importance of "the art of medication."[52]

Such "drugs" definitely do not fit in with our conventional views of why drugs work. We may not mind it when our minds fool our bodies, as with sugar substitutes; indeed, for the most part, we like the idea of the mind controlling the body—in the case of pain, through stoicism, or a discipline that actually diminishes the pain experience. So it is not that the links between body and mind are in themselves threatening. We feel no threat when these links are made apparent to us—when, for example, a symbol (such as an image on a billboard or in a song) causes us to become hungry or sexually aroused—because no loss of control is involved. But we do not like the idea of our minds affecting our bodies when someone is influencing our minds without our awareness or consent, as happens in Ader's experiments. We call this "brainwashing" (a term used often by CPC patients). We very probably would not like to receive a dummy pill unknowingly, even if we knew we would enjoy the same benefits as if the pill contained active ingredients with fewer negative side effects.

In short, issues of control play a major role in our uneasy reactions to some of the phenomena that challenge our conceptualization of the separation between the body and mind. Since pain is aversive, when we cannot get rid of it we are frustrated by our lack of control, and any suggestions about mind over matter can easily appear to be a cruel joke.

A patient obsessively maintained that his pain was real—that his physical problems were making him crazy, not the other way around: "I'll take a lie detector test to show them I'm not lying."

"*Do you think they think you're* lying?"

"They think my mind is deluding me."

This man was an extreme case; his fellow patients considered him delusional (although they did not use the term), and staff members indicated that admitting him had been a mistake. Although patients made valiant efforts to help him, overall his presence during the few days he was on the unit was deeply disturbing to the rest of the community, for he embodied one of their worst nightmares—a flagrant case of precisely what they joked about and struggled with in their efforts to understand their own pain and benefit from the program: Do staff members and other patients see me as I'm seeing him? Their discomfort forcefully illustrates the stigma of "all-in-your-head" pain.

One reason so many people—sufferers, their families, primary physicians, neurobiology researchers—are invested in seeing pain as a sensation is the fact that any evidence of the mind playing a mediating role is seen as decreasing the organicity of a pain experience, which increases its potential stigma. When "real" pain is simply defined as communication about a nociceptive stimulus producing tissue damage, we have an uncomplicated model that neither challenges our ideas about mind/body separation nor complicates our notions about who deserves sympathy for bodily injury. Yet chronic pain is not this simple. That such a model leaves out an extremely important aspect of chronic pain— it stigmatizes, despite its invisibility—is increasingly being recognized. Kleinman addresses the question of why the image chronic pain patients present is viewed as so menacing and why pain patients are cast so often as modern pariahs: he suggests that chronic pain has almost become "an icon of cultural delegitimation of our society's priorities and practices."[53]

Nina, the evening nurse, illustrated the CPC position on psychogenic pain quite adroitly. When asked about the links between perceived physical and emotional pain she spoke of energy that had to "come out" one way or another. When she had a headache, she said, she did not merely notice pain, she would ask herself about whether something was bothering her: "Usually if I can take it to that, the headache will go away."

The headache would go away because of insight. But while staff members may have had psychogenic pain, none of them had had psychogenic chronic pain. As Thomas reminded the group, he had had terrific pain from a car accident, but his pain went away—implying he did not need to hang onto his pain as patients did. Hence evaluating CPC's effect on patients with respect to the issue of reducing perceived stigma and building self-esteem is complicated, for an important part of the CPC message was getting patients to shift to a more internal locus of control approach to their pain[54]—accept more responsibility for their pain and how they coped with it. Getting patients to make this shift required inducing guilt. Some components of the CPC program worked to build patients' self-esteem, but, given its message that body and mind are closely interconnected, a downside risk was that when a person in a great deal of intractable pain accepted that psychogenic factors were playing a role in her pain and yet the pain did not go away or even diminish, she could feel even more guilty and stigmatized. As a young man noted, CPC said both "accept yourself the way you are," but also, "you have to change."

A reductionist, hyperpositivist position toward chronic pain can cause additional pain because of the stigma that results from being labeled neurotic in a crude and dismissive way. The issue is not body-mind interaction, which occurs constantly with no stigmatizing consequences. Nor is it an issue of the mind controlling the body, which is often seen as desirable.[55] Stigma results when the mind is seen as controlling the body in an unconscious and unwanted way.[56] The generally accepted definition of neurotic (unwanted behavior that we cannot eliminate) is a reasonable one, and stigma will continue to be apportioned to those so labeled. My issue is not with these facts, but with a hyperbiological paradigm that at times rather cavalierly dismisses complex problems by locating them in the individual and pigeonholes these individuals into either-or diagnostic categories such as "organic," "functional," "imaginary," and "hysterical."

Some part of this stigma can be traced to the liminal nature of pain and pain patients. Mary Douglas has argued that what is anomalous or ambiguous is often seen to be unclean and defiling. Similarly, Victor Turner maintains that "the unclear is unclean."[57] While hardly "abominations," as the Old Testament terms "betwixt-and-between" creatures or manufactures (e.g., cotton and linen must not be combined in a garment), chronic pain sufferers who lack a clearcut diagnosis are indeed in an ill-defined state and perhaps suffer some discrimination because of this. When the established biomedical boundaries separating mind and body do not seem to apply to a given case, especially with respect to moral responsibility (as in alcoholism and chronic fatigue syndrome), this analysis argues that people perceive a kind of danger emanating from it; when this sense of danger is projected onto the source of the fear, the source becomes stigmatized. The danger comes from an erosion of their confidence in the reliability of their image of the world—its structure and meaning. It seems reasonable to conclude that part of the stigma reported by CPC patients stemmed from their possessing just such a liminal, unclear status.

Given that we are talking about feelings felt by sentient human beings, then (except for newborn infants) all pain will have meaning in the sense that it is culturally and socially informed. There are many demonstrations of how the meaning of a nociceptive event affects the accompanying pain experience. Henry Beecher found that wounded soldiers on the battlefield at Anzio during the Allies Italian campaign in 1943 requested less medication than expected because their pain meant a ticket home with honor.[58] That pain might be at least somewhat welcome in a battlefield and other situations (such as religious ordeals) does not indicate masochistic tendencies, but reflects the fact that pain may be welcome if it is the route to a desired end.

People in chronic pain struggle with its meaning. In part this is because they have been socialized to see pain as a sensation, basically a physical event, accompanied by an emotional response. Yet pain's meaning cannot be so confined. Indeed, pain defies all attempts to specify its meaning; in the words of one sufferer, "It is impossible to define physical pain, one cannot describe it; it is only a matter of experience. One cannot speak of pain with a capital P. It is a succession of seconds, a succession of minutes, and this is what makes it so hard to withstand."[59]

As with any illness, pain can be a means of communication: a way to express ideas, anxiety, demoralization, suffering, and a host of other feeling states.[60] What, in fact, is the meaning of pain in this expanded sense?[61] Separating "the pain experience" per se from experiences that accompany pain but are not considered to be part of the actual pain itself presents a considerable challenge for pain sufferers or those around them.

Severe unending pain often seems to involve increased suffering because of a kind of meaninglessness to it—beyond the knowledge that "I'm hurtin' for certain," as Fred put it. Discussions with patients indicated that their intractable pain cried out for explanation, because of both its intensity and its ability to create anxiety and fear; the available explanations for why they suffered so much were not satisfactory.

To begin with, patients could not answer the question "Why me?" In addition, questions like "What caused this?" "Will it get worse?" and "How long will it last?" often brought only vague responses from clinicians. While most types of chronic pain have a name, many sufferers find that little information lies behind the label. Also, because pain can come to totally dominate one's existence, many sufferers attempt to use their pain as a sort of lens to interpret their life stories, but the very meaninglessness of many cases of chronic pain can make this a more difficult task than it might be, for example, for someone with an inherited disease. Additionally, when pain is a main component in sufferers' attempts to create a new sense of self (because chronic pain has such extensive consequences for their daily life and their life vision), meaninglessness or confusion may persist because all available explanations seem to say such unacceptably negative things. Finally, uncertainty about the future can also contribute to a feeling of meaninglessness. Will one continue to deteriorate? Will the pain-diminished self meet the "challenge" of pain and grow from the suffering, or will the pain go away and the pre-pain self return?

Many authors writing on pain have puzzled over the almost contagious spread of what has come to be called chronic intractable pain. Why such an epidemic is raging is indeed puzzling, and to explain it requires using the notions both of cultural construction and social production of disease.[62] To analyze the cultural construction of this particular disease we would have to understand all the ways chronic pain now exists as a category in the minds of the general population and health care professionals. The medical profession now fully acknowledges pain in its own right, and this has led to significant changes in training, practice, and medical ethics. Pain management is now a medical specialty with all the accompanying paraphernalia: journals, professional societies, international meetings, pressure groups to increase funding, and so forth.[63] Treating pain has always been of concern to medicine, of course, but as many authors point out, the medical profession did not until recently identify pain, acute or chronic, as a topic in its own right. This fact seems most remarkable, given that pain is by far the most frequent presenting symptom. As noted above, Porter suggests that taboos provide a partial explanation. Yet it is in the attention currently being given to chronic pain that we can see most clearly the cultural processes of constructing new meanings out of existing material. Thomas Csordas points out that the anomaly of chronic pain reveals how the very notions of "disability" and the "natural course" of illness are cultural categories in which political and biological definitions are being contested in a fundamental way.[64]

The social production of disease (referred to as the "manufacture of illness" by McKinlay[65]) has to do with all the contributing factors in society that produce a particular type of ill health. Clearly this concept overlaps with that of "cultural construction"; however, the distinction is useful if we do not insist on rigid boundaries between them. An inquiry into the social production of chronic pain would examine all the ways in which activities in the workplace, on the highways, during leisure time, and so forth, result in events that immediately or later on lead to chronic pain problems—in other words, a broadly-based epidemiology of chronic pain. When we consider the high rate of disability due to chronic pain in the United States, especially in comparison to certain other countries,[66] we would have to consider the contributions made by current insurance and litigation practices. We would look at the ways in which pain has been medicalized, resulting in what Kleinman calls a new "bureaucratized object and . . . standardized commodity: *the pain patient.*"[67] And, of course, we would have to analyze the influence of the industries that manufacture and promote devices and drugs to test and treat pain, paying special attention to their misuse by health care professionals and the public. Finally, we would have to examine more general values that play a role in the incidence of chronic pain, such as our notions that we are entitled to compensation if our pain and suffering are someone else's fault, that surgery is usually preferable to long-term conservative measures, and that it is appropriate to medicate ourselves against almost every form of dysphoria. We are very ambivalent toward opioid medications. On the one hand, substantial numbers of people in pain are undermedicated because unwarranted fears about addiction make hospital and federal review boards worry about looking too lenient with narcotics prescriptions (unfortunately, often the most undertreated are those who cannot speak for themselves or have exceptional difficulty being heard—infants, the aged, the mentally ill, the dying, minorities).[68] On the other hand, our culture's ready approval of popping pills and consuming mind-altering substances contributes to the substantial numbers of people who end up abusing such substances, both legally and illegally.

Perhaps the most fundamental puzzle of all is the way pain is associated with so many disparate images. On the one hand, pain is so protean, its role in shaping the human condition so vast, that any boundaries we try to place on it are arbitrary and recede when we examine them closely. Nevertheless, we try to understand it using our analytical tools of classification, analogical modeling, and statistical analysis and our creative faculties to produce fiction, poetry, and painting about it. Yet our own pain provides us with one of the most immediate, real, direct experiences we can have, one that is anything but abstract or metaphorical. As one sufferer puts it, "There is no transcendence. I have found no creativity, no meaning in this."[69] Indeed, as Scarry eloquently points out, pain can be all we experience, blotting out, at least momentarily, everything else. In severe pain, we can easily lose the ability to find meaning and easily lose our trust that we can overcome obstacles and, if not triumph, then at least survive; as Kirmayer says, "how can we claim to encompass all possible worlds of meaning in the permutations of language when bodily pain and suffering up-end our orderly lives and drive us to the most desperate gestures of faith?"[70]

Hence grasping the entire meaning of pain, despite pain's core reference to bodily experience, is a challenge. If we enlarge our concept of pain to include unembodied pain—emotional pain such as grief when it has little bodily involvement,[71] we have a concept that stretches far and wide, one dominating much of the West's cultural production, for the mainspring of all novels and plays, tragic and comic (virtually all humor is ultimately based on someone's pain), is pain of one kind or another.

Finally, a concept of pain that includes what we might call metaphorical pain covers even vaster territory. Examples include the pain of knowing one is a sinner in the Christian context or the pain of knowing one is going to die, the kind of pain we experience that other animals do not experience, and which, therefore, is a fundamental part of being human.

Puzzle 6: Pain Is Beneficial

A final puzzle, which has received a great deal of attention in this book, has to do with the advantages of pain and suffering. Because this study is set in a pain clinic, I have concentrated on notions about possible gains—to the sufferers or those around them—from being in pain, but the issue is far broader than that. Although pain might be aversive, we do see it as the means to many worthwhile ends. "Pain is simultaneously viewed as an evil in itself, yet also, potentially, the most powerful instrument for bringing about good."[72] Several scholars have examined the question why some forms of suffering bring pleasure (aesthetic pleasure, perhaps, or the pleasure of enlightenment) to sufferers or those who behold suffering—the tubercular *Belle Dame aux Camélias* perhaps being the best example.[73] Another possible benefit involves seeking pain, despite its aversiveness, as the means to a hoped-for end: the philosophy underlying a "no pain, no gain" strategy sees pain as a teacher and disciplinarian who requires secular ordeals in the gym or religious ordeals in the wilderness.

Much of the literature on pain points out that to be impervious to pain would be disastrous for both the individual and the species.[74] Porter states: "Yet if, to the physician, pain has been seen as protective, to the layperson it has been seen as evil, sickening and sinister."[75] Physicians also find pain sickening and sinister when they suffer it themselves, as the many accounts by physician-patients attest.[76]

Of particular interest is what we might call "authorized" pain. Clearly, being in authority can, at times, require doling out pain of one kind or another. This is seen as "good" or "useful" pain—or at least necessary for getting the job done. (Note that when authorized beneficial pain is spoken of it is, not surprisingly, almost always pain felt by others, sayings like "this hurts me more than it does you" notwithstanding.)

What is most interesting about authorized pain is the fact that institutions (states, chiefdoms, churches, extended families) and the officials representing them (warlords, patriarchs, popes, mothers-in-law), bolstered by the ideologies legitimating those institutions and offices, produce and justify numerous kinds of pain that seem to us unnecessary. Attempting to understand why is undoubtedly a good endeavor, whether we speak of horrific public executions, female genital operations, torture, rape, genocide,[77] or all the other seemingly infinite number of ways to suffer.

Surely suffering and pain are humanity's lot, and giving top priority to eliminating and avoiding pain would make us such poor parents, letting such hopelessly immature individuals out into the world, that the species probably *would* be threatened after a generation. Yet, though we can agree that pain is unavoidable, a lot of pain seems very avoidable. Without question, people in positions of authority constantly inflict a great deal of unnecessary pain on their fellow humans (although in just which cases pain is indeed unnecessary is often subject to debate). This issue has drawn a great deal of attention in fields as diverse as philosophy, jurisprudence, religion, and sociology. Obviously some pain is deliberately caused by people who ought to know better, but who are angry or envious or vengeful or greedy and simply abuse their authority. But much of what seems to be unnecessary pain is produced by people with good intentions, who believe either that they are not causing pain (as occurred not too long ago when clinicians used no anesthesia while performing medical procedures on infants), or that the pain they are causing is necessary as a means to a desired end—the justifications for countless examples of authorized pain—"the rule of thumb" in nineteenth-century marital law; nineteenth-century cliterodectomy operations; policies affecting the homeless in our cities; the "development" of the third world and the delivery of foreign aid; treatment of the deinstitutionalized mentally ill; our foreign policy in Latin America and just about everywhere else; ethnic cleansing; and so forth.[78] Michel Enaudeau asks:

After extermination or "Gulag" camps, how are we to regard the suffering of peoples and individuals? And when death or the threat of death reaches a climax, i.e., theodicy or ideology, in the name of what is suffering endured or accepted? What is left of pain but its hateful uselessness?[79]

This question, of course, leads into the debate on cultural relativism. What can we say of a system of social control so effective that an individual can die, willingly and peacefully, living out its construction of the world, as does the South Asian widow who hypothetically succeeds in dying blissfully on her husband's funeral pyre? It is paradoxical that while we admire the mind-over-matter discipline of fakirs in India who control their breathing and heartbeats to an impressive extent, we probably do not much admire the widows whose blissful deaths probably enlist rather similar psychophysiological mechanisms. Whether we feel feminist outrage or are simply uneasy about just how voluntary or painless such deaths are, the existence of cultural mandates so internalized that they allow individuals to do such extreme violence to themselves tests our tolerance for cultural diversity. Yet to refer to entire cultures as "sick" begs the question. And the examples are legion, kamikaze pilots being a familiar one.

The most perplexing set of examples of this particular mind/body puzzle, which is the puzzle of free will, involves situations where individuals have internalized the need to undergo authorized pain or injury. In the most bizarre examples, bodily pain is controlled, perhaps even nonexistent, but what we might call extreme existential pain—death— occurs. Despite what appears to be admirable control over their bodies, the widows still end up as dead bodies. Yes, their culture says such a fate is necessary, but surely the lessons we can learn from these examples are fundamentally different from those we learn from the fakirs.

In a certain sense we can see CPC as an arena in which the very grand issue of theodicy was addressed and struggled over—our culture's understanding of why we must suffer and why some people suffer more than others. At CPC, ironically a facility designed to treat chronic pain, a topic of constant debate was whether the authorized pain deliberately inflicted by the staff on patients was, in fact, necessary. The behavioral policies followed at CPC were often justified by a "*this* pain is good for you" kind of sentiment. Clearly, some of CPC's deliberate, authorized pain was indeed necessary, as it is in all rehabilitation efforts. But it has required an entire book to explore the question whether the remaining amounts of authorized pain were justified or not. "Necessary for whom?" is the question asked by those who write on medicine as an institution of social control.[80] This issue is of particular interest in the case of CPC because of the extremely unhappy situation of those pain sufferers who sought help there, the conflicting discourses they encountered, and the ambiguities and confusions resulting from gaps in knowledge about certain aspects of pain and its management. CPC, with its "tough love" and confrontation, provides an excellent example of the problems of working through the question of whether authorized, deliberately inflicted pain is necessary.

At times I have been quite critical of CPC policies, but I do not want to sound sanctimonious: I have enormous respect for the clinicians I observed who, when being candid, were the first to admit that at times they were "playing God," were "in a crapshoot," had limited knowledge, and who also questioned certain CPC policies. For example, some CPC staff members were uneasy about incoming patients' lack of information about what actually went on. Kenneth said that although one reason for this was that the referring health care professionals were ignorant, another was that patients were simply not told, and he wondered whether it was really ethical not to tell people. But, he said, on the other hand, there were a lot of people who benefited from being at CPC who had denied the fact that they had had any problem other than a physical one, and once they had been admitted they really did benefit. Although he had misgivings, the policy might be justified in terms of therapeutic value.

A second example comes from Naomi, discussing the CPC policy of openly criticizing patients receiving disability payments. Was receiving such payments morally wrong or therapeutically wrong? She said that she hesitated to judge them morally—who was she to judge them if they were accepting something that might be rightfully theirs after all, even if they had been working under the table? But if their belief system somewhere unconsciously had been telling them such behavior was wrong, then some inward stress might have been complicating their pain. Once again, a staff member, hesitant about defining patient behavior as moral or immoral, was quite willing to justify authorized pain in the form of public embarrassment as potentially therapeutic.

CPC staff members at times were very judgmental indeed toward disability payments, saying that people who were "paid to be in pain" did not get better. Edward was admitted worrying about this issue, describing himself as "threatened," worrying about his medical bills, defensively saying he had a "real thing." Edward became a CPC convert, but his roommate, Kurt, changed from being a "happy-go-lucky guy" to someone so "down in the dumps" that Edward felt he had to "keep both eyes on him half the time." Edward approved of CPC's trying to "goad" and "push" Kurt into thinking about doing something with the rest of his life instead of just collecting his retirement and working under the table. Edward's account admirably conveys some of the dynamics of the CPC operation and some of the cultural and social conditions that form the seedbed from which policies like CPC's grow. The fact that Kurt was most definitely not a convert is not in itself proof that the policy was not effective, for, as we have seen, others like him were converts. And he did improve, discarding his neck brace and increasing his range of motion. But the massive amount of "tough love" directed at him during his stay resulted in his feelings being deeply wounded; as Edward said, "He really did not like the whole idea of playing a game"—being told up until the last day that he would be discharged with no limitations. CPC staff members assumed Kurt was motivated to continue to be in pain because of financial gains and he and his wife assumed that CPC misled him, humiliated him in front of other patients, and in general deliberately caused him much unnecessary distress out of simple meanness and misguided psychotherapeutic theory. When he and his wife talked with me a month after he left CPC, they were still bitter about having been "lied to" and manipulated regarding the degree of his physical limitations. Edward, the caring, observing roommate, had extremely complex reactions because, first, he was comparing Kurt's case to his own and, second, being sharp as a tack, he did not miss any of the dilemmas introduced by the ongoing drama.

The issue of authorized unnecessary pain is not, finally, about individuals in authority, such as CPC staff members, insofar as they are well-intentioned; it is about the system in which they operate. Kurt's case is perplexing because it embraces so many of the dilemmas of chronic pain, especially its treatment. Most of his misery had been produced by factors far beyond the control of CPC (e.g., his work-related accident and the medical encounters that followed before he came to CPC). CPC staff members thought his attitude and choices were wrong and used rather extreme—certainly ethically questionable—means to get him to change. As individuals, their motives were undoubtedly complex, but they *were* trying to help. Kleinman writes of a "poisoned clinical atmosphere" in many settings where chronic pain is treated, in which trust and support are replaced by suspicion and accusation.[81] He is critical of the behaviorist discourse, which he finds stereotyped, overly focused on pain as a problem of an *individual,* and dehumanizing.[82] Many CPC patients did indeed feel as if they were suspected and accused, and many of them blamed individual staff members for being uncaring, but these people were not mean or uncaring. Any criticism surely must focus on the underlying premises of this approach as practiced at places like CPC in the mid-1980s, in particular its rather simple-minded exclusion of many of the determinants of chronic pain and its crudely postulated mechanisms of considering *how* an inducement such as perceived financial gain operates in a pain sufferer's motives and consequent behavior.

Conclusions

Pain is a congeries of puzzles because it is so protean and because so many of its disparate meanings conflict with one another. Pain is an experience we want to avoid and want our loved ones to avoid, as well as something intimately associated with several other deeply aversive topics such as disability, death, weakness, and failure. Yet pain is also spoken of as beneficial, and we authorize inflicting it in cases where we want to punish (the etymology of the word refers to this function), or take vengeance, or simply teach our children many of the basic facts of life they need to learn to be able to survive and thrive. This book has been about one of the most disturbing pain puzzles: severe pain that does not go away. It is also about what attempts to deal with it tell us about our society and culture.

It is unusual at the end of a book to find a list of puzzles rather than conclusions that tie everything up. It is useful, after so many words on pain, to remember how many authors who write on pain need to comment that, in the end, one cannot and perhaps should not, attempt to contain, categorize, or measure pain with words. Some pain is indeed "unspeakable." Kleinman speaks of both anthropologists and clinicians possibly finally admitting "there are no words!" Scarry speaks of pain's "inexpressibility." Steiner, speaking of Nazi death camps, contends that "abominations may be so excruciating, physiologically and psychologically, as to be beyond the healing power of words, and even perhaps the redemptive capacity of art."[83] Recall what Morris writes of chronic pain:

Such inexplicable pain is not simply too complex or too severe to be contained within language. As one medical treatment after another fails, chronic pain becomes an experience about which there is increasingly nothing to say, nothing to hope, nothing to do. It is pure blank suffering.[84]

In short, the concept of chronic pain seems to be as intractable as its reality. We will not, of course, really conclude that all we can say about chronic pain is that it is "pure, blank suffering," for we will continue our effort to understand it better. But given that our understanding is far from complete, such a notion helps remind us that those who suffer do so for many reasons, and that sometimes the best of intentions does not prevent us from administering pain which, authorized though it might be, is most definitely not therapeutic.

Coda : A Note on Approach

Taking an Ethnographic Perspective

"Ethnography" refers to both a period of intensive long-term fieldwork and the resulting write-up. While anthropologists collect data in many ways, participant-observation is the hallmark of the anthropological enterprise; it is a critical boundary that separates anthropology from other social and behavioral sciences.

Participant-observation involves spending large amounts of time observing and talking to people in their own surroundings. The researcher learns the language and plunges into local activities as completely as possible, for example, attending rituals, "hanging out" and gossiping, washing clothes at the river with other women. This approach evolved at a time when the vast majority of anthropologists carrying out field research went to exotic locales and studied "primitive" peoples, and is still used, with certain modifications, in a wide range of research settings. Participant-observation has numerous advantages. First, it is virtually the only way to conduct research with people who do not use a written language. Second, speaking a language as well as possible increases the chance of making sense of what is happening in the native speakers' terms, and this is as true of the linguistic variability accompanying occupational, class, and ethnic differences as it is for entire languages. Although ethnographic research has been conducted by interviewing people using an interpreter, problems of translation arise, as well as the possibility that the interpreter is telling the anthropologist what the interpreter wants to go on the record, rather than an accurate and comprehensive version of an informant's responses.

Third, over time the researcher becomes less intrusive, less a stranger. People are more comfortable; they come to know and, hopefully, like the researcher and in general develop a sense of understanding and trust toward the individual and the research that greatly aids the investigation. Fourth, there is no need to rely only on what people say about what happened, for the participant-observer actually witnesses at least some of it. It is useful to observe an event, talk to several people afterward about what went on, and then compare notes. At times people will consciously or unconsciously misrepresent what went on, and having observed a given event oneself is a good check on the distortions that inevitably creep into accounts of an event.

Fifth, the researcher, being "there" all the time, observes not only the ceremonies but the preparations for them and the mopping up afterward. This includes not only customary behavior, but behavior that breaks the rules.

Traditional anthropological fieldwork involves immersing oneself, taking in large amounts of vastly different kinds of data. The range and abundance of such "raw" experience and observation help provide a context for more formally acquired information—gathered through structured interviews, for instance.

Being on "their turf" has other advantages. The members of the culture continue to arrange and live their lives on their own terms. Much of this activity does not involve conscious thinking, and often the most valuable information comes from observing precisely those ways of doing and seeing that are unquestioned by the people being studied. Ward Goodenough has commented that to write a good ethnography one must get to the point of knowing the rules for appropriate behavior in that culture.[1] Clearly, a lot of this must be learned first hand, for most of us cannot verbalize much of our understanding of the world in response to direct questions. More recent work has criticized statements like Goodenough's for implying that learning rules is all that matters, whereas the researcher should be concerned with questions about how and why people's activities make psychological sense to them, and that learning about people and culture must occur to a considerable extent through direct experience, not with the distancing and objectivity of the scientific method as practiced by social scientists. For example, the researcher should learn through senses other than seeing and hearing—by smelling or acquiring habitual body postures, for instance.[2] The anthropologist effectively becomes a data-gathering instrument, and a variety of alterations in her or his experiences (emotions, proprioception, etc.) become a way of knowing. As Susan Harding states, "the only certain evidence of the reality that preoccupies ethnographers, of shared unconscious knowledge, is experiential."[3]

Proponents of such "total immersion" fieldwork also argue that this approach tears the researcher away from familiar routines and unexamined assumptions: abrupt, at times violent, changes, it is argued, enable the anthropologist to acquire new languages and habits more quickly and completely. Fieldwork is often called a "rite of passage" not only because it marks an important career stage for the pre-dissertation anthropologist but also because it recalls the painful, disorienting practices in initiation rites that function to eradicate familiar habits and expectations. Such violent ritual practices have been said to be a far more effective way to inscribe a new social status and teach new concepts and behaviors than when an initiate learns new knowledge with a minimum of affect and bodily participation.[4]

Those who favor long-term, intense, "experience-near" fieldwork see it as a way to achieve a profound, multidimensional knowledge not available to someone who visits a community for a few days or weeks or who is closely tied to a more scientific research methodology. Not only is one more likely to learn secret or esoteric knowledge, one will learn the kinds of knowledge not immediately available even to the possessors of that knowledge and which cannot, therefore, be acquired by an outsider through direct interrogation. Bourdieu's notion of habitus (repetitive, unconscious, mundane practices) is pertinent here. Virtually all anthropology's ancestral figures have contributed to the extensive debates in the social sciences over the issue of how to interpret a postulated meaning that is not readily available to the consciousness of the members of the community being studied. Examples are Marx's "false consciousness," Gramsci's hegemony, and Bourdieu's *doxa* (unquestioningly accepted authoritative discourses and practices).[5]

None of the above is intended to imply that the researcher should jettison attempts to be objective and achieve validity, and the literature on fieldwork endlessly discusses the best mix of scientific approaches (stressing objectivity, replicability, predictability) and experiential, empathic, intuitive approaches ("getting under the native's skin").

The disadvantages of participant-observation are fairly obvious. First, it takes a huge amount of time, some of it spent inefficiently. Second, anthropologists want to stick their noses into things, and people do not always like this when they experience it, which is why it is crucial to inform potential subjects about a study and gain their permission. Often the information people are most reluctant to reveal is precisely what the investigator most needs to understand the phenomena being studied. In this instance, the agendas of investigator and investigated are simply opposed; what is important is that there be an understanding that this might occur as part of an agreement made prior to the investigation. Third, it is sometimes difficult to explain to the people being studied (and to university committees approving a researcher's informed consent procedures) exactly what a participant-observer wants to do and why. At times people draw their own quite inaccurate conclusions about the researcher's goals, and some of these mistaken notions can lead to unwanted consequences. Fourth, the anthropologist's presence *will* affect the interaction being studied. And finally, it can be difficult to demonstrate adequately why readers should accept conclusions based solely on participant-observation. "Since I was there, my perceptions are accurate," is not a very reassuring, objective-sounding statement, no matter how forcefully it is put. This is why researchers always rely on other techniques, such as censuses, archival work, genealogies, projective tests, and structured interviews.[6] Other drawbacks to doing ethnographic research apply more generally to many kinds of social science research (for example, the issue of respecting and maintaining privacy), and are mentioned when pertinent elsewhere in this book.[7]

An ethnographic approach in a medical setting not only allows for rich, contextualized data but can also show how changes occur—that is, one can study the *process* of change. Retrospective interviews or questionnaires cannot provide information on how new norms emerge for either an individual or a group, especially in a situation involving long-term interaction. Quantitative data or qualitative results of interviews clarify such questions, but only ethnography can provide the all-important context; only ethnography permits intensive observation of all members of an interacting group over time.

Doing the Research

In several respects, CPC turned out to be a nearly ideal fieldwork situation. I was in a small, face-to-face community, able to get to know everyone; the people I was studying most intensively, the patients, spent all their time at one place—a *very* unusual situation in an industrialized society. As any researcher will affirm, maintaining contact with urban dwellers can be extremely difficult. Furthermore, unlike patients in hospital wards (but like those in mental hospitals and drug and alcohol treatment centers), patients at CPC interacted intensely with one another and with the staff, and an ethnographic approach ensured that I would be privy to much of this interaction. And, given the rate of patient turnover, at the end of the research I had a respectable sample size.

In addition, some of the top CPC staff (Dr. B, Kevin, Naomi) knew me and supported the study in every way. Having been a patient, I already had a considerable amount of knowledge under my belt regarding how CPC functioned.

My dual role of former patient and social scientist had advantages—in terms of access, ease of obtaining patient permission, and prior knowledge of the program—that far outweighed the disadvantages. All researchers have personal reasons for choosing a particular topic, and many anthropologists choose a site because they are familiar with it. I felt my best course was to be as self-aware and as cautious as I could about possible distorting influences.[8]

In other ways the research was nervewracking. "Getting into the field" is almost always difficult in fieldwork, especially in settings like CPC. Both anthropologists and sociologists have written extensively about how hard it can be to gain the confidence of those in authority, to explain one's intentions adequately, to obtain everyone's consent. There were constraints on my interactions with the patients; given the considerable divide between patients and staff (and a few newly-admitted patients' outright suspicion of me), the last thing I needed was to seem to pry, and a question as innocuous as asking someone's age might seem like just that. Furthermore, because many patients indicated they were fed up with the quantity of tests and questionnaires administered during their first week, I did not want unduly to burden them further. I soon realized, in part from talking with patients early on, that if I was to be accepted I had to blend in as much as possible. Consequently after the first week I abandoned my clipboard, and all note-taking, apart from scheduled interviews, took place hurriedly during trips to the women's room in the hospital's business office next door. I wondered whether the folks in that office thought I had a chronic bladder infection. (See Appendix 2 for interview protocols.)

I was always in a precarious position doing this kind of research, for had I antagonized even one patient to the point of bringing a formal complaint, I could have been denied access to the unit so long as that person was there, and then have had to undergo the slow process of integrating myself again. Hence it was necessary to be very diplomatic and constantly to let people know that, while I was indeed studying CPC, I was not doing individual case studies. Demographic and other characteristics of pain center populations were available in various published studies, so I concentrated interview time—always at a premium—on issues unique to my research.

I began going to CPC in February 1986. Four frustrating months were spent in the waiting area outside the front office where Dr. B, Rhonda, and various clerical personnel worked. Following guidelines specified by the hospital's committee on human subjects, which required that I be introduced to each patient by a staff member rather than introduce myself, Rhonda would introduce me to prospective patients who had just completed an evaluation appointment with herself and Dr. B. I would explain the research and ask whether they were willing to sign a consent form. Almost all of them did.

The need to obtain permissions before beginning fieldwork had to do with the nature of my study and the constraints imposed by the hospital. Since mine was a study of the patient community, I needed access to the entire group of patients. CPC decided that a patient's admission to the unit should not depend on his or her willingness to participate in the study. The process took so long because there was little congruence between the evaluation session and admission to the program; some patients waited a year or more between the two. In addition, some patients were evaluated by telephone interviews and some—arriving in ambulances—were admitted directly following their evaluation before I was able to meet them.

While "entering the field" slowly had its advantages, that four-month period was discouraging. Since the front office was disorganized and often ran very late, I lost a lot of time. And the distance between evaluations and admissions meant that many pain sufferers who consented to being studied did not actually participate; several were admitted and discharged during this four-month period. (Some came to chat with me—at times bringing other curious and gregarious patients—and express disappointment that they could not participate.)

When I had signatures for all but seven patients on the unit, I asked Georgia, a PRA, to ask them if they would mind my talking to them. All consented and gave their permission over the next two days. By my first day actually on the unit I was more than ready.

I spent the next eight months on the unit as participant observer, finishing in February 1987. I conducted 196 interviews with 136 patients (60 of them twice) and 20 staff members. I observed 173 patients overall. Throughout this period I also talked with family members who came to visit, and to former patients who had returned for follow-up interviews with Dr. B or, sometimes, just to visit with current patients.

I was on the unit as much as possible, morning and afternoon five or six days, and at least three evenings, a week. I was present at all activities except private sessions with therapists, group therapy sessions, psychomotor sessions, and the discharge planning meetings each patient had with his or her team. (Teresa, the patient we met in Chapter 1, invited me to her discharge planning meeting.)

As noted, intensive "saturation" fieldwork has several advantages. Being on the unit so much of the time meant that most patients became comfortable with my presence and I came to know some of them surprisingly well. The vast majority of patients were open about themselves and supportive of what I was trying to do. Although I tried hard not to act like a staff member or seem to be on "their side," many newly-arrived patients assumed I was one more staff member with one more form to fill out. "Seasoned" patients would work hard at overcoming newcomers' initial misgivings about talking with me, saying things like "oh, *she's* Ok"; once Davie said, "Jean's blood" (as in blood kin).

For the most part I tried to be open as well, but on more than one occasion I had to be less forthcoming than I would have liked as a result of conflicts in the role I was playing. Some of these conflicts confront every field researcher; some were unique to my situation. Because I was part of a fairly small and intense group, there was no possibility of being only an unobtrusive social scientist or impartial observer. But although I cannot know all the effects I had on individuals or on the functioning of the unit, I heard few complaints, and many patients and staff indicated they found me an asset despite my marginal and ambiguous status.

All patients agreed to the study, as required by the hospital, and the vast majority agreed to be interviewed as well. Most of those who hesitated misunderstood my goals, were suspicious of my motives, were concerned about invasion of privacy or embarrassment, or felt they did not have enough time. Four patients simply did not believe me; according to other patients, they assumed I was some sort of company spy. However, several patients who seemed to understand quite well what I was doing still had reservations. My impression was that these individuals (eight in all) knew just how sneaky social scientists can be; unlike most of those who were initially suspicious, these were people very much like me in terms of social class, educational background, and occupation. With two exceptions, these patients also opened up after two or three weeks. One who did, Eleanor, about my age, came to me after a run-in with Dr. S saying, "OK, *now* I'm willing to talk to you!" I had the impression that she had been uncomfortable with the differences between her status and mine in that setting, but now saw me as a possible confidante. The patients I did not interview either did not want to be interviewed, dropped out before I could interview them, or were so old and infirm that an interview seemed inappropriate.

The eight months of intensive participant observation went remarkably well in almost every respect. I had expected a rockier road, given the stress and confusion of patients in the new surroundings, their pain and demoralizing previous experiences, the intensity of the program, and the use of confrontational therapies. Kevin, the head psychologist, warned me early on that patients sometimes projected issues they were having trouble with onto people in their immediate environment, and that I might be a target. I certainly was manipulated by various patients, but I was never the focus in any of the instances of acting out that I witnessed. Perhaps my fence-straddling and ambiguous identity kept me from being a lightning rod. It also may simply have been a matter of luck.

Although I still have not entirely figured out why I got along so well with almost everyone, I know some of the reasons. Many patients told me that they welcomed the opportunity to talk to someone who was neither staff nor fellow patient because "I can tell you things and it won't go anywhere else." They also liked the fact that I did not attend staff meetings and did not read their medical records. As Kotarba found for the chronic pain sufferers he studied, most CPC patients were eager to talk about themselves and their problems.[9] Many recently arrived patients were in a state of shock and talked to me about what was bewildering them. In addition, even when a patient was resisting discussion of a sensitive topic (a problem between a staff member and a patient, say, or criticism of the program) with Dr. S or in an encounter group, I often heard about such issues by "hanging out" with patients in the solarium.

Finally, most patients enthusiastically supported my research. One man commented at the end of our discharge interview, in which we had continued to discuss the horrendous story begun in the intake interview: "The ironic part of it is that no one knows anything about this, about the personal part, the agony of it. And I feel I want to get it off my chest here. I didn't get a lawyer or sue or anything, I just want to get the anger out. I've told you more than I've told anyone, to help the research."

I tried to be as friendly and helpful as possible toward the staff, and they treated me like a fellow professional, with the reserve accompanying that kind of relationship. Most considered the research I was doing worthwhile and came to like me as a person. For the most part, they were circumspect in my presence, as was proper, although I did pick up tidbits fairly regularly. I tried hard to avoid becoming coopted into the staff's way of looking at things, always a danger for social scientists working in medical settings. This is why I postponed interviewing staff members until I had finished the participant observation portion of the study. I found my anxieties about cooptation were justified, for when I began interviewing the staff the shifts in my perspective were striking. These were welcome signs of empathy, but given the clear lines of cleavage between staff and patients and my interest in having as patient-focused a study as possible, the decision to postpone staff interviews had been prudent.

When I finished my research and attended a staff meeting to thank them and say good-bye, they presented me with a card signed by all and a beautiful pair of earrings, a gesture that meant a great deal to me.

No doubt, both patients and staff at times felt I was hearing things I should not be hearing. I tried to resolve this issue by being scrupulous about confidentiality and reassuring staff members and patients that I was a responsible person who was doing a worthwhile project. That they understood this came across in mordant comments made after incidents at which I had heard quite an earful. Both staff members and patients knew they could ask me not to be present at a meeting, and this did happen from time to time; however, several times staff members were asked to leave a patient community meeting and I was allowed to stay, which made me feel very accepted (although also somewhat apprehensive about how staff members would react).

All in all, as is the case for my field research in the Northwest Amazon, CPC fieldwork was a peak experience of my life. I was never bored. I felt privileged to be at CPC because I was able to get to know a succession of fascinating people. Although chronic pain sufferers are often seen by clinicians as a "difficult" population, "losers" and "crocks,"[10] I became engrossed with their stories, their personalities, and the drama of their experiences at CPC. The research was anything but depressing — a question frequently asked by my friends — ghastly as many patient stories were. Had I met some of these individuals on the outside, on the subway, for instance, we would have perceived each other as having very little in common. Yet at CPC I connected strongly even with those most unlike me, for example, men from rural Maine with long hair, tattoos, and stories about their trucking days. They were in CPC because of pain, and I was there because I wanted to hear about it.

Ethan, effusive and very fond of metaphors, said he had loved having me there, as someone who was aware of the program, in her right mind and "able to think as quickly and as sensibly as I can." Talking to me was "like a coffee break." He continued: "I can talk to you and go back into this because you don't shatter the head set. You know what the head set is and you have managed to walk so slowly into the stream that you have not disturbed the flow of the water. When my friend comes in to visit, it's like a rhinoceros moving into the stream and there's waves and turbulence and the water gets all muddy and it's like, 'no! I don't want that!'"

As I return again and again to the fieldnotes and interview transcripts, I am often strongly moved by my memories of the research, especially enjoying recalling patients' personalities, humor, uniqueness, *humanity*. Whatever was creating the connections worked both ways, and I have concluded that this mysterious process is the main reason why the research proceeded as smoothly as it did.

Appendix 1: CPC Patients and Staff

All names are pseudonyms; within each category they are listed by name in alphabetical order. The descriptions of individual patients that follow are non-verbatim, and are provided by the patients themselves.

Ann Cooper	Mid-fifties; medical secretary; lower back and leg pain following job-related injury in 1976; three disk surgeries, bone fragments lodged in sciatic nerve; angina; stress related to two recent deaths in the family
Adrienne Fonseca	Mid-thirties; computer operator; temporo mandibular joint disorder and arthritis in neck, becoming severe in 1983; worried about upcoming major jaw surgery; medication dependency
Agnes Huang	Mid-twenties; student; ruptured disk; post-herpetic neuralgia; legally blind
Alice Pantanella	Early fifties; pain for 4 1/2 years following a car accident; became depressed following second car accident; stressful marriage followed by death of husband; over-medicated
Amy Simeone	Mid-fifties; registered nurse; pancreatitis since 1969 (diagnosed 1975) following gall bladder surgery; other medical conditions; medication dependency
Amalie Swanson	Early thirties; graduate student; lower back pain for many years, two episodes of incapacitation, surgery in 1982; most recent incapacitation began eight months previously; marital stress
Anita Hayes	Mid-thirties (not interviewed)
Arlene Ford	Early fifties; housecleaner; lower back pain from injury in 1984 resulting in degenerative disk; bursitis; other medical problems
Audrey Dorfman	Early forties; lower back pain that worsened following a spinal fusion and removal of two disks
Beth Fitzgerald	Seventy-three; lower back and leg pain not relieved by laminectomy in 4th and 5th vertebrae for arthritic spurs and removal of a disk in April 1986; pain and numbness in the genital-anal region; incontinence

Caroline Lawrence	Early sixties; long-term lower back pain; spasms in rectal muscle since 1984, acute since December 1985. Abused with enemas as a child
Cathy Michod	Late thirties; lupus erithematosis and four years of lower back pain from pinched nerve
Catherine Sutton	Mid-sixties; nun; lower back, hip, right side pain from arthritis and disk deterioration; some shoulder pain
Daphne Gerardin	Mid-thirties; occupational therapist; neck, shoulder, and back pain resulting from work-related accident; tendinitis and bursitis in both shoulders resulting from eight months wearing a collar
Denise Harburger	Late thirties; research scientist; headaches, neck, shoulder, and back pain and numbness from whiplash injury in a car accident in 1983
Diane Himmel	Early forties; migraines for ten years; marital problems
Dolores Kavanaugh	Sixty; hip, leg, and ankle pain in right leg due to degeneration from several sprains; severe back pain since 1984; two surgeries, complications following surgery to remove disk
Dora Hatch	Mid-fifties; factory worker; neck, back, arm, and leg pain since 1984 following injury from badly pulled muscles, bulging disk, and fibrosis; arthritis
Doris Regent	Early fifties; real estate agent; back pain from herniated disk and continuing deterioration of lower spine following a head-on car accident in 1983
Edith Hanrahan	Early forties; clerical worker; neck, arm, and back pain following car accident in 1984; "stress for 20 years"; over-medicated
Eileen Dorfman	Early thirties; lower back pain and migraines for two years; several surgeries; had been a CPC patient the previous year; medication dependency (overdosed twice, at least once intentionally); incest victim
Eleanor Dowling	Mid-forties; lower back and leg pain from herniated disk, beginning in 1985; temporary relief from facette injections, no relief from rhizotomy
Elsa Swan	Mid-thirties; clerical worker; neck, shoulder, arm, and back pain beginning in high school, aggravated by several minor car accidents and a job-related injury
Emily Houston	Twenty-one; headaches since childhood; severe head pain due to injury; epilepsy following surgery at sixteen to correct congenital brain condition; previous CPC patient
Emma Tomlinson	Mid-sixties; secretary; pain since 1985 from partially amputated thumb following injury; lower back pain
Faye Bennett	Mid-forties; damaged lumbar region of spine following car accident in 1984; thoracic outlet syndrome
Felicia Turner	Mid-sixties; university administrator; generalized pain in right leg and hand from thalamic syndrome caused by aneurism in thalamus in 1983
Florence Gifford	Late sixties; ruptured disk from falling downstairs back-

	ward; post-herpetic neuralgia in shoulder, chest, and arm; osteoporosis in back and hip
Gloria Lopez	Mid-forties; pain since 1983 from fibromyalgia and neck pain from disk problems; medication dependency
Hannah Epstein	Late sixties; back and leg pain since approximately 1978 following injury; arthritis; other medical conditions; laminectomy
Helen Emerson	Early fifties; nurse's aide; diabetes; heart condition; job-related back injury in 1969; injured back again lifting bedridden husband; ruptured disc diagnosed in 1984; medication dependency; multiple pain problems; depression, especially following death of husband two years previously
Hope Douglas	Late forties; hospital laboratory aide; temporo mandibular joint disorder beginning with surgery for pyorrhea, aggravated by cervical strain following car accident; severe pain following second surgery for pyorrhea
Imogene Felice	Late fifties; working on college degree; six years of spastic colitis; insomnia
Joanna Fiorella	Mid-fifties; housewife; lower back and leg pain, severe since 1984, some due to degenerative arthritis; 3-day cycles of headaches since childhood
Kami Ferguson	Early forties; neck, arm, and lower back pain from degenerative disk disease following car accident in 1969; 13 back surgeries (several fusions that did not take); severe pain due to fall three months previously
Karen Grey	Late forties; operating room registered nurse; pain due to work-related back injury in 1977; medication dependency
Karlia Fontaine	Early thirties; student; eleven years of back pain beginning with a fall; surgery in 1984; had been a CPC patient in 1983
Kate Glazer	Late thirties; public relations agent; pain on left side, neck, arm, and back following a car accident in 1976, complicated by a second accident in 1982
Katherine Dohrn	Late forties; twenty years of shoulder pain; ten years of lower back pain; scoliosis; surgery in 1980; broken Harrington rod one year later
Kitty Hardy	Mid-forties; neck and back pain; unsuccessful surgery; irritable bowel syndrome; medication dependency
Laura Cassidy	Mid-sixties; multiple medical problems; stomach ulcer; back, left shoulder pain from arthritis, osteoporosis, broken shoulder, and surgery for lung cancer in 1985; over-medicated; insomnia
Laverne Gilligan	Late forties; housewife and part-time student; lower back and leg pain, some disk involvement, resulting from bad fall
Marcella Erickson	Early thirties; student; back and wrist pain from three accidents beginning in 1984

Mary Rourke	Mid-thirties; registered nurse; back and neck pain from car accident in 1984; one surgery to repair ruptured disk; aggravated by second car accident in 1985 and second surgery
Nadine Green	Late forties; three years of lower back pain following rupture of two disks and subsequent surgery following work-related accident
Nancy Underwood	Mid-forties; pain from chronic urinary and vaginal infections, medical procedures to dilate urethra; pain in coccyx; marital stress
Natasha Ellison	Late twenties; migraines since 1969; medication dependency
Navidad Montoya	Late thirties; pain "in T-8 on the left side" following work-related accident as laboratory technician in 1984
Nelia England	Late thirties; registered nurse; back and leg pain and numbness for 9 months from herniated disk; fall downstairs in 1984 probably involved
Nell Esposito	Late thirties; migraines and vertigo following an inner ear infection four months previously; marital stress
Netty Auclair	Late forties; special education teacher; pain since 1982 following work-related injury that ruptured two disks; several hospitalizations; medication dependency
Noel Edwards	Mid-thirties; five years of migraines and temporo mandibular joint disorder
Nora Heath	Late fifties; clerk in department store; migraines since 1971; medication dependency; marital stress
Norma Frazer	Mid-thirties; college instructor; fourteen months of neck spasms relieved for a while by traction, but became acute one month prior to admission; insomnia; overmedicated; marital stress
Olivia Valente	Late twenties; migraines and dizziness since 1980
Ondine Edelstein	Mid-thirties; migraines
Pauline Glover	Mid-thirties; emergency-room aide; neck, back, hip, and leg pain since 1983 following car accident
Rachel Murphy	Mid-thirties; studying to become a nuclear therapy technician; cycles of pain, burning, swelling, and weakness in the arms and hands, no clear diagnosis ("some kind of myopathy"); medication dependency; marital stress
Rebecca Stewart	Late forties; assistant manager in a bank; pain and numbness in left side of neck and arm and hand originating in a car accident in 1984; unsuccessful surgery to remove ruptured disk; post-operative infection, other medical problems
Roberta Singer	Mid-thirties; executive in an athletic-shoe company; Olympic skiier; back pain since 1974; head, side, and right leg pain since 1985; Epstein-Barr syndrome; medication dependency
Rosemary McFarland	Twenty-three; store clerk; migraines since age five; insomnia; recreational drug user since age thirteen
Ruth O'Malley	Late forties; multiple pain problems throughout body,

	worsening during previous two years; insomnia; going through a divorce
Sandra Glynn	Late thirties; one year of lower back pain from spondylosis, scar tissue, decompression of sciatic nerve; surgery six months previously in 1986 did not help
Sarah Larson	Early fifties; neuropathy in feet, some lower back pain; had been a CPC patient the previous year; many medications for various other medical conditions
Selma Johnson	Late thirties (not interviewed)
Sharon Pansini	Mid-thirties; temporo mandibular joint disorder; marital problems
Susan Conroy	Mid-forties; intermittent history of lower back pain and sciatica since 1966; developed severe bladder interstitial cystitis, lost her job
Sylvia Goldin	Early fifties; university administrator; lower back pain from disk problems, not relieved by surgery; some congenital abnormalities in spine; complications from medication
Terry Kaplan	Late thirties; skiing instructor; back pain began with car accident in 1982 producing spinal leak; recovered after three surgeries; injuries sustained in second car accident led to unsuccessful bone fusion in back; further surgery installed Knott-rod fusion, complicated by fall on ice; medication dependency
Teresa Gilman	Mid-thirties; artist; lower back pain initiating in motorcycle accident in 1972 producing herniated disk; several hospitalizations, pain increased with complicated pregnancy and birth; unsuccessful spinal laminectomy for bone spurs, arthritis
Thelma Jasonides	Mid-seventies; housewife; neck, and head pain; several medical conditions; marital stress
Trudy Fermin	Early forties (not interviewed)
Ursula Niewolski	Mid-thirties; registered nurse; hip dislocation at age twelve; pain "on and off" since then; on crutches; at CPC for second time; medication dependency; depressed
Valerie Belanger	Late forties; middle-management; pain since 1973; ruptured disk; complications (pneumonia) following laminectomy; acute episode 6 months previously; ulcer for one year; chronic pain from other injuries; family stress
Wendy Cantor	Late thirties; lower back pain since childhood; several extensive surgeries and two years of brace and bed rest
Yvonne Friedman	Late thirties; psychotherapist; cluster headaches since childhood; medication dependency
Zelda Greenberg	Mid-thirties; lower back and leg pain since 1984 from herniated disk beginning with a fall; insomnia

PATIENTS — MEN

Barry Lyons	Late thirties; partial quadriplegic due to diving accident in swimming pool in 1984; low back pain since 1985
Ben Case	Mid-forties (not interviewed)
Christopher Fields	Early forties; pain in jaw and cheeks, twitching in legs, ringing in ear (from having it cleaned); dizziness
Chuck Caulfield	Early forties; furniture mover; lower back and leg pain resulting from job injury in 1984
Davie Black	Mid-forties; manual laborer; migraines and back, leg, neck, arm pain, related to broken back, brain injury, and surgeries resulting from explosion at work
Dick Macdonald	Early twenties; migraines, nausea, and dizziness since 1983
Edgar Leger	Mid-forties; emergency room manager, fast-food franchise manager; lower back pain since 1970 following combat injury in Vietnam war and iatrogenic complications; medication dependency
Edward Vaillant	Mid-forties; ruptured disk in 1981 from work-related injury; surgery unsuccessful; back pain increased following being blown through a door in a building that caught fire and blew up; medication and alcohol dependency
Eric Fisher	Mid-thirties; complications from two years of blocked infected pancreatic duct; several long-term hospitalizations
Ethan Hill	Thirty-nine; salesman; lower back pain beginning at age twenty, becoming severe in 1977; slight bulge in 2 disks, no satisfactory diagnosis; medication dependency at one time
Evan Hathaway	Early forties; seven months of muscle pain in lower back and legs
Felix Campbell	Seventy-three; thirty-five years of pain due to three cervical herniated discs; scar tissue and adhesions following two laminectomies; arthritis; medication dependency
Floyd Knopf	Mid-thirties; computer programmer and software manager; abdominal pain for eleven years and lower back pain following an injury in 1981
Frank Emile	Mid-fifties; gastro-intestinal pain following femoral bypass surgery in 1985; arteriosclerosis; rectal fistula; prostatitis; complications from graft; ultimate diagnosis of severed nerve following exploratory surgery (to search for cause of pain), causing pain in rectal area
Franklin Austin	Mid-twenties; student; lower back and leg pain from sports injury in 1984; ruptured disk, two others bulging; unsuccessful surgery three months previously; colitis
Fred Hardy	Late twenties; migraines since 1983; medication and alcohol dependency
Gabriel Blanchard	Late forties; back and leg pain from ruptured disk

	beginning in 1979; four spinal surgeries; infection following one surgery; arachnoiditis
George Beckwith	Fifty-five; junior technician in hospital operating room; arm and hand pain since 1981 from being hit by a door on the job; unrelieved by nerve blocks; chronic nausea
Harry Walter	Late forties; lumber and paper mill worker; four years of arm and elbow pain from job-related accident not relieved by surgery; lower back pain from herniated disk not relieved by surgery; insomnia
Harvey Blake	Late twenties; manual laborer; pain since 1982 from costo-chondritis—Tietze's syndrome, a rare condition involving chest cartilege hardening; pain worsened following being hit on the chest and being thrown through a wall by an angry body builder
Henry Bolton	Mid-thirties; manual laborer; muscle pain in chest, lower back pain
Herbert Lupone	Mid-seventies; pain since 1983 from post-herpetic neuralgia, peripheral neuropathy, and several other medical problems; insomnia
Homer Grigoriadis	Late thirties; food service worker; penetrating ulcer since 1974; infection and pneumonia following surgery; further surgery to remove scar tissue; bile duct bypass in 1986; medication dependency
Ian Edwards	Mid-fifties; executive; lower back pain for forty years, greatly increasing following surgery for aneurism in right leg seven months previously; diagnosis of pinched nerve; three further surgeries
Ira Gross	Late thirties; abdominal pain and nausea, improved following reconstructive surgery in 1986; gastectomy in 1975; medication dependency
Karl Hill	Mid-thirties, three years of lower back pain from congenital fusion and work-related accident
Keith Williams	Twenty-seven; warehouse supervisor; lower back and leg pain from work-related injury in 1984 rupturing three disks; pain somewhat relieved by two surgeries
Kenny Fonseca	Mid-sixties; carpenter; pain since 1975 on left side, especially arm and shoulder, following a stroke
Kent Elliot	Late thirties; clinical psychologist; pain for 1 1/2 years; 2 surgeries for herniated disk; thoracic outlet syndrome; bone spurs, cynosis in neck
Kurt Hawkins	Mid-forties; manual laborer; neck, arm, and back pain from work-related injury that broke neck and damaged disk in 1981; neck and back surgery unsuccessful, collapsed lung during back surgery; developed bone spur in foot from walking incorrectly to favor neck
Mark Irving	Early forties; archaeologist; lower back pain since 1984; scar tissue from laminectomy and fusion
Marvin Magliano	Late twenties; several years lower back pain from herniated disk; four surgeries
Ned Wilson	Late forties; bus driver; headache and temporo-

	mandibular joint disorder since age seventeen which worsened in recent years; medication dependency; marital stress
Noah Kahn	Late forties; nine months of lower back pain from herniated disk; spinal fusion did not relieve pain; insomnia
Norman Bonilla	Mid-thirties; pain in upper back following compression fracture of two vertebrae resulting from work-related injury that healed incorrectly; recovering alcoholic
Ralph Wilson	Mid-forties; food service worker; bladder pain for several years
Randall Keller	Sixty-six; pain and numbness in penis and anus; medication dependency at one time
Roy Deleo	Late sixties; retired machinist; leg pain following work-related accident in 1979; two surgeries to remove scar tissue
Samuel Troy	Late fifties; arthritis in neck, back, knees, hands, ankles, and feet; medication dependency
Scott Theriault	Mid-thirties; paraplegic from diving accident; lower back, buttock, and leg pain; recovering alcoholic
Simon Walsh	Late seventies (not interviewed)
Steven Laronde	Mid-thirties; manual laborer; back and leg pain from ruptured disk and scar tissue; spinal stenosis beginning with injury in work-related accident in 1982; damaged bladder due to medications; medication dependency
Terence Richard	Mid-forties; M.D.; neuritic pain since 1984 in thighs and knees, not relieved by surgery; insomnia
Tim Rowe	Late thirties; pain in knees; several sports injuries; 19 or 20 surgeries, beginning in 1966; pain became severe in 1983; back pain; medication dependency; previous CPC patient
Toby Reynolds	Early forties; university professor; shoulder, neck, and upper back pain following surgery to repair a sports injury in 1984; iatrogenic ulcer and rectal fistula, both surgically repaired
Tom Hicks	Mid-fifties; architect; arm and shoulder pain following bad fall in 1983 that broke arm; developed thoracic outlet syndrome; scar tissue from two surgeries for rib resection
Umberto Santini	Late forties; meatpacker; lower back and leg pain from work-related accident in 1982; three spinal surgeries, scar tissue and nerve damage; spinal fusion

STAFF

Beverly Corey	Patient rehabilitation associate
Donna Grady	Patient rehabilitation associate
Evelyn Walton	Physical therapist supervisor
Fredericka Thompson	Physical therapist
Georgia Burns	Patient rehabilitation associate

Jennifer Bell	Secretary in head office
Kenneth Sutherland	Physical therapist
Kevin Jefferson, Ph.D.	Head psychologist for first half of study
Laurel Copeland	Social worker
Linda Warren	Registered nurse
Martha Dowling	Registered nurse (left during period of research)
Matthew Hyman	Psychologist
Naomi Fields	Patient coordinator (registered nurse)
Nina Cummings	Registered nurse
Neil Meyer, Ph.D.	Head psychologist for last three months of study
Nicole Monteaux	Intern specializing in movement therapy
Nathan Levy	Patient rehabilitation associate
Pam Howard	Social worker (left during period of research)
Polly Emery	Patient rehabilitation associate
Raquel Cannon	Psychologist conducting weekly psychomotor sessions
Rhonda Murray	Clinical assistant to Dr. B (registered nurse)
Robert Katz	Social worker (left during period of research)
Sonia Mueller	Registered nurse
Tracy Jones	Physical therapist
Thomas Michaels	Psychologist (left during period of research)
Vera Stouffer	Physical therapist
Veronica White	Registered nurse

DIRECTOR AND CONSULTANTS

Ethan Bernstein, M.D.	Director (Psychiatry, Neurology)
Robert Andrews, M.D.	Consulting Neurologist
Henry Stevens, M.D.	Consulting Psychiatrist
William Oliveira, M.D.	Consulting Internist

Appendix 2: Interview Questions

1. Why did you decide to work with chronic pain patients?
2. What do you particularly like about working with this population?
3. How does working here differ from other places you have worked or might work?
4. What is your definition of pain? Of chronic pain?
5. How do patients on the unit differ from the people out on the street with chronic pain?
6. What are some of the most frustrating features of your work?
7. What is your model of chronic pain syndrome?
8. Please comment about the degree of heterogeneity in the staff regarding their views about maintaining health, disease, and treatment.
9. What are the most typical types of patients admitted here?
10. What don't you like about working with this population?
11. Are patients well enough informed about the program when they are admitted?
12. Why are people so resistant to psychogenic explanations of pain?
13. What is your opinion about the amount of confrontation on the unit?
14. How does chronic pain differ from other types of chronic diseases?
15. In your opinion, how many patients leave significantly improved?
16. How many patients leave with their pain significantly reduced?
17. What parts of the program could be improved?

PATIENT INTAKE

1. Why did you come to CPC? Why did you choose CPC in particular? What did you know about the program? What were your expectations of the program? Have there been any surprises?
2. Describe your pain problem. What caused it? What have been the consequences? What have you tried to do to get rid of the pain?

3. What do you think is the cause of your pain?
4. What is the most frustrating thing about your pain?
5. What do you hope to get out of your stay here?
6. What do you think about the multidisciplinary feature of CPC?
7. What are your reactions to CPC so far?
8. What do you think of the therapeutic community aspect of the program? What do you think of the other patients? How do you feel about being on a unit with 20 other people in chronic pain?
9. What do you think of the staff so far?
10. What's working for you so far?
11. Have you had a group therapy session yet? What do you think of it?
12. Why do some patients improve and others don't?
13. Any questions you have for me?

PATIENT DISCHARGE
1. How is your pain now?
2. Which of your original goals were met and which ones weren't?
3. Were there any surprises during your stay? Any ups and downs?
4. What was your experience being in a residential community of about 20 people, all of whom have chronic pain?
5. Has your model of pain, of your pain, changed?
6. How many people in your group have been significantly helped by the program? How many people have had a significant reduction in pain, do you think?
7. Has your body image changed? Your self image?
8. Any ways the program could be improved?
9. Why is there such a range of outcomes in this program?
10. Anything I should have asked about but didn't?
11. Any questions of me?

Notes

Chapter 1. A Baffling Phenomenon

1. The varied perspectives in this discourse are one reason the experimental work on pain sometimes contributes very little directly to our understanding of the lived reality of severe chronic pain. Melzack, for example, points out that, while highly formal psychophysical laws that describe the relationship between sensation and stimulus energy can be discovered when rats or students are involved in pain experiments in artificial laboratory chambers, in the normal world perception and behavior differ significantly, with a multitude of contributing factors (1996: 130). However, the development of the gate-control theory of pain developed by two experimental researchers, Melzack and Wall (1965, 1973, 1983; Melzack 1996) revolutionized thinking about pain. Baszanger describes the theory and its impact on explanatory models of pain prevalent at the time (1998: 54–57). Recent thinking sees sensory, motivational, and cognitive processes occurring in parallel *interacting* systems at the same time (Baszanger 1998: 54, discussing Melzack and Wall 1973).

2. Hilbert quotes a pain sufferer who remarked that a positive diagnosis of "even cancer" would be positive in the sense of good news, because it would provide a special form of relief (1984: 368).

3. Baszanger (1998: 93). Federico (1996: 252) gives a maximum of 60 million; also see Bonica, ed. 1990.

4. "Study Says 1 in 5 Americans Suffers from Chronic Pain," *New York Times*, Friday, October 21, 1994. The Nuprin Report found some 32 percent of the adult U.S. population suffering from back pain alone (as cited in Sternbach 1986). According to Deyo et al. (1991), chronic low back pain afflicts more than 4 million Americans; of these nearly 50 percent are disabled (1991, as cited in Kidd and North 1996: 174).

5. Frymoyer and Cats-Baril (1991). Also see Osterweis et al. (1987).

6. International Association for the Study of Pain (1979). Other discussions of the definition of pain include Merskey (1986), Diller (1980), and Melzack and Torgerson (1971). Diagnostic uses are described by Gaston-Johansson and Allwood (1988). D. Morris discusses the definition of pain (1991: 16) and the plethora of terms for types of pain (70). Finally, Priel et al. (1991) look at an expanded notion of the meaning of pain with respect to physician-patient interaction.

7. As quoted in Porter (1994: 104); he provides no reference for the quotation.

8. Merskey and Bogduk (1994: xi).

9. Note that, as Bonica pointed out in 1953, persistent pain does produce serious psychophysiological reactions that "may precipitate or aid in perpetuating a biologically harmful or eventually even destructive process" (quote from Baszanger 1998: 28).

10. See Black (1979) and Merskey and Bogduk (1994: xi–xii). Melzack and Wall (1983), and Brand and Yancey (1993) describe the biological usefulness of pain, and Baszanger (1998: 32) provides a nice summary of earlier thinking about whether pain is a physiological or pathological sensation. Because of this "beneficial" role, pain, especially chronic pain, can confound our notions of disease and health. Criteria for distinguishing between pain as an ally and pain as an enemy are sometimes obscure. On one hand, everyone would probably agree that pain is a negative feeling: in the West we believe that only masochists want to feel pain. On the other hand, pain is a normal response to an abnormal situation. This good/bad contradiction can be difficult to maintain—as mothers who must talk their children into going to the dentist will affirm. Because pain is experientially negative, intellectual effort is required to think of it as good. Actually *experiencing* a pain as good, or welcome (as in "no pain, no gain" aerobics) is probably even more difficult but possible. People welcome pain when they know it will bring a gain greater than the cost of the pain—consciously, as in religious ordeals or heightened sexual arousal, or unconsciously, as occurs when pain symptoms are produced or amplified because of the interpersonal or environmental advantage they provide. Sacks offers an interesting discussion of cases in which a disease state results in a feeling of well-being (1985: 89). Damasio (1994) presents examples of patients with pain from tissue injury that lacks affective symptoms; these cases are highly unusual and involve people with rare tumors, or rare surgery, or who have recovered from rare types of strokes.

11. This is not to say this issue is unproblematic within the pain treatment community; as with nearly everything in pain research and treatment, debate continues over the acute versus chronic distinction. Loeser (1991; 1996: 103, 106), for example, understands the difference to be a radical one, providing abundant evidence of the harm done to patients whose physicians continue to apply a "broken part" diagnosis, that is, to see a case of chronic pain in terms of the acute model. A near-opposite position is taken by Staats (1996: 118, 119), who, stating that "pain is pain" and that nonmalignant pain is treated with a bias against biomedical therapies, argues for a greater convergence between treatment of cancer pain and nonmalignant types of pain (very few multidisciplinary pain centers accept cancer pain patients). Another dispute concerns whether chronic pain is to be defined with reference to adaptive or maladaptive behavior. In this scheme, people who suffer pain but adequately adapt to it are to be seen as fundamentally different from "chronic pain patients" or people with "chronic pain syndrome" who do not adapt successfully. This scheme does not rely on kinds or qualities of pain itself nor on the notion of duration as a defining characteristic (see Baszanger 1998: 90).

12. Merskey (1976: 712), Knoll (1975: 367).

13. Recent research indicates that anesthetics based primarily on hypnotic drugs and analgesic-based anesthetics have different effects on hormonal responses to surgical stress. It is likely that some patients *do* experience pain under anesthesia. A particularly interesting example of a gray area is "twilight sleep," an analgesic used during 1914 and 1915 for childbirth. A mixture of scopolamine and morphine, it induced a state where the body—with gestures, screams, and verbal cries—appeared to be registering extreme acute pain, but the patient did

not remember the experience. This presents an enigma: did these patients experience pain but have no memory of it? If so, as Morris (1991: 160) asks, is pain we cannot remember still pain? Or were their minds only semiconscious, in a state that allows us to conclude that they were not "experiencing" the pain, and therefore that what occurred was not pain? (Miller 1979; Leavitt 1980: 149). Whether pain-inducing stimuli occurring under anesthesia may be recorded at some deeper level of consciousness is currently being debated in the fields of neurology and the psychology of perception.

14. Baszanger (1998: 48) provides a useful discussion of specificity theory and how Melzack and Wall's gate control theory (1973, 1983) replaced it.

15. This type of pain is technically known as deafferentiation pain. See Loeser (1991: 215–16).

16. Melzack (1989, 1996).

17. Sullivan (1995: 11). Also see Melzack and Wall's discussion of this problem (1973: 206).

18. See Loeser (1996: 104) on the dangers of overreliance on physical indicators obtained from imaging technologies such as X-ray and CT and MR scans when treating pain.

19. Loeser (1996: 102).

20. Long comments:

Physicians in training generally do not understand these patients, have little patience with them, and manage them poorly. Such pejorative phrases as *pain patient* and *pain turkey* are often heard in their conversations. As a rule, they show little compassion for these patients and poor understanding of the complexities of the problems, particularly drug-seeking behavior. Patients complain about them and they complain about the patients. (1996: 17–18)

He maintains that "this peculiar prejudice" of non-pain specialists against pain patients and their therapists is unique to the problem of pain (1996: 19). Keefe et al. (1996: 96) similarly note that physicians will use terms like "crocks" or "losers" for patients who are considered to exhibit excessive pain behavior during observation. "Pain behavior" can be loosely defined as any behavior the person exhibiting the behavior or someone observing it sees as a response to pain. However, the tighter definition supplied by some behavioralist researchers is behavior that has developed over time to decrease or avoid pain which subsequently does not require the presence of pain to appear because it has been consolidated by a reinforcer (e.g., rest, attention, taking drugs). See Baszanger (1998: 74–79) on pain as learned behavior.

21. In-depth studies by social scientists of pain centers include Baszanger (1998; see also 1986, 1989, 1990, 1992), Cademenos (1981), J. Clark (1984), and Corbett (1986). Other social science authors writing about chronic pain include Bates (1996), Croissant (1996), Csordas and Clark (1992), Fagerhaugh and Strauss (1977), and Kotarba (1981).

22. Taricco (1996: 110). Also see Kotarba (1981) and Aronoff and Evans (1982: 4) on the increase of funding. Taricco states that pain clinics would not exist without modern-day health insurance, particularly the liability component (1996: 10). Inpatient facilities, in particular, sprang up partly because third-party carriers were at first reluctant to pay for outpatient care. Pain centers claim that their programs are, in the long run, less costly than many of the alternatives open to chronic pain sufferers.

23. Taricco (1996: 112).

24. Present-day medically oriented centers are often affiliated with hospital anesthesiology departments; among their most frequently used interventions are trigger point injections, peripheral nerve blocks or epidural steroid injections, drugs (analgesics, antidepressants), and surgery (see Osterweis et al. 1987: 240). On the history of pain centers, see Lipton and Wells (1983) and Baszanger (1998).

25. Four basic models are used to explain chronic pain; the following description has been modified from Bates (1996). The *biological* model, while it may mention psychological and sociocultural factors, is primarily concerned with ascertaining the nature of tissue damage and reducing pain by mechanical or chemical means. The *psychodynamic* model views chronic pain as an expression of personal and interpersonal problems, among them depression, unmet dependency needs (sometimes resulting from childhood abuse or neglect), and particular personality features such as introversion (Egan and Katon 1987; Knoll 1975; Menges 1981; Merskey 1987; Swanson 1984). The *cognitive* model is based on the fact that pain is a psychological phenomenon, and focuses on the contributing factors to the subjective experience of pain. Treatment attempts to reduce the perception of pain or distract the sufferer by redefining the experience (e.g., with imaging techniques) or providing a greater sense of control (e.g., with biofeedback). Finally, the *behavioral* model sees chronic pain sufferers as people who have been so rewarded for pain behavior that it has become a conditioned response: "[R]egardless of its source, pain eventually develops a life of its own by interacting with environmental factors that reinforce pain behavior" (Osterweis et al. 1987: 238). Treatment is targeted at reducing or eliminating pain behavior (e.g., groaning) and increasing "well behavior" (e.g., getting out of bed). Fordyce complains that, prior to the behavioral model, psychological factors contributing to pain were seen as imaginary symptoms or motivated by hysterical, hypochondriacal, or malingering tendencies—mind-based problems which, he maintains, are not implied by the behavioral model (1996: 39). Other discussions of the behavioral model include Fordyce (1976), Sternbach (1984), and Turner and Clancy (1988). Note that these are *models* of pain; treatment approaches in behavioral pain centers employ cognitive-behavioral techniques. Turk et al. (1983) and Keefe (1982) present comprehensive discussions of the behavioral approach at the time of my research; both articles describe a variety of pain centers. Keefe and Lefebvre (1994) discuss centers currently employing a combination of cognitive and behavioral therapy.

All four models have implications for assigning responsibility for chronic pain (and for responding to criticisms of "blaming the victim"). The biological model is least concerned with responsibility, largely because the cause of the pain is usually seen in proximate, seldom in ultimate, terms. Within the psychodynamic approach, responsibility can seem vague, or shifts because the responsible agent is often ultimately an external force—an abusive parent or spouse, for example. This type of explanation often makes pain sufferers defensive ("all I know is that I didn't want to have this pain") because they understand that the more precise the assessment of the ultimate cause, the more likely the more proximate causes involve mental processes. Cognitive approaches maintain that many factors influence pain, not all of which are directly controlled by the individual. Pain sufferers, however, are likely to respond defensively when they understand an implication of this model: logically, if mental processes can relieve pain, mental processes may have produced pain.

Of the four models, the behavioralists come in for the most criticism, because their message is that pain is in part the result of learned associations between the experience and the benefits (attention, financial benefits, etc.) the pain sufferer receives when he or she expresses the pain. These benefits are known as "secondary gain"—the interpersonal or environmental advantage supplied by a symptom(s). (Primary gain diverts the patient's attention from a more disturbing problem [Hahn 1995: 26], and tertiary gain involves someone other than the patient seeking or achieving gains from the patient's illness [Bokan et al. 1981: 331].) Critics note that this model shows little concern with pain itself and instead serves the needs of others—the physician, the family, the economy—by concentrating on eliminating deviant behavior (Bates 1996: 30; also see Kleinman 1992: 169–70; Edwards 1984). Discussing the history of chronic pain treatment in the latter half of the twentieth century, Baszanger (1998) describes two models: the traditional approach to treating chronic pain, which reads pain in the body, and a new approach, which "reads and listens to pain through the patient's experience" (7). The treatment goal of the first approach is to cure pain; the the second approach focuses on managing pain by getting the patient to modify her experience of pain (6). She points out that theoretically and in practice there is no unified concept of chronic pain, which is unattainable at this point in time. Pain journals publish articles with completely opposing points of view side by side. She notes that Bonica attempted a compromise between the points of view in the revised (1990) edition of his 1953 "bible" of pain treatment (8, 94).

26. Mattingly's (1998) discussion of how occupational therapists create stories to help bring about therapeutic goals (which she calls "therapeutic emplotment") is one attempt to answer such *how* questions.

27. The creation of a new medical specialty required a new name: "dolorology," subsequently replaced by "algology," both terms referring to the study and treatment of pain. But the latter term has not taken hold either; Lippe (1996: 309) provides a rare example of current use.

28. And partly because of the ambiguous nature of chronic pain: "some pain persists for a long time after the cause has been identified and appropriate treatment has been applied. In other cases, the etiology remains obscure or even unknown; in still others, it accompanies the evolution of a disease that has been duly identified but for which there is currently no treatment" (Baszanger 1998: 4).

29. I have written on this issue of the "real" in Jackson (1992, 1994a), and on how a single patient's view on what is "really" wrong can shift in Jackson (1994b). Baszanger (1998: 277) provides an example of this discourse of the "real."

30. Kleinman, Eisenberg, and Good (1978: 251).

31. Kleinman (1995: 32).

32. Exceptions are Brody (1987), Kleinman (1988), Fagerhaugh and Strauss (1977), and Frank (1974).

33. Scarry (1985).

34. Parsons (1958); Mechanic (1972).

35. The "meaning-centered approach" has a broader focus than the traditional interest in semantics, although semantics, together with phenomenology (Schutz 1970), and hermeneutics play major roles in its formulation. Ricoeur's notion (1971) of the work of daily life as a text to be read is a provocative way to look at people's experiences and the sense they make of them. B. Good (1994) and Mattingly (1998) provide examples of this approach in clinical settings.

36. Cademenos (1981); Bakan (1968), and Vrancken (1989).

37. See, e.g., D. Morris (1991: 244), Honkasalo (1998), and Kleinman (1988).

38. See, e.g., Berliner and Salmon (1979), Moyers (1993), and Goleman and Gurin 1993.

39. See Gramsci (1971), Williams (1977); also Ortner (1989–90) and Willis (1977). For a review of the concept as used in medical anthropology, see Csordas (1988) and other articles in the special issue on critical medical anthropology in Frankenberg (1988a).

40. All names have been changed. Although the speaker is identified for some of the quotes, only a few patients are discussed enough at length to qualify as case studies. Brief sketches of patients are found in Appendix 1; these are very truncated, and their main purpose is to provide an overview of the kinds of problems patients had.

41. The reader will also notice that staff generalizations about chronic pain patients are not completely consistent.

42. See M. Clark (1996: 65–67), Cohen (1996b: 131–35), and Kerns (1996: 184–87) for discussions on attempts to model the complex nature of chronic pain.

43. Escobar (1995: 110). Although he is concerned with deconstructing the "expert discourses" of development experts, much of what he says is applicable to the pain literature.

44. Shorter's discussion of what is "really wrong" with pain sufferers illustrates a variant of Foucault's notion of the medical gaze (1992: 285–99; cf. Foucault 1973).

45. See Young's review (1982); also see Taussig (1980), Frankenberg (1988a), Scheper-Hughes and Lock (1987), Lock and Scheper-Hughes (1990), Singer (1990), and B. Good (1994: 56–62).

46. See Cohen (1996a: 78; also 1996b: 134) on how constructs that make complex phenomena more manageable create blind spots. Keefe et al. (1996: 92) critique overly simplistic concepts of pain behavior.

47. B. Good 1994: xv.

48. Goffman (1963).

49. This literature pays special attention to the fieldworker as a mediator between the society being studied and its representation in published texts. These issues are discussed in Lewin and Leap (1996), Jackson (1986), Kondo (1986), Marcus and Fischer (1986), and Abu-Lughod (1993: 29–42). Kotarba (1977) has written reflexively about his chronic pain condition in the context of his research on chronic pain.

50. Abu-Lughod (1986), Kondo (1986), and the entire issue of Cerroni-Long (1995). Behar (1993) discusses similar issues. Other insightful discussions of "insider/outsider" include Narayan (1993), Ohnuki-Tierney (1984), and Kim (1990). The latter three writers are mainly concerned with being non-Westerners studying communities in their native countries; however, they share with Kondo, Abu-Lughod, and me the ambiguity of having two identities while doing fieldwork and dealing with the consequences of employing hegemonic scholarly discourses they were trained in but are also questioning.

51. See B. Turner (1992); Featherstone et al. (1991); Martin (1987), Jacobus et al. (1990); Kirmayer (1992).

52. Baszanger (1998), Bates (1996), M.-J. Good et al. (1992), Kleinman et al. (1997), D. Morris (1991), and Sheridan (1992). Many articles and books written by pain clinicians begin by mentioning literary or historical references to pain.

53. For reasons of consistency, I have altered the terminology in the quotations in this book to reflect current rather than mid-1980s usage (for example, "workmen's compensation" is now "workers' compensation"). A term used in 1985–86, temporomandibular joint pain, is now temporo mandibular joint disorder or temporo mandibular pain dysfunction syndrome. See Dworkin and LeResche (1992) and Mersky (1986).

54. For examples of this kind of approach, see Mishler (1984), West (1984), and Fisher and Todd (1983).

55. D. Morris (1991: 71) states that "Americans today probably belong to the first generation on earth that looks at a pain-free life as something like a constitutional right. Pain is a scandal." Melzack (1974: 277) agrees that Western culture considers a goal of ultimate panacea of complete pain relief for everyone to be reasonable. We often encounter statements that the problem of pain has been solved (Baszanger 1998: 29). Also see Knoll (1975).

56. See Streltzer and Wade (1981), Rosenthal (1994), and Hershkopf (1994). Baszanger (1998: 330), citing a study by Besson (1992), states that fears about drug dependency are unfounded: of 10,000 patients treated with morphine, none became drug dependent.

57. On the preference for both patients and physicians for invasive treatments, see Carron et al. (1985).

58. See Kotarba and Seidel (1984: 1396).

59. Debates over appropriate surgery continue. Loeser (1996: 104), one of the more outspoken critics, notes that the rate of surgery for low back pain in a specific country is directly related to the number of orthopedic and neurological surgeons practicing there.

Chapter 2. Summer Camp? Boot Camp? An Introduction to CPC

1. All names are pseudonyms.

2. D. Clark describes some therapeutic communities as "grubby" (1977: 559).

3. Compare these reactions to CPC with Clark's description of a hypothetical visitor to a therapeutic community: "It will stir him up and within one day he will find himself exhilarated, infuriated, puzzled, challenged and perplexed" (1977: 559).

4. Psychomotor is group therapy in which a patient, with the leader's help, sets up a drama and plays a role, with fellow patients playing other parts.

5. Flor et al. found a mean duration of seven years (1992 as cited in Turk 1996: 268).

6. Most CPC staff members felt the program should be at least five or six weeks. Kenneth, a physical therapist, spoke of the speed-up from six weeks to four: "Part of [the program involves] authority and pushing people, which is necessary in many ways, especially given the little time we have. So the fact that it's four weeks is a real assault and battery on a patient. One week, the first week, they are just getting used to being up 10 or 12 hours a day, and people coming in and prodding and poking, and they have to be in groups on time. And no one has real time to get used to it, and suddenly it's four weeks and they are out."

7. Behavioral approaches, promoting the goal of helping patients take more responsibility for their own lives and health care, were first introduced in pain centers in the late 1960s and 1970s. The first ones encountered resistance from the medical establishment. Physicians were reluctant to refer patients to these

centers in part because their programs were represented as superior to conventional medical approaches to treating pain. Some also had doubts concerning the advisability and effectiveness of some of the approaches used. For example, Bonica and Butler (1978: 62) complain of an "internationally known orthopaedic surgeon (who knew nothing about our facility) referred to [our facility] as 'treatment by committee.'" Staff members in these centers also criticized the use of operant conditioning techniques. ("Operant" basically means "learned," and "operant pain" refers to pain that exists because a patient has learned a "pain habit": see Fordyce 1977: 279. Operant conditioning, then, involves teaching patients to "unlearn" their pain habits.) Bonica and Fordyce (1974: 311) discuss staff dissatisfaction.

8. D. Clark (1977: 559).

9. Kennard and Clemmey (1976: 35). A great deal of discussion in the literature concerns how to define "therapeutic community" (see Bloor et al. 1988). The phrase "milieu therapy" is a much looser concept; such a setting will be a small face-to-face residential community using some therapeutic community approaches: a "ward or hospital treatment setting that provides an effective environment for behavioral changes through re-socialization and rehabilitation" (Wilson and Aronoff 1978: 479). However, as such wards lack the "permissive, egalitarian, democratic, and communalistic" characteristics of the early examples of therapeutic communities, according to D. Clark, they are not examples of a "therapeutic community proper" (1977: 554). The therapeutic community *movement* is finished (see Manning 1976b: 278; Clark 1977: 562). Although I never heard the phrase "reality confrontation" used at CPC, the concept describes its philosophy and practice.

10. Bloor and McKeganey (1986: 68).

11. Although CPC downplayed the medical model, some patients nevertheless needed diagnostic work and basic medical treatment. Although policies were fairly clear cut, patients struggling to have their pain recognized as resulting from organic causes were envious of the medical attention others were receiving and concluded that the lack of attention to diagnosis and orthodox hospital procedures in their particular case indicated that the staff thought *their* pain was "all in their head."

12. Obviously, the training and specialties of the treatment team significantly influence which patients are admitted to a pain center program. Several authors point out that perhaps "multidisciplinary pain center" is a misnomer, given that directors' philosophies determine the treatment options available in them. Belzberg (1996: 74) questions whether even one truly multidisciplinary pain center exists, as those he is familiar with lack a truly broad approach that would include different fundamental perspectives on pain problems.

13. These disagreements among CPC staff are mirrored in the literature. Turk (1996: 258) cites surveys that find chronic pain patients more likely to suffer greater levels of emotional distress, have work-related injuries, report greater health care use, report more constant pain, indicate more negative attitudes about the future, take opioid medications, have had surgery, report greater functional impairment. However, neither duration of pain, nor pain location, nor demographic factors differentiate patients in pain centers from community samples of chronic pain patients: "Rather, the most significant discriminators are previous treatments, impairment in functioning, and psychosocial difficulties." Long, discussing patients at the Johns Hopkins pain center, reports profiles that differ substantially from most of those reported in the literature. If

comorbid anxiety, depression, and "personality vulnerabilities" (lifelong traits that are not clearcut personality disorders but probably complicate patients' reactions to their pain, treatments received, and so forth) are factored out, these patients look like "any patient with a chronic disease" (1996: 15–17).

14. A "pain-prone personality" is considered to be a person likely to somatize or overly focus on a pain experience. Some specialists feel that people with pain prone personalities are more likely to engage in behavior that results in pain (e.g., "accident-prone") than the average person.

15. Debates abound in the literature over criteria for selecting those patients most likely to profit from a pain center program. Some recommend rather stringent standards—those with a "still salvageable spine," for instance. However, other authors are more inclusive and think treatment should not be refused to, for instance, injured workers with pending litigation or disability claims, stating that some can return to acceptable levels of health behavior (i.e., functioning reasonably well in the various domains of one's life) and that an exclusionary policy means these individuals face an endless struggle to gain recognition of their "sickness" (Brena et al. 1979: 51; quotation marks in original). They further argue that this would allow collection of the data needed to call for improvements in current laws on disability payments, because at present the system rewards pain and illness behaviors.

16. See Chap. 1, n. 1.

17. Corbett (1986) provides an example of a "million dollar workup."

18. All team members collected and shared information on the patient during team conferences, which the staff members found extremely helpful. Patient opinion of this pooling of information is captured by the expression they sometimes used: "betrayal of confidence." Pooling of information by staff is characteristic of therapeutic communities.

19. See Alperson (1974).

20. In fact, acupuncture acts on the transmission of nerve impulses triggering pain in much the same way as transcutaneous electrical nerve stimulation (Baszanger 1998: 63).

21. In this respect CPC exemplified an approach to pain treatment (and other medical problems) that began in the 1950s characterized by a new "medical gaze" that took into consideration the patient's view, and that involved two subjects rather than an inquiring subject (physician) and an object that was acted upon (patient). See Baszanger (1998: 6).

22. Finer (1983: 196).

23. Several patients compared one nurse to "Nurse Ratched," a character in Ken Kesey's novel *One Flew Over the Cookoo's Nest* (1962), which, interestingly, was based on his experiences in California hospitals that paid lip service to Maxwell Jones's ideas about therapeutic communities (see D. Clark 1977: 558).

24. See Manning (1976a: 135–36) on high staff turnover in therapeutic communities in clinical settings. D. Clark discusses how the therapeutic community approach puts great strain on staff, and the negative effects of high patient and staff turnover (1977: 562). Cademenos (1981) also notes high staff turnover in the pain unit he studied.

25. See, e.g., Caudill et al. (1991), Loeser et al. (1990), and many of the contributors to Cohen and Campbell (1996).

Chapter 3. The Painful Journey

1. Note that today some of these patients' use of analgesics to keep functioning would not be considered "drug-seeking behavior" or indication of a medication dependency (Judith Spross, personal communication, November, 1997).

2. See M.-J. Good (1992) on "work as a haven from pain."

3. See Fagerhaugh and Strauss (1977: 241).

4. Morris (1991: 65–68) discusses the invisibility of chronic pain and the way we sometimes suspect people who say they are in pain but exhibit no pain behavior. Cademenos (1981) reports a patient saying he wished he could wear a badge that said "Chronic Pain."

5. Loeser (1991: 214; cf. also 215, 217, 223).

6. See, for example, Pilowsky (1978: 206).

7. For example, Campbell, a surgeon, states that Fordyce and other psychologists make a dangerous assumption when they accept referring clinicians' assertions that the patient has no structural lesion for the ongoing pain problem (1996: 31).

8. Sarno (1976: 150). Compare Frank's example of a young psychiatrist in psychoanalytical training who said: "Even if the patient doesn't get better, you know you're doing the right thing" (1961: 125).

9. Fordyce (1978: 52, 54). He has maintained this basic position (see, e.g., Fordyce 1996).

10. As quoted in Schaeffer (1983: 25).

11. For example, pain specialist Paul Latimer says the physician should want the patient to report less pain (quoted in Schaeffer 1983: 25; see also 1982). Examples of newer thinking about chronic pain that shows why "*either* organic *or* emotional" models need to be discarded, given the plasticity of the central nervous system, can be found in Melzack (1996), Liebeskind (1997), and Fields and Basbaum (1989).

12. See Sternbach (1978: 247) on the doctor having "the role of a double agent, ostensibly working for the patient, but really working for his [the doctor's] sources of income, since the doctor's reports go to every agency that pays his bills."

13. See Kotarba and Seidel (1984).

14. The volume edited by Cohen and Campbell (1996) provides many examples of such disagreements.

15. Wall, a pain specialist, notes that many physicians would just as soon wash their hands of patients who fall into the category of chronic pain syndrome (as cited in Benedetti 1974: 265).

16. See D. P. Gordon (1983).

17. Hilbert (1984).

18. See Stewart (1990) on the evolution of the concept of somatization.

19. See Young (1980) on stress, and Kleinman (1982: 121) on neurasthenia.

20. Davie's complaint reflects an important debate in the pain literature: whether certain psychological and environmental elements are cause or effects of chronic pain (cf. Baszanger 1998: 94).

21. Except for a few returning patients who had previously left against medical advice or were back for a "retread" because of new problems.

22. Cf. Bloor et al. (1988: 191, 142–45) on therapeutic communities' use of "disembodied surveillance" techniques of pooling information to form a collective staff view of residents and the recording of the results in their files.

23. A parallel to this is found in the practice of a pain clinic studied by Baszanger which would anesthetize a painful region of the body to show a patient that her painful sensations were abnormal, since, when pinched or pricked, she felt nothing (1998: 158).

24. Bloor et al. (1988: 59).

25. See Tipton (1982) on the human potential movement. Many of the psychotherapeutic approaches developed in the 1970s, especially encounter groups, also contained elements of "reality confrontation" similar to CPC's approach.

Chapter 4. "Getting with the Program"

1. For convenience, the various approaches are catalogued as educational; psychotherapeutic; tough love, confrontation, and psychological manipulation; and love and acceptance. These are somewhat arbitrary divisions; for example, some of the material discussed in the sections on education or tough love could be included in the section on psychotherapeutic approach.

2. Patients who experienced the surveillance component of CPC's approach had a particularly hard time: "All of a sudden you are hit by all these things that they dig up in your past, and I really don't see why they have to be watchdogs, and that's exactly how I feel they are. You are being constantly watched, constantly observed: what you say, how you say it, how you walk."

3. Compare Bloor et al.'s (1988: 97) discussion of Cooley's notion of "the looking glass self."

4. See Young's discussion of similar complaints made by veterans at a VA hospital: "You know how to open us up, but that's all" (1995: 190).

5. Sarno, director at another pain clinic, also describes his program as confrontational, and, interestingly, adds that patients are less resistant if a medical doctor rather than a psychiatrist does the confronting (1976: 149).

6. See Chap. 2, n. 7.

7. Note that such confrontational techniques characterized many human potential movement programs (including approaches used in intentional communities—communes) that were formed during the 1970s and 1980s. See Tipton (1982), esp. 176–231. Zablocki (1980), Felton (1972), and Yablonsky (1965) discuss some precursors.

8. See Bloor (1981) on how staff members in a therapeutic community capitalize on patients' complaints about inconsistencies by making them occasions for therapeutic work.

9. See Chap. 3, n. 24.

10. However, some patients had little or no difficulty with any part of CPC's approach to medications—not deceleration (any type of pain medication, including aspirin, was decelerated if staff members felt there were signs of psychological dependency), or fixed schedules, or even the near-universal prescribing of doxepin. Although many fought (or fantasized about fighting) that policy, some later agreed it had been good for them. Helen, the woman who had arranged to have three physicians unknown to one another prescribing pain medications from three different pharmacies, said at the end of her stay: "I think it's a fabulous program. Why doesn't [Dr. B] lecture to orthopedic surgeons and tell them pills are not the answer? Maybe he does, and the doctors don't attend to him, or they're just in it for the bucks."

11. The evening session on reflexology taught by Beverly was another example. Some of the men would jokingly sexualize the demonstration.

12. Georgia mentioned Kaufman (1976) and Matthews-Simonton et al. (1978).

13. See Cousins (1979).

14. See Siegel (1986).

15. See Angell (1985) for a clear-headed discussion of this issue.

16. See Goffman (1961).

17. Bloor et al. (1988: 97). These authors also use Berger and Luckmann's (1967) term "nihilation" to describe this self-fulfilling aspect of staff work.

Chapter 5. Building and Resisting Community

1. Main (1946), as cited in D. Clark (1977: 553).

2. Jones (1953). See Rapoport's study of this community, the Belmont unit (1960).

3. Bloor et al. (1988: 201). Many kinds of institutions claim to be therapeutic communities; some are residential and some operate as outpatient units. So varied are these institutions that some authors accord the name to any institution that claims it. Bloor et al. focus on the therapeutic process rather than how these communities are organized. See also Weppner (1983).

4. Bloor et al. (1988: 59, emphasis in the original). The authors draw a distinction between communities that stress "reality confrontation" ("the repeated reflection back to the resident by both staff and fellow residents of their view of his or her conduct"), which provides the impulse toward change, and communities characterized by careful manipulation and control of the residents' social environment and education that are supposed to lead to behavioral change—"instrumentalism" (1988: 59–60). CPC had elements of both.

5. Rapoport (1960).

6. I neglected to ask the psychologists with Ph.D.s what they thought of this practice. See D. Clark (1977: 561).

7. See Manning (1976a: 133, 135).

8. As Bloor et al. (1988: 9) point out, heterogeneity is found in all therapeutic communities, and the assumption that residents experience common problems that will benefit from common solutions can be challenged. When CPC patients said things like "my case is different," they were suggesting that the fact that they shared pain with other patients was relatively inconsequential, as they did not share other characteristics that would qualify them to participate in such a program.

9. He also said: "I thought, 'Oh, here are going to be twenty people who hurt, most of whom have probably been leading substantially diminished sex lives and are going to be away from their partners. And it's going to be like a college dorm with everybody screwing everybody'—and this is the most asexual group of people I've ever seen!"

10. Compare Bloor et al. (1988: 62) discussing how psychiatric patients are supposed to contrast their old "unreal" social relationships on the outside with the new, warm relationships they find in the therapeutic community.

11. Compare Young's (1995) discussion of veterans' "war stories" in a unit treating post-traumatic stress disorder.

12. See Sharp's discussion of a dissident clique of residents in a halfway house community (1975, as cited in Bloor et al. 1988: 145).

13. A few patients told me they had struggled with a drug dependency secretly following admission.

14. Specialists distinguish addiction, which involves behavior, and chemical dependency, which is physiological and can be eliminated through detoxification. This distinction was not understood by most CPC patients.

15. This is a classic example of Bloor et al.'s "reality confrontation" (1988).

16. See Bloor et al. (1988: 105) on "patient therapists."

17. See Bloor (1981: 366) on how "reality confrontation" by fellow patients is more effective than staff confrontation.

18. See Bloor et al. (1988: 115) on residents of therapeutic communities who feign improvement.

19. This is not to deny substantial individual and cultural variation in pain expression; see Zola (1966), Zborowski (1952, 1969), and Bates (1996).

20. While therapeutic communities are sometimes found in prisons, the vast majority are located in treatment centers residents have chosen to join. Exceptions are communities serving retarded or disturbed children and adolescents. See Goffman (1961) on total institutions, which control a great deal of their residents' lives. Examples are prisons, monasteries, and the locked wards of mental hospitals. Some intentional communities, such as the Oneida community of the nineteenth century, are total institutions.

21. Kanter (1972).

22. See Hayden (1976) on the tension between participation and authority in intentional communities.

23. V. Turner (1969: 95).

24. However, as Bloor et al. (1988: 179) point out, democracy is one of the creative "myths" of any therapeutic community practice. Because patient governance was so minimal, CPC would qualify as a treatment program that took a "therapeutic community approach" rather than being a "therapeutic community proper"; see D. Clark (1965), as cited in Bloor et al., 1988: 28).

25. Bloor et al. (1988: 97) discuss such self-fulfilling aspects of staff redefinitional work; also see Sharp (1975). Getting patients to be responsible for keeping fellow patients in treatment is found in a number of therapeutic communities.

26. That CPC staff members, despite their goal of encouraging patient independence, at times socialized patients into a "passive patient" role is a situation reminiscent of Alexander's (1981) insightful discussion of Bateson's double bind theory as applied to kidney dialysis patients, or Friedson's (1961) analysis of doctors as parent figures encouraging passivity and dependence. Estroff (1981) also refers to a double bind in her study of a mental health community in which patients are encouraged to get better but also encouraged to remain patients. Also pertinent is Young's discussion of how patients in a program for veterans suffering post-traumatic stress syndrome are not allowed to interpret their symptoms or their progress if this interpretation differs from staff's construction of what their problem is; such opinions are interpreted as "resistance" (1985: 116). See Bloor (1981: 362–363) on how staff in a day hospital spoke of how patient culture can "vitiate" therapy. Also see Mishler (1984).

27. Foucault (1973), Bloor et al. (1988).

28. And on the darker side, Charles Manson, Mel Lyman of the Fort Hill commune in Boston and Los Angeles, and Charles Dederich, the founder of Synanon, all of whom seriously abused the authority they were granted. See Felton (1972).

29. See Bloor et al. (1988: 12) on "personal and collective liberation from a

pathogenic society." Note that Plato's *The Republic* (one of the earliest known intentional communities, albeit a fictional one) states that it is necessary to reject part of one's culture and invent a new one. This characterization does not apply to those therapeutic communities for children based on a family model.

30. Plato's *Republic* stressed self-awareness and self-knowledge, mainly as a way to determine appropriate work.

31. Quoted in V. Turner (1969: 94).

32. See van Gennep (1960) for the classic account of rites of passage.

33. Herdt, ed. (1982).

34. See Herdt, ed. (1982) and Kanter (1972).

35. Twilight is a temporal liminality, a swamp a geographical one, lungfish a zoological example; hermaphrodites express sexual liminality. Liminality necessarily occurs when we impose classification systems on the natural world; in the social world, liminality occurs when people pass from one class in a given system into another. Why liminality is so often heightened and emphasized, why it is a conspicuous feature in the symbol system of every culture, and why it is so often accompanied by heightened affect is the topic of a great deal of discussion in the anthropological literature on symbol systems. A functionalist social-structural explanation would suggest that liminality reveals gaps and confusions in rules and classifications; symbol and ritual therefore highlight liminality as a way of appropriating threatening ambiguity to illustrate just how important clarity and lack of ambiguity are. In this view, society needs to order experience by classifying the universe—to allow its members to think and interpret and for the society's own ends as well. Such an approach allows individual members not only to "make sense" of the myriad stimuli assaulting their senses, but to judge some as more beautiful or better than others. Since this goal is achieved by highlighting some attributes of certain phenomena and ignoring others, the argument goes, confusion and conflict threaten in instances of boundary-straddling. Gluckman (1963) argues that ritual and formal behavior in general serve to keep potentially confused, ambiguous, and conflictive roles distinct by highlighting their differences. Also see Babcock (1978).

A functionalist psychological explanation would note that "betwixt and between" phenomena disturb one's sense of order and purpose and are hence paid attention to, because the resulting sense of control relieves anxiety. Crocker (1973) and B. Morris (1987) discuss various social, cognitive, and affective/emotional theories explaining why, under certain circumstances, liminality is highlighted and exaggerated. See V. Turner (1967, 1969) for further discussion of liminality.

36. V. Turner (1969: 95); van Gennep (1960).

37. The period prior to admission can also be seen as a liminal state for some pain sufferers: those whose lives were so dominated by pain that their previous roles as parent, worker, lover, hobbyist, citizen, etc., had fallen into disuse. Goffman (1961) discusses strippping and leveling processes in residential institutions that directly cut across the various social distinctions with which the recruits enter. See van Gennep (1960: 20) on thresholds.

38. See Schieffelin (1976, 1985); Atkinson (1987).

39. Cf. Kennard and Clemmey (1976: 50) on patients in therapeutic communities seeing fellow patients as like themselves.

40. V. Turner (1969: 128).

41. See V. Turner (1969: 95). He also speaks of sacredness of neophytes, which I did not encounter at CPC.

42. V. Turner (1969: 103).
43. V. Turner (1969: 95).
44. See note 9.
45. See Jackson (1990b,1995).

Chapter 6. "Winners": CPC Converts

1. Manning (1976a: 126).

2. Rawlings (1981: 11) lists several of the defensive, self-justifying ways used by therapists in a therapuetic community to dismiss negative findings in a follow-up study of ex-patients.

3. See Rawlings's social constructionist discussion (excessive, in my opinion) of why it is impossibile (her term is "absurd") for an ethnographer to evaluate the success rate of a therapeutic community. There are no "facts" to evaluate because "the only facts in this case are the practical accomplishment of the research procedure." Such an endeavor results in the ethnographer concealing "the organisation he sets out to discover, since he is essentially competing and collaborating with the people whose activities constitute the organisation." (1981: 13, 16). Frank made a related point a generation ago: "Psychotherapy is the only form of treatment which, at least to some extent, appears to create the illness it treats" (1961: 7). Also see Obeyesekere (1985: 149).

4. This subheading is only half ironic. See Baszanger (1998: 163) on how physicians and patients in a pain center negotiate improvement in such a way as to constitute it.

5. See Long (1996: 17), Turk (1996), Flor et al. (1992).

6. Assessing improvement is even harder for treatment clinics because of "the well-known fact that you can't accurately assess compliance by having the providers of patients' care ask them about compliance in the very setting in which they are being treated" (Kleinman, 1982: 165). Cohen (1996: 137) also mentions the potential investigator bias in studies carried out by clinician investigators who are devoting their careers to pain centers.

7. Cohen believes that seeing chronic pain as a syndrome in its own right helps legitimate pain as a focus of treatment. The drawbacks are a tendency to homogenize what is a very heterogeneous category of patients, and logically flawed, circular syndromic diagnoses based on negative findings: "Here the proverbial emperor is wearing no clothes" (1996: 135).

8. For example, Painter et al. (1980) found 75 percent of patients who successfully completed treatment had maintained their gains a year later. Aronoff (1982: 100) reports 75 percent improvement. These figures do not include patients who leave early. One study of 200 patients at the Mayo Clinic found 18 percent leaving within the first ten days (Swanson et al.,1979). Caudill et al. (1991) project substantial savings in utilization of health care for the first two years following pain sufferers' participation in an outpatient behavioral medicine program. What determines who stays and who leaves (and how many are later readmitted) are important questions not adequately covered in the literature.

9. Sarno (1976: 149).

10. Fordyce locates success in the disappearance of pain behaviors: with these gone, he affirms, there is no pain problem; besides, it "is moot as to whether there has been a corresponding reduction in 'pain' " (1978: 67).

11. Latimer, as quoted in Schaeffer (1983: 25).

12. Staff kept informed about former patients through several sources. CPC patients returned one month after discharge for a meeting with Dr. B, and some were advised to join a weekly psychotherapy group he ran. Some former patients visited CPC periodically just to chat with staff members and patients. Finally, a self-help group of former patients, run by Dr. B, held monthly meetings at the hospital.

13. See Sugarman's discussion of "concept house" (a type of U.S. therapeutic community to treat drug dependence) dropout rates of 30% to 60% (1975: 153); Bloor et al. discuss debates about treatment efficacy in therapeutic communities where dropout rate is high (1988: 174).

14. Heirich (1977), as cited in Snow and Machalek (1984: 170). On surrendering to a higher power, see James (1963 [1902]: 223, 226).

15. See Sugarman's comparison of the kind of therapeutic community called a "concept house" and religious sects:

> the total dedication to moral and spiritual improvement of members; the use of public confession and mutual criticism; the elimination of privacy; the hierarchy of authority based on moral and spiritual superiority; the procedures for mortification of deviants and for periodically generating states of ecstatic love and joy within the group. (1975: 141)

16. See W. Clark (1958), as quoted in Snow and Machalek (1984: 172) on demonstration events. James offers a standard definition of conversion: "the process, gradual or sudden, by which a self hitherto divided, and consciously wrong inferior and unhappy, becomes unified and consciously right superior and happy" (1963 [1902]: 189). Snow and Machalek (1984: 168) discuss the literature on degrees of change.

17. Also see Young (1985: 112–14), who, discussing a veterans' hospital that treats post-traumatic stress syndrome, suggests that patients in the program, many of whom want to stay in the hospital, are not in fact helped by the therapy. Rather, he says, they learn verbal behavior that gives an impression of improvement.

18. For example, decisions about further surgery: "If I said, 'well, I'll hang out here three more weeks, and if [things don't work out], I'll go have that surgery.' You can't, you can't do that. I had to make up my mind that if I came through the door [to CPC] surgery was out. But I hear a lot of that; they know they can go back to the drugs or go back to the doctor. As long as they think that they have a choice other than this, then I think that's different from realizing 'I *have* to do this if I want to get on with my life.'" This statement contains what I call "conversion language": it speaks of a highly meaningful period in one's life during which one converts to a new belief and cautions against returning to past attitudes and behaviors.

19. Brown (1977: 115), as cited in Snow and Machalek: (1984: 174).

20. Snow and Machalek (1984: 175).

21. In my case, I improved, but I was not a convert.

22. Levine (1980: 146–51), as cited in Snow and Machalek (1984: 180).

23. See, e.g., Heffner (1987: 70). Frank (1974: 137) notes that a sudden religious conversion is usually preceded by a period of misery, characterized by tormenting self-doubts.

24. James considers "the way in which emotional excitement alters"—the role

of change in a man's "*habitual centre of his personal energy*" (1963 [1902]: 195, 196, emphasis in the original) to be crucial to conversion.

25. Cf. James: "getting so exhausted with the struggle that we have to stop, — so we drop down, give up, and *don't care* any longer . . . there is documentary proof that this state of temporary exhaustion not infrequently forms part of the conversion crisis" (1963 [1902]: 212, emphasis in the original).

26. See Loeser (1991) on confusion concerning the meanings of tissue damage, acute vs. chronic pain, suffering, pain behavior, impairment and disability.

27. See Kleinman (1988: 121) and Havens (1986) on paradox in therapy.

28. Frank (1961: 84, 95, 143).

29. See Palazzoli et al. (1978) on paradoxical therapy; Tipton (1982) on the human potential movement; Frank (1961) on ritual healing.

Chapter 7. Me/Not-Me: Self, Language, and Pain

1. In fact, eye blinks are one of only a few behaviors we can call true reflexes; most behavior we see as reflexes "occurs only after inputs have been analyzed and synthesized sufficiently to produce meaningful experience" (Melzack 1996: 136).

2. Nociception is a useful concept, but it, too, is tricky. Why should whatever proximate cause that initiated a pain experience, rather than all the other causes, be seen as *the* cause? We privilege the time a given pain experience begins and its location (e.g., the low back) because we think of pain in terms of tissue damage and because our models of causation are linear, chronological, and simple: *a* cause, followed by *an* effect.

3. See Goldberg (1976) and Stoltenberg (1989) for examples of this kind of argument. For an analysis of notions about unmanly characteristics and higher incidence of ill health, see Warwick et al. (1988).

4. Many studies have looked at sex and gender differences in illness; see, e.g., Marcus et al. (1983). Kirmayer (1988) critiques biomedicine's "hidden values" with respect to assumptions about sex differences.

5. Scarry (1985: 52).

6. B. Good (1992: 45).

7. My use of the phrase "lifeworld" derives from phenomenology. See Leder (1990: 60–102) on the unexperienced body being the normal state. Also see Buytendijk (1974), a precursor of Leder.

8. Merleau-Ponty puts it this way:

> . . . if I say that my foot hurts, I do not simply mean that it is a cause of pain in the same way as the nail which is cutting into it, differing only in being nearer to me. . . . I mean that the pain reveals itself as localized, that is constitutive of a "pain-infested space." "My foot hurts" means not "I think that my foot is the cause of this pain," but "the pain comes from my foot" or, again, "my foot has a pain." (1962: 93)

Note that pre-objective, pre-abstract pain is most definitely not precultural (see Schutz 1971: 212–18).

9. See Csordas (1990); also Leder (1990).

10. Despite the fact that the IASP definition was published in 1979, despite the

gate control theory's having been in existence for thirty years (in which psychological factors, "which were previously dismissed as 'reactions to pain' were now seen to be an integral part of pain processing" [Melzack 1996: 132]), ample evidence exists that people, experts and lay alike, continue to see pain as a sensation with subsequent emotional input—as Sullivan points out, the "ghost" of the pain sensation continues to lurk about (1995: 11). A recent attempt to distinguish acute and chronic pain illustrates this point: Loeser states that acute pain, suffering, and pain behaviors "follow tissue damage. Of course prior experience, culture, age, sex and a myriad of other factors influence the pain behavior" (1991: 221). This model, although sophisticated, nonetheless sets up an overly simple cause-and-effect progression that begins with tissue damage and allows prior experience to influence only the pain *behavior*. Various authors have attempted to meet the challenge of rethinking this model. Cademenos's statement that "every sensation is already pregnant with meaning" (1981: 46) is an example of such an attempt. Sullivan, who addresses this issue comprehensively, states that "We [mistakenly] want to make the relation between a person and his or her pain simple and universal, and bring in the complexity later as emotional reaction" (1995: 12), but that "Pain is experienced in terms of the pain concept; it is not experienced raw and then interpreted conceptually" (9). And: "Does it make sense to say that my relation to pain is always one of having and that all the diversity of pain experience arises from my different reactions to this 'having pain'?" (12).

11. Public Radio International (n.d.: 11).

12. Bakan (1968: 84) also notes that pain is always experienced as something phenomenally ego-alien.

13. B. Good (1992: 39).

14. B. Good (1992: 39).

15. A patient speaking on the Public Radio International broadcast said something similar: "So it's sort of like another me almost that has this pain, but the real me of course doesn't" (n.d.: 2).

16. See Estroff (1993) on the distinction between "having" a disease and "being" a disease—the latter a variant on the "pain subjectified" theme. Cademenos also discusses the modes of being and having—the experience in pathology of "being had": "Everything I have also has me" (1981: 62). He sees healing in terms of the ability "to reconcile the experiences of both being and having an onerous body" (142). Patients in the clinic he studied, as did those at CPC, spoke of getting to the point where "I have pain but it doesn't have me" (159).

17. See Copp (1985).

18. Cademenos (1981: 152,164). See his example of a patient with a leg in excrutiating pain who objectified and repudiated his leg while simultaneously feeling his inalienable ownership of it (1981: 81).

19. Honkasalo's (1998) interviews with pain patients also generated this theme.

20. D. Morris (1991: 73). He also comments that "As one medical treatment after another fails, chronic pain becomes an experience about which there is increasingly nothing to say, nothing to hope, nothing to do. It is pure blank suffering" (78). An oft-quoted passage from Virginia Woolf expresses the same idea:

> English, which can express the thoughts of Hamlet and the tragedy of Lear, has no words for the shiver and the headache. . . . The merest schoolgirl, when she falls in love, has Shakespeare or Keats to speak her mind for her; but let a sufferer try to describe a pain in his head to a doctor and language at once runs dry. (1947: 11)

And here is the medical historian Roy Porter:

> Indeed, the very notion of a syntax of pain has been culturally and morally problematic. Over the centuries, it has often been argued that physical outrages or emotional injuries may be so terrible that to translate them into words may obscenely traduce and degrade them; we talk after all of "unspeakable" atrocities. Silence may be more eloquent than speech. "The rest is silence": great playwrights like Shakespeare have recognised that the dramatic presentation of tragedy is readily trivialised by descriptive vocabulary. In the depths of his pain, the words King Lear utters are "Howl, howl, howl, howl, howl." (Porter 1994: 108)

Reynolds Price notes that *King Lear* contains the lines:

> The worst is not
> So long as we can say "This is the worst."

He concludes that at the actual worst, "presumably, we'll be mute as rocks. Or howling, wordless, or humming nonsensical hymns to any conceivable helper" (1995: 160). Also see Das's discussion of the "fractured relation to language" documented for the many survivors of prolonged violence "for whom it is the ordinariness of language that divides them from the rest of the world" (1997: 76).

21. Csordas (1993: 23).

22. Scarry (1985: 43).

23. See Melzack (1975); Melzack and Katz (1992). The McGill Pain Questionnaire elicits the subjective experience of pain by having subjects rate their experience using words describing the sensory, affective, and evaluative aspects of pain. Sullivan, citing work by Holroyd et al. (1992), concludes that the McGill Pain Questionnaire "is to be commended for calling our attention to the multidimensional character of the pain experience but criticized for reifying these dimensions as universal" (1995: 10). Diller notes that language can produce culturally modulated differences in pain perception, and exert a powerful influence on conscious attention, "but probably also on semi-conscious and unconscious aspects of our species' cognitive abilities to deal with meaning" (1980: 24–25).

24. For example, Liebeskind disagrees with the International Association for the Study of Pain's definition of pain, maintaining that pain in an experimental setting can be emotionless (in Barsky et al.1998: 186).

25. See Johnson (1987) on how the body is encoded in language; Kirmayer (1992) argues that Johnson's model pays inadequate attention to the role of emotions and culture. See M. Jackson (1989) on the priority given to visual perception.

26. See Croissant (1996) for a discussion of attempts to "objectively" diagnose lower back pain by measuring muscular fatigue using EMG signals.

27. The film *The Return of Dr. Fritz* has remarkable footage documenting such phenomena (Greenfield and Gray 1988).

28. However, Goleman (1989) discusses evidence that some surgical patients hear—and remember what they hear—during anesthesia. See Sullivan (1995) for a discussion of the nature of pediatric pain.

29. See Bushell on ascetic "virtuosos" who self-inflict pain and apparently induce "hyperstimulation analgesia" (1995: 560).

30. In anthropology this issue has been addressed most fruitfully in discus-

sions of the epistemological status of interpretations of rituals which are rejected by participants in the ritual. See, e.g., Charsley (1987), Wagner (1984), Lewis (1980), and La Fontaine (1985: 12).

31. On "real" pathology, see B. Good (1994: 10) and Kirmayer (1988).

32. B. Good (1992: 40).

33. This is the point made by Sontag (1977) regarding attributing psychological causes to cancer.

34. Scarry (1985: 11). Since the primary meaning of pain always refers to something experienced in the body, I am calling unembodied pain "emotional pain" or "metaphorical pain." Speaking of a nonembodied emotional pain as metaphorical pain is not, by any means, intended to suggest that such an experience is somehow less real, or less overwhelming, or involves less suffering.

35. See Swanson (1984). For a still-useful discussion of pain as both sensation and emotion, see Buytendijk (1962). William Styron (1990) maintains that all states of depression involve embodied pain.

36. B. Good (1992: 38).

37. See Leder (1990).

38. All references to Hilbert in this chapter are from (1984).

39. Merleau-Ponty (1962: 140).

40. Merleau-Ponty (1962: 140).

41. Scarry says that "pain comes unsharably into our midst as at once that which cannot be denied and that which cannot be confirmed" (1985: 4). These reported feelings of *communitas* about pain would seem to contradict this idea. See Sullivan for an extended critique of Scarry's position. The two positions can be reconciled if we keep in mind that whatever a given pain's meaning for me, it is derived from language and culture, which we share with others — and that the pain I am feeling this instant cannot be your unmediated experience. Das (1997) also discusses this issue.

42. Schutz (1971: 232).

43. Scarry (1985: 30). It is important to note that metaphors are also abundantly used by patients who manage to reduce the experience of pain; Reynolds Price's contrast between experiencing his pain as a bonfire and, later, as a small campfire (n.d.) is an example. Later in the broadcast he speaks of visualizing a rotary switch which, when turned down, helps decrease consciousness of a part of the body (see also Price 1995: 154–58).

44. Schutz (1971: 233).

45. B. Good (1992: 41) speaks of the dissolution of these building blocks. Schutz's (1971: 215–16) discussion of *durée* is applicable here. Also see D. Morris's (1991: 71) discussion of how chronic pain is structurally similar to a nightmare.

46. Keyes (1985: 164–65).

47. Schutz (1971: 233).

48. B. Good (1992: 136).

49. However complex their relations, the pain-full world does articulate with the everyday lifeworld. For example, as noted above, the preobjective, pre-abstract world is nonetheless a world with cultural meaning, the meaning provided in part from the everyday world of "working" (Schutz 1971: 212–18). A non-pain example of a crossover between worlds is Oliver Sacks's (1984) description of "musicking" himself down a cow path after an injury.

50. Note that this decline occurred in talk about what patients considered to be their physical pain; talk about other problems in their lives occurred

throughout their stay. If anything, for many, the longer they stayed, the more they talked about these problems.

51. B. Good (1992: 40).

52. Kirmayer (1992: 324).

53. B. Good (1992: 29).

54. A great deal of literature deals with language as creator and instantiator; we could start with the beginning of the Old Testament and never stop. See Veena Das's moving discussion of men inscribing slogans on "enemy" women's bodies during the partition of India and Pakistan (1997: 83–85) to create the two nations. She also describes a novel in which a father's speech gives life to his horribly violated daughter: "and though she may find an existence only in his utterance, he creates through his utterance a home for her mutilated and violated self" (1997: 77).

55. However, as many authors point out, this is not the whole story. Cademenos notes that "Pain is paradigmatic of all human intersubjectivity, and its recognition cuts across all cultural barriers. We are more certain of its reality in others than of anything else in them" (1981: 73). He notes that "Even the most abhorrent forms of torture are based on the torturer's ability to apprehend the exquisiteness of the pain he is inflicting upon his victim" (73). Das also discusses how we manage to move out of the "inexpressible privacy and suffocation of [our] pain" (1997: 70), referring to Wittgenstein's notion of a "language game," which Kirmayer describes as "a metaphor Wittgenstein uses to explicate the different ways in which knowledge is acquired and used. It roots meaning in social interaction and technique or praxis" (1992: 338; also see Sullivan 1995). In this "game," Das says, a statement like "I am in pain" "makes a claim asking for acknowledgment, which may be given or denied. In either case, it is not a referential statement that is simply pointing to an inner object" (1997: 70). As many linguists have pointed out, speech acts are rarely simple communications about referential information, something especially true about pain-sufferers' speech about pain—one reason why Wittgenstein devised the notion of "game" using the example of pain (the other reason is pain's reputation as the quintessentially private inner state). Wittgenstein wished to remind philosophers of the intersubjective and social nature of all inner states. Clinicians need reminding from time to time, too: Keefe and Dunsmore note that nonverbal communication about pain, when seen by clinicians as a conscious effort to communicate pain, can "enrage" clinicians, for nonverbal pain behavior should be "unintentional" pain communication (as such it is presumably a far more reliable source of information about "the pain sensation" than speech) (as cited in Sullivan 1995: 11).

56. Kirmayer (1992: 323, 324).

57. Scarry (1985: 28). Also see Foucault's discussion of power and language in (1972: 50).

58. See Gramsci 1971.

59. See Rosaldo (1984: 143).

60. Note that I am including here individuals at CPC who suffered severe chronic pain from well-known causes. Although in one sense they already had a "name"—a diagnosis of arthritis, for instance—they still searched for words that describe their condition more comprehensively, the words that would account for why they, unlike some other arthritis sufferers, suffered *so much*.

61. B. Good (1992: 39).

Chapter 8. Conclusions: The Puzzles of Pain

1. For example, contrary to earlier assumptions, severe pain *can* kill you, not only because the accompanying depression at times leads to suicide, but as Bonica showed in the 1950s, severe chronic pain produces a number of serious psychophysiological reactions that impede healing or cause damage. See *New York Times* (1994), Liebeskind (1994), and Clinton (1992). Attitudes toward medications have changed, and many new medicines have been developed to treat pain and depression.

2. Kirmayer states:

Mind-body dualism is so basic to Western culture that holistic or psychosomatic medical approaches are assimilated to it rather than resulting in any reform of practice. Distress is dichotomized into physical and mental, real and imaginary, accident and moral choice. The duality of mind and body expresses a tension between the unlimited world of thought and the finitude of bodily life. It provides a metaphoric basis of thinking about social responsibility and individual will. (1988: 83)

3. See Anderson and Anderson (1994).

4. Some ordeals do not in fact threaten body integrity as much as they seem to; firewalking is an example. Some ascetic traditions attempt to control not only pain but all affect, positive as well as negative (see Bushell 1993, 1995).

5. Liebeskind (1998) is an exception.

6. Anderson and Anderson (1994: 130).

7. See Natali (1994: 4).

8. This refers to the biological substratum characterizing *homo sapiens* (a substratum most appropriately seen in terms of establishing potentialities and setting limits), and the variability that separates breeding populations (see B. Turner 1992: 16). Wide variation in pain behavior in response to nociceptive stimuli has been extensively documented.

9. Sullivan (1995: 7).

10. Natali (1994: 4).

11. Melzack and Wall (1983: 27).

12. Melzack (1996: 130). For a recent example of the debate in the popular press, see Goode 1999.

13. Melzack (1996: 134, 137).

14. Sullivan (1995: 11, 12).

15. Kirmayer (1992: 328, 330), Sullivan (1995: 13), Melzack (1996: 129).

16. Price (1995).

17. Menges (1981: 93).

18. See D. R. Gordon (1988) and Young (1980).

19. See Kuhn (1970). I am using "paradigm" loosely. Kuhn speaks of it in terms of scientists' underlying premises about that portion of the world they are conducting research on; my usage refers to the dominant view of the body in the West. Haddox (1996: 298–303) enlists the notion of paradigm shift in pain research and treatment. Melzack (1996) also uses Kuhn to discuss shifts in how pain is conceptualized.

20. Cannon (1942); also see Hahn (1995: 89–94).

21. See Bushell (1993) on psychoimmunology, Harrington, ed. (1997) on placebo.

22. Loeser (1996: 102) provides a trenchant critique of single-cause explanations of chronic pain. Attempts to devise more comprehensive explanatory models can be found in Cohen (1996b), Keefe et al. (1996), and Kerns (1996).

23. Brodwin (1992) provides an example of a pain sufferer relying on her pain to express herself emotionally to her family and friends.

24. For example, Boureau (1994: 61). Note that this issue, like so many others in the literature, is contested; Staats, for example, argues that although cancer pain and noncancer pain may have different etiologies, their pathophysiologies may be quite similar, "mediated by the same peripheral nociceptors, modified at the level of the spinal cord, and involving psychological processes" (1996: 120). He argues that psychologically sophisticated pain management programs could help these individuals.

25. As we saw in Chapter 1, defining chronic pain is fraught with difficulty, in part because some specialists want to reserve the phrase for people who have "complicated" pain, which means they exhibit what clinicians see as maladaptive behavior. The debate over whether to think of chronic pain in terms of pain itself (linked to a "nociceptive problem") or (maladaptive) behavior has been neither won nor allowed to wither away. As not all persistent pain develops into an illness, a problem arises concerning how to distinguish these two populations. A fascinating dispute over terminology in the pain literature (examples of championed phrases include "chronic intractable benign pain syndrome," to be contrasted with "chronic benign non-neoplastic pain") is outlined in Baszanger (1998: 89–91).

26. Scarry (1985: 4). An extensive literature in philosophy deals with this issue.

27. See Porter (1994: 108).

28. See Gramsci (1971). Williams discusses hegemony as a process involving renewal, recreation, defense, and modification of a form of dominance which is "continually resisted, limited, altered, challenged by forces not at all its own. We have then to add to the concept . . . the concepts of counter-hegemony and alternative hegemony" (1977: 112–13).

29. See Scott (1985), also Kleinman (1992: 187).

30. See Bourdieu (1972: 164–71), also D. R. Gordon (1988).

31. See Eisenberg et al. (1993) on the surprisingly high frequency of use of "unconventional medicine" in the United States. Goleman and Gurin have edited an excellent volume on mind-body medicine (1993).

32. The current interest in the immune system illustrates such shifts, for part of this discussion concerns how the immune system is affected by inputs from the mind. Most interesting is the degree to which immune-system images have penetrated into the public imagination, including ideas about mental and emotional processes strengthening or weakening the immune system. See Martin (1990, 1994) and Felber (1993).

33. Loeser (1991: 215).

34. See, e.g., Casey et al. (1994).

35. Boureau (1994: 64).

36. For example, kindling theory—which holds that repeated abuse during childhood can build up depressed reactions until the depression is neurologically self-sustaining—argues that the brain becomes "rewired" as if the person had been born that way. The brain is seen as the bearer of mental illness, but it has now become an intersection for social and biological influences (see Dumit 1997).

37. Dumit (1997: 96).

38. See Dumit (n.d.: 1). The following discussion is taken from Dumit (1997, n.d., forthcoming).

39. See Melzack and Wall (1983: 28–29) and Anderson and Anderson (1994: 124–27).

40. Zborowski (1952, 1969).

41. See Bates and Edwards (1992), Bates (1996), and Lipton and Marbach (1984).

42. Notions about "primitive" people and people in the lower classes having a higher pain threshold have a long history. See Leavitt's discussion of supposed class differences in childbirth pain (1980).

43. Much of the literature dealing with gender and pain focuses on women; see Lack (1982), Crook (1982), Celentano et al. (1990), and Reid et al. (1991). With some exceptions, this is a relatively new field, much of it influenced by the women's health movement.

44. Porter (1994: 103). Baszanger refers to pain prior to the creation of a "world of pain" beginning in the 1950s as a "shadow area of medicine, a blind spot in medical knowledge" (1998: 2). Note, however, that Bakan (1968: 58) argues that pain has played a central role in the religious thought of Western civilization, Eve's punishment of childbirth pain and the crucifixion being two salient examples.

45. Kirmayer (1988: 83).

46. Porter (1994: 103).

47. Liddy (1980).

48. Duby (1994: 74).

49. See Wissler (1921: 264), as cited in Melzack and Wall (1983: 31–32).

50. Comments following a paper on "Conditioning in Pharmacotherapies," at a workshop on biobehavioral pain research, Rockville, Md., January 18–21, 1994 (Ader 1994). Also see Ader (1997) and Harrington's discussion of the debate about classical conditioning's role in the placebo effect (1997: 5–7).

51. Moerman (1979).

52. Moerman (1979: 61). Also see papers in Harrington, ed. (1997).

53. Kleinman (1992: 181).

54. Buckelew et al. (1990).

55. Note that the issue of just how desirable is an attitude of "mind over matter" with respect to the body is much more complex than can be addressed here. A countervailing theme is also apparent in the West, one exemplified by Freud's theories on sexuality and the cause of neurosis, Nietzsche's invective against the "despisers of the body," Foucault's concerns with how the state controls the body, Marx's longing for the "species being" who does not experience conflict between mind and body in work, and various members of the Frankfurt school (see B. Turner 1991: 14–15).

56. As Kirmayer (1988: 71, 81) points out, while psychiatric disorder may not be seen as someone's fault, the personhood of the sufferer is diminished; he or she is seen as mentally weak.

57. See Douglas (1966: 67–72); V. Turner (1967). On chronic pain stigma see Lennon et al. (1989) and Jackson (1995).

58. Beecher (1946, 1956). But see Blank (1994) writing on the experience of Israeli soldiers in the Six Day War.

59. Quoted in D. Morris (1991: 16), who cites Herzlich and Pierret (1987: 87).

60. Brodwin (1992) gives a tightly argued analysis of pain as performance.

61. This is what Kleinman (1982) is referring to when he discusses the meaning of pain.

62. See Hahn (1995: 77–80). My use of the terms "construction" and "production" differs somewhat from his model.

63. Baszanger's (1998) book is about the invention of pain medicine, which she refers to as the creation of a "world of pain."

64. Csordas (1994: 145).

65. McKinlay (1986).

66. See Osterweis et al. (1987) for discussions of pain in the United States.

67. Kleinman (1992: 170), emphasis in the original.

68. See Felber (1999).

69. As reported in Kleinman (1992: 179).

70. Kirmayer (1992: 324).

71. No bodily involvement is a purely hypothetical situation. Even actors, when told to represent a given emotion, exhibit measurable parasympathetic and orthosympathetic reactions in keeping with the emotion being portrayed (see Vincent 1994: 20).

72. Porter (1994: 102).

73. See Sontag (1977).

74. See Melzack and Wall (1982: 15–19), Natali (1994: 5), Vincent (1994: 24), Porter (1994: 110), Enaudeau (1994: 143, 145).

75. See Porter (1994: 110).

76. See Hahn (1995: 234–61).

77. On public executions see Foucault (1979: 32–69); on female genital operations see Walley (1997); on torture, see Scarry (1985) and Daniel (1994); on rape see Sanday (1990), Brownmiller (1975), and the chapter on women in Desjarlais et al. (1995); on genocide see Kuper (1981).

78. On infant pain see Anand and McGrath (1993); on cliterodectomies see Ehrenreich and English (1978: 111); on the homeless mentally ill see Desjarlais (1996); on third-world "development" see Farmer (1992), Escobar (1995), and Danaher (1994); on foreign aid see George (1977); on treatment of the deinstitutionalized mentally ill see Estroff (1981).

79. Enaudeau (1994: 145).

80. See Zola (1972); Clark (1983).

81. Kleinman (1992: 181).

82. Kleinman (1992: 185); also see Corbett (1986) and Kotarba and Seidel (1984). Taussig (1980) provides an extremely trenchant critique of behaviorist approaches and the way biomedicine constructs the "non-compliant" patient.

83. Kleinman (1992: 191), Scarry (1985: 3). Quote from Steiner as cited in Porter (1994: 108); see also Langer (1996).

84. D. Morris (1991: 78).

Coda: A Note on Approach

1. Goodenough (1957).

2. See Stoller (1989).

3. Harding (1987: 180).

4. Anthropologists who discuss such phenomenological learning in the field

include Jean Briggs's work on the Inuit (1970) and Michael Jackson's look at African systems of thought (1989).

5. Bourdieu (1977).

6. I have discussed some of these issues in Jackson (1990a, 1990b, and 1997).

7. Many of the methods, goals, and benefits of participant observation in a hospital setting are spelled out in Sudnow (1967: 5–7).

8. Zola (1982) discusses similar issues in connection with his research on disability.

9. Kotarba (1977).

10. See D. P. Gordon (1983).

Bibliography

Abu-Lughod, Lila. 1986. *Veiled Sentiments: Honor and Poetry in a Bedouin Society.* Berkeley: University of California Press.

———. 1990. "The Romance of Resistance: Tracing Transformations of Power Through Bedouin Women." *American Ethnologist* 17: 41–55.

———. 1993. *Writing Women's Worlds: Bedouin Stories.* Berkeley: University of California Press.

Ader, Robert. 1994. "Conditioning in Pharmacotherapies." Paper given at NIH Workshop on Biobehavioral Pain Research, January 18–21, Rockville, Md.

———. 1997. "The Role of Conditioning in Pharmacotherapy." In Anne Harrington, ed., *The Placebo Effect: An Interdisciplinary Exploration.* Cambridge, Mass.: Harvard University Press: 138–65.

Agnew, D. C. and Harold Mersky. 1976. "Words of Chronic Pain." *Pain* 2: 73–81.

Alexander, Linda. 1981. "The Double-Bind Between Dialysis Patients and Their Health Practitioners." In Leon Eisenberg and Arthur Kleinman, eds., *The Relevance of Social Science for Medicine.* Dordrecht: D. Reidel: 307–32.

Alperson, Erma Dosamantes. 1974. "Carrying Experiencing Forward Through Authentic Body Movement." *Psychotherapy: Theory, Research and Practice* 11, 3: 211–14.

Anand, K. J. S. and P. J. McGrath, eds. 1993. *Pain in Neonates.* New York: Elsevier.

Anderson, Robert T. and Scott T. Anderson. 1994. "Culture and Pain." In *The Puzzle of Pain.* Reading, UK: Gordon and Breach: 120–38.

Andrews, Edward Deming. 1963. *The People Called Shakers: A Search for the Perfect Society.* New York: Dover.

Angell, Marcia. 1985. "Disease as a Reflection of the Psyche." *New England Journal of Medicine* 312, 24: 1570–72.

Aronoff, Gerald M. 1982. "Pain Units Provide an Effective Alternative Technique in the Management of Chronic Pain." *Orthopaedic Review* 11: 95–100.

———. 1983. "The Pain Center as an Effective Alternative Treatment for Intractable Suffering and Disability Resulting from Chronic Pain. *Seminars in Neurology* 3, 8: 377–381.

———. 1984. "Psychological Aspects of Nonmalignant Chronic Pain: A Multidisciplinary Approach." *Resident & Staff Physician* (August): 3–14.

Aronoff, Gerald M. and Wayne O. Evans. 1982. "Evaluation and Treatment of Chronic Pain at the Boston Pain Center." *Journal of Clinical Psychiatry* 43, 8: 4–9.

Aronoff, Gerald M., Wayne O. Evans, and Pamela L. Enders. 1983. "A Review of Follow-up Studies of Multidisciplinary Pain Units." *Pain* 16: 1–11.

Atkinson, Jane. 1987. "The Effectiveness of Shamans in an Indonesian Ritual." *American Anthropologist* 89, 2: 342–55.

Babcock, Barbara A., ed. 1978. *The Reversible World: Symbolic Inversion in Art and Society.* Ithaca, N.Y.: Cornell University Press.

Bakan, David. 1968. *Disease, Pain, and Sacrifice: Toward a Psychology of Suffering.* Chicago: University of Chicago Press.

Barsky, Arthur, Isabelle Baszanger, Laurence Bradley, Kenneth Casey, C. Richard Chapman, Richard Gracely, Jennifer Haythornwaite, Jean Jackson, Mark Jensen, Francis J. Keefe, John Liebeskind, Henrietta Logan, Patrick McGrath, Deborah B. McGuire, Ronald Melzack, David Morris, Stephen G. Post, Donald Price, Fenella Rouse, Judith Spross, Mark Sullivan, Dennis C. Turk, Lynn Underwood, Father Clement Zeleznik. 1998. "Perspectives on Pain-Related Suffering: Presentations and Discussion." *Advances in Mind-Body Medicine* 14, 3: 167–203.

Baszanger, Isabelle. 1986. "Les maladies chroniques et leur ordre négocié." *Revue Française de Sociologie* 27: 3–27.

———. 1989. "Pain: Its Experience and Treatments." *Social Science and Medicine* 29, 3: 425–34.

———. 1990. "Emergence d'un groupe professionnel et travail de légitimation: le cas des médecins de la douleur." *Revue Française de Sociologie* 31: 257–282.

———. 1992. "Deciphering Chronic Pain." *Sociology of Health and Illness* 14, 2: 181–215.

———. 1998. *Inventing Pain Medicine: From the Laboratory to the Clinic.* New Brunswick, N.J.: Rutgers University Press.

Bates, Maryann S. 1996. *Biocultural Dimensions of Chronic Pain: Implications for Treatment of Multi-Ethnic Populations.* Binghamton: State University of New York Press.

Bates, Maryann S. and W. T. Edwards. 1992. "Ethnic Variations in the Chronic Pain Experience." *Ethnicity and Disease* 2, 1: 63–83.

Beecher, Henry K. 1946. "Pain in Men Wounded in Battle." *Bulletin of the U.S. Army Medical Department* 5: 445–54.

———. 1956. "Relationship of Significance of Wound to the Pain Experience." *Journal of the American Medical Association* 161: 1609–13.

Behar, Ruth. 1993. *Translated Woman: Crossing the Border with Esperanza's Story.* Boston: Beacon Press.

Belzberg, Allan J. 1996. "Commentary on Chapters 2–5." In Mitchell J. M. Cohen and James N. Campbell, eds., *Pain Treatment Centers at a Crossroads: A Practical and Conceptual Reappraisal.* Seattle: IASP Press: 69–76.

Benedetti, G. 1974. "Psychological and Psychiatric Aspects of Pain." In John J. Bonica et al., eds., *Recent Advances on Pain: Pathophysiology and Clinical Aspect.* Boston: Charles C. Thomas, 1974: 256–73.

Berger, Peter L. and Thomas Luckmann. 1967. *The Social Construction of Reality.* New York: Anchor Books.

Berliner, H. S. and J. W. Salmon. 1979. "The Holistic Health Movement and Scientific Medicine: The Naked and the Dead." *Socialist Review* 9: 31–52.

Besson, Jean-Marie. 1992. *La douleur.* Paris: Odile Jacob.

Black, Richard G. 1979. "Evaluation of the Complaint of Pain." *Bulletin of the Los Angeles Neurological Society* 44, 1–4: 32–44.

Blank, Jon W. 1994. "Pain in Men Wounded in Battle: Beecher Revisited." *IASP Newsletter* (January–February): 2–4.

Bloor, Michael. 1981. "Therapeutic Paradox—The Patient Culture and the Formal Treatment Programme in a Therapeutic Community." *British Journal of Medical Psychology* 54: 359–69.

Bloor, Michael and Neil P. McKeganey. 1986. "Conceptions of Therapeutic Work in Therapeutic Communities." *International Journal of Sociology and Social Policy* 6: 68–79.

Bloor, Michael, Neil McKeganey, and Dick Fonkert. 1988. *One Foot in Eden: A Sociological Study of the Range of Therapeutic Community Practice.* London: Routledge.

Bokan, John A., Richard K. Ries, and Wayne J. Katon. 1981. "Tertiary Gain and Chronic Pain." *Pain* 10: 331–35.

Bonica, John J., ed. 1990. *The Management of Pain.* 2nd ed. Philadelphia: Lea & Febiger.

Bonica, John J. and Stephen H. Butler. 1978. "The Management and Functions of Pain Centres." In Mark Swerdlow, ed., *Relief of Intractable Pain.* Amsterdam: Elsevier/North-Holland Biomedical Press.

Bonica, John J. and Wilbert E. Fordyce. 1974. "Operant Conditioning for Chronic Pain." In Bonica et al., eds., *Recent Advances on Pain: Pathophysiology and Clinical Aspects.* Boston: Charles C. Thomas.

Bourdieu, Pierre. 1977. *Outline of a Theory of Practice.* Cambridge: Cambridge University Press, 1977.

Boureau, François. 1994. "Pain Treatment Centres." In *The Puzzle of Pain.* Reading, UK: Gordon and Breach: 61–70.

Brand, Dr. Paul, and Philip Yancey. 1993. *Pain: The Gift Nobody Wants.* New York: HarperCollins.

Brena, Steven F., Stanley L. Chapman, and L. Allen Bradford. 1979. "Conditioned Responses to Treatment in Chronic Pain Patients: Effects of Compensation for Work-Related Accidents." *Bulletin of the Los Angeles Neurological Society* 44, 1–4: 48–52.

Briggs, Jean. 1970. *Never in Anger: Portrait of an Eskimo Family.* Cambridge, Mass.: Harvard University Press.

Brodwin, Paul. 1992. "Symptoms and Social Performances: The Case of Diane Reden." In Mary-Jo DelVecchio Good et al., eds., *Pain as Human Experience: An Anthropological Perspective.* Berkeley: University of California Press: 77–99.

Brody, Howard. 1987. *Stories of Sickness.* New Haven, Conn.: Yale University Press.

Brown, Richard H. 1977. *A Poetic for Sociology.* New York: Cambridge University Press.

Brownmiller, Susan. 1975. *Against Our Will: Men, Women, and Rape.* New York: Simon and Schuster.

Buckelew, S., M.S. Shutty Jr., J. Hewett, T. Landon, K. Morrow, and R.G. Frank. 1990. "Health Locus of Control, Gender Differences and Adjustment to Persistent Pain." *Pain* 42, 3: 287–94.

Bushell, William C. 1993. "Psychophysiological and Cross-Cultural Dimensions of Ascetico-Meditational Practices: Special Reference to the Christian Hermits of Ethiopia and Application to Theory in Anthropology and Religious Studies." Ph.D. dissertation, Columbia University.

———. 1995. "Psychophysiological and Comparative Analysis of Ascetico-Meditational Discipline: Toward a New Theory of Asceticism." In Vincent L. Wimbush and Richard Valantasis, eds., *Asceticism.* New York: Oxford University Press: 553–75

Buytendijk, F. J. J. 1962. *Pain: Its Modes and Functions.* Trans. Edna O'Sheil. Chicago: University of Chicago Press.

————. 1974. *Prolegomena to an Anthropological Physiology*. Pittsburgh: Duquesne University Press.

Cademenos, Stavros. 1981. "A Phenomenological Approach to Pain." Ph.D. dissertation, Brandeis University.

Campbell, James N. 1996. "Pain Treatment Centers: A Surgeon's Perspective." In Mitchell J. M. Cohen and James N. Campbell, eds., *Pain Treatment Centers at a Crossroads: A Practical and Conceptual Reappraisal*. Seattle: IASP Press: 29–38.

Cannon, Walter. 1942. "'Voodoo Death." *American Anthropologist* 44: 169–81.

Carden, Maren Lockwood. 1971. *Oneida: Utopian Community to Modern Corporation*. New York: Harper and Row.

Carrier, James G., ed. 1995. *Occidentalism: Images of the West*. Oxford: Clarendon Press.

Carron, Harold, Douglas E. DeGood, and Raymond Tait. 1985. "A Comparison of Low Back Pain Patients in the United States and New Zealand: Psychological and Economic Factors Affecting Severity of Disability." *Pain* 21: 77–89.

Casey, Kenneth L., S. Minoshima, K. L. Berger, R. A. Koeppe, T. J. Morrow, and K. A. Frey. 1994. "Positron Emission Tomographic Analysis of Cerebral Structures Activated Specifically by Repetitive Noxious Heat Stimuli." *Journal of Neurophysiology* 71, 2: 802–7.

Cassell, Joan. 1991. *Expected Miracles: Surgeons at Work*. Philadelphia: Temple University Press.

Caudill, Margaret, Richard Schnable, Patricia Zuttermeister, Herbert Benson, and Richard Friedman. 1991. "Decreased Clinic Use by Chronic Pain Patients: Response to Behavioral Medicine Intervention." *Clinical Journal of Pain* 7: 305–10.

Celentano, D. D., M. S. Linet, and W. F. Steward. "Gender Differences in the Experience of Headache," *Social Science and Medicine* 30, 12: 1289–95.

Cerroni-Long, E. L., ed. 1995. *Insider Anthropology*. National Association for the Practice of Anthropology *Bulletin*. Arlington, Va.: American Anthropological Association.

Chapman, C. Richard. 1978. "Pain: The Perception of Noxious Events." In Richard A. Sternbach, ed., *The Psychology of Pain*. New York: Raven Press: 169–202.

Chapman, C. Richard, Anders E. Sola, and John J. Bonica. 1979. "Illness Behavior and Depression Compared in Pain Center and Private Practice Patients." *Pain* 6: 1–7.

Charmaz, Kathy. 1991. *Good Days, Bad Days: The Self in Chronic Illness and Time*. New Brunswick, N.J.: Rutgers University Press.

Charsley, Simon. 1987. "Interpretation and Custom: The Case of the Wedding Cake." *Man* 22: 93–110.

Clark, Candace. 1983. "Sickness and Social Control." In Howard Robby and Candace Clark, eds., *Social Interaction: Readings in Sociology*. 2nd ed. New York: St. Martin's Press: 346–65.

Clark, D. H. 1965. "The Therapeutic Community: Concept, Practice, and Future." *British Journal of Psychiatry* 111: 947–954.

————. 1977. "The Therapeutic Community." *British Journal of Psychiatry* 131: 553–64.

Clark, Jack A. 1984. "The Conversational Art of Diagnosis: The Social Construction of Medical Facts." Ph.D. dissertation, University of Colorado, Boulder.

Clark, Michael R. 1996. "The Role of Psychiatry in the Treatment of Chronic Pain." In Mitchell J. M. Cohen and James N. Campbell, eds., *Pain Treatment*

Centers at a Crossroads: A Practical and Conceptual Reappraisal. Seattle: IASP Press: 59–68.

Clark, Walter Houston. 1958. *The Psychology of Religion: An Introduction to Religious Experience and Behavior.* New York: Macmillan.

Clinton, Jarrett J. 1992. "From the Agency for Health Care Policy and Research." *Journal of the American Medical Association* 267, 3: 2580.

Cohen, Mitchell J. M. 1996a. "Introduction to Chapters 6–10." In Mitchell J. M. Cohen and James N. Campbell, eds., *Pain Treatment Centers at a Crossroads: A Practical and Conceptual Reappraisal.* Seattle: IASP Press: 77–78.

———. 1996b. "The Pain Center: Centerpiece of Comprehensive Medicine?" In Cohen and James N. Campbell, eds., *Pain Treatment Centers at a Crossroads: A Practical and Conceptual Reappraisal.* Seattle: IASP Press: 125–42.

Cohen, Mitchell J. M. and James N. Campbell, eds. 1996. *Pain Treatment Centers at a Crossroads: A Practical and Conceptual Reappraisal.* Seattle: IASP Press.

Copp, Laurel Archer. 1985. "Pain Coping Model and Typology." *Image: The Journal of Nursing Scholarship* 17, 3: 69–72.

Corbett, Kitty K. 1986. "Adding Insult to Injury: Cultural Dimensions of Frustration in the Management of Chronic Back Pain." Ph.D. dissertation, University of California, Berkeley.

Cousins, Norman. 1979. *Anatomy of an Illness as Perceived by the Patient: Reflections on Healing and Regeneration.* Toronto: Bantam Books.

Crocker, Christopher J. 1973. "Ritual and the Development of Social Structure: Liminality and Inversion." In James D. Shaughnessy, ed., *The Roots of Ritual.* Grand Rapids, Mich.: William B. Eerdmans: 47–86.

Croissant, Jennifer L. 1996. "Pain, Fatigue, and Sites of Knowledge." Paper presented at the American Anthropological Association 95th Annual Meeting, San Francisco, session on "Body Work/Body Talk: Refiguring the Body in Anthropological Discourse."

Crook, Joan. 1982. "Women with Chronic Pain." In Ranjan Roy and Eldon Tunks, eds., *Chronic Pain: Psychosocial Factors in Rehabilitation.* Baltimore: Williams and Wilkins: 68–78.

Crue, Benjamin L. 1975. "Some Philosophical Considerations of Pain—Suggestion, Euthanasia, and Free Will." In Crue, ed., *Pain: Research and Treatment.* New York: Academic Press: 401–13.

Csordas, Thomas J. 1988. "The Conceptual Status of Hegemony and Critique in Medical Anthropology." *Medical Anthropology Quarterly* 2, 4: 416–21.

———. 1990. "Embodiment as a Paradigm for Anthropology." *Ethos* 18, 1990: 5–47.

———. 1993. "Somatic Modes of Attention." *Cultural Anthropology* 8: 135–156.

———. 1994. Review of Mary-Jo DelVecchio Good, Paul E. Brodwin, Byron J. Good, and Arthur Kleinman, eds. *Pain as Human Experience: An Anthropological Perspective. Social Science and Medicine* 39, 1: 145–50.

Csordas, Thomas J. and Jack A. Clark. 1992. "Ends of the Line: Diversity Among Chronic Pain Centers." *Social Science and Medicine* 34: 383–93.

Damasio, Antonio R. 1994. *Descartes' Error: Emotion, Reason, and the Human Brain.* New York: Putnam.

Danaher, Kevin, ed. 1994. *50 Years Is Enough: The Case Against the World Bank and the International Monetary Fund.* Boston: South End Press.

Daniel, E. Valentine. 1994. "The Individual in Terror." In Thomas J. Csordas, ed., *Embodiment and Experience: The Existential Ground of Culture and Self.* Cambridge: Cambridge University Press.

Das, Veena. 1997. "Language and Body: Transactions in the Construction of Pain." In Arthur Kleinman, Veena Das, and Margaret Lock, eds., *Social Suffering*. Berkeley: University of California Press: 67–92.

Desjarlais, Robert. 1996. "The Office of Reason: On the Politics of Language and Agency in a Shelter for 'the Homeless Mentally Ill.'" *American Ethnologist* 23, 4: 880–900.

Desjarlais, Robert, Leon Eisenberg, Byron Good, and Arthur Kleinman. 1995. *World Mental Health: Problems and Priorities in Low-Income Countries*. New York: Oxford University Press.

Deyo, R.A., D. Cherkin, D. Conrad, and E. Volin. 1991. "Cost, Controversy, Crisis: Low Back Pain and the Health of the Public." *Annual Review of Public Health* 12: 141–46.

Diller, Anthony. 1980. "Cross-Cultural Pain Semantics." *Pain* 9: 9–26.

Douglas, Mary. 1966. *Purity and Danger: An Analysis of the Concepts of Pollution and Taboo*. London: Routledge and Kegan Paul.

Duby, Georges. 1994. "Physical Pain in the Middle Ages." In *The Puzzle of Pain*. Reading, UK: Gordon and Breach Arts International: 71–80.

Dumit, Joseph. 1997. "A Digital Image of the Category of the Person: PET Scanning and Objective Self Fashioning." In Gary Lee Downey and Joseph Dumit, eds., *Cyborgs and Citadels: Anthropological Interventions in Emerging Sciences and Technologies*. Santa Fe, N.M.: School of Americas Research Press: 83–102.

———. n.d. "Biology Is Elsewhere: Brain Imaging, New Social Movements, and Cutting-Edge Evidence." Manuscript.

———. forthcoming. "When Explanations Rest: 'Good-Enough' Brain Science and the New Biomental Disorders." In Margaret Lock, Alberto Cambrosio, and Allan Young, eds., *Intersections: Living and Working with the New Medical Technologies*. Cambridge: Cambridge University Press.

Dworkin, Samuel F. and L. LeResche. 1992. "Research Diagnostic Criteria for Temporomandibular Disorders: Review, Criteria, Examinations and Specifications, Critique." *Journal of Craniomandibular Disorders: Facial and Oral Pain* 6: 301–54.

Edwards, Rem B. 1984. "Pain and the Ethics of Pain Management." *Social Science and Medicine* 18, 6: 515–23.

Egan, K. and Wayne J. Katon. 1987. "Responses to Illness and Health in Chronic Pain Patients and Healthy Adults." *Psychosomatic Medicine* 49: 470–81.

Ehrenreich, Barbara and Deirdre English. 1978. *For Her Own Good: 150 Years of the Experts' Advice to Women*. New York: Doubleday.

Eisenberg, David M., Ronald C. Kessler, Cindy Foster, Frances E. Norlock, David R. Calkins, Thomas L. Delbanco. 1993. "Unconventional Medicine in the United States: Prevalence, Costs, and Patterns of Use." *New England Journal of Medicine* 328, 4: 246–52.

Enaudeau, Michel. 1994. "On Pain, in Brief." In *The Puzzle of Pain*. Reading, UK: Gordon and Breach: 139–46.

Escobar, Arturo. 1995. *Encountering Development: The Making and the Unmaking of the Third World*. Princeton, N.J.: Princeton University Press.

Estroff, Sue E. 1981. *Making It Crazy: An Ethnography of Psychiatric Clients in an American Community*. Berkeley: University of California Press.

———. 1993. "Identity, Disability, and Schizophrenia: The Problem of Chronicity." In Shirley Lindenbaum and Margaret Lock, eds., *Knowledge, Power and Practice: The Anthropology of Medicine and Everyday Life*. Berkeley: University of California Press: 247–86.

Fabrega, H. and S. Tyma. 1976. "Culture, Language, and the Shaping of Illness: An Illustration Based on Pain." *Journal of Psychosomatic Research* 20: 323–37.

Fagerhaugh, Shizuko Y. and Anselm Strauss. 1977. *Politics of Pain Management: Staff-Patient Interaction.* Menlo Park, Calif.: Addison-Wesley.

Farmer, Paul. 1992. *AIDS and Accusation: Haiti and the Geography of Blame.* Berkeley: University of California Press.

Featherstone, Mike, Mike Hepworth, and Bryan S. Turner, eds. 1991. *The Body: Social Process and Cultural Theory.* London: Sage.

Federico, John V. 1996. "The Cost of Pain Centers: Where Is the Return?" In Mitchell J. M. Cohen and James N. Campbell, eds., *Pain Treatment Centers at a Crossroads: A Practical and Conceptual Reappraisal.* Seattle: IASP Press: 249–56.

Felber, Daniel. 1999. "Easing Pain the Hard Way." *New York Times,* January 16.

———. 1993. "The Brain and the Immune System." In Bill Moyers, ed., *Healing and the Mind.* New York: Doubleday: 213–38.

Felton, David, ed. 1972. *Mindfuckers: A Source Book on the Rise of Acid Fascism in America.* San Francisco: Straight Arrow Books.

Fields, Howard L. and Allan I. Basbaum. 1994. "Endogenous Pain Control Mechanisms." In Patrick D. Wall and Ronald Melzack, eds., *Textbook of Pain.* Edinburgh: Churchill Livingstone: 206–17.

Finer, Basil. 1983. "Update: Psychosomatic Organization Based on Hypnosis in Persistent Pain." *Persistent Pain* 1: 193–203.

Finneson, Bernard E. 1976. "Modulating Effect of Secondary Gain on the Low Back Pain Syndrome." In J. J. Bonica and D. Albe-Fessard, eds., *Advances in Pain Research and Therapy,* vol. 1. New York: Raven Press: 949–52.

Fisher, Sue and Alexandra Dundas Todd, eds. 1983. *The Social Organization of Doctor-Patient Communication.* Washington, D.C.: Center for Applied Linguistics.

Flor, H., T. Fydrich, and D. C. Turk. 1992. "Efficacy of Multidisciplinary Pain Treatment Centers: A Meta-Analytic Review." *Pain* 49: 221–230.

Fordyce, Wilbert E. 1976. *Behavioral Methods for Chronic Pain and Illness.* St. Louis: Mosby Press.

———. 1977: "Operant Conditioning: An Approach to Chronic Pain." In Ada K. Jacox, ed., *Current Concepts of Pain and Analgesia.* New York: Current Concepts: 275–83.

———. 1978. "Learning Processes in Pain." In Richard A. Sternbach, ed., *The Psychology of Pain.* New York: Raven Press: 49–72.

Foucault, Michel. 1970. *The Order of Things: An Archaeology of the Human Sciences.* New York: Random House.

———. 1972. *The Archaeology of Knowledge.* New York: Harper and Row.

———. 1973. *The Birth of the Clinic: An Archaeology of Medical Perception.* New York: Random House.

———. 1979. *Discipline and Punish: The Birth of the Prison.* New York: Vintage.

Frank, Jerome. 1961. *Persuasion and Healing: A Comparative Study of Psychotherapy.* Baltimore: Johns Hopkins University Press.

———. 1974. *Persuasion and Healing.* New York: Schocken.

Frankenberg, Ronald. 1988. "Gramsci, Marxism, and Phenomenology: Essays for the Development of Critical Medical Anthropology." *Medical Anthropology Quarterly* 2, 4: 324–459.

Friedson, Eliot, 1961. *Patients' Views of Medical Practice.* New York: Sage.

Frymoyer J. W. and W. L. Cats-Baril. 1991. "An Overview of the Incidences and Costs of Low Back Pain." *Orthopedic Clinics of North America* 22, 2: 263–71.

Gaston-Johansson, Fannie and Jens Allwood. 1988. "Pain Assessment: Model Construction and Analysis of Words Used to Describe Pain-Like Experiences." *Semiotica* 71, 1, 2: 73–92.

Gennep, Arnold van. 1960. *The Rites of Passage.* Trans. Monika B Vizedom and Gabrielle L. Caffee. London: Routledge and Kegan Paul.

George, Susan. 1977. *How the Other Half Dies: The Real Reasons for World Hunger.* Montclair, N. J.: Allanheld, Osmun and Co.

Gluckman, Max. 1963. "Rituals of Rebellion in South East Africa." In Gluckman, ed., *Order and Rebellion in Tribal Africa.* London: Cohen and West: 110–37.

Goffman, Erving. 1961. *Asylums: Essays on the Social Situation of Mental Patients and Other Inmates.* New York: Doubleday.

———. 1963. *Stigma: Notes on the Management of Spoiled Identity.* Englewood Cliffs, N. J.: Prentice-Hall.

Goldberg, Herb. 1976. *The Hazards of Being Male: Surviving the Myth of Masculine Privilege.* New York: Signet, 1976.

Goleman, Daniel. 1989. "Doctors Find That Surgical Patients May Still 'Hear' Despite Anesthesia." *New York Times,* Oct. 26: 21.

Goleman, Daniel and Joel Gurin, eds. 1993. *Mind Body Medicine: How to Use Your Mind for Better Health.* Yonkers, N.Y.: Consumer Reports Books.

Good, Byron, 1992. "A Body in Pain—The Making of a World of Chronic Pain." In Mary-Jo DelVecchio Good et al., eds., *Pain as Human Experience: An Anthropological Perspective.* Berkeley: University of California Press: 29–48.

———. 1994. *Medicine, Rationality, and Experience: An Anthropological Perspective.* Cambridge, Cambridge University Press.

Good, Byron and Mary-Jo DelVecchio Good. 1981. "The Semantics of Medical Discourse." In Everett Mendelsohn and Yehuda Elkana, eds., *Sciences and Cultures.* Sociology of the Sciences 5. Dordrecht: D. Reidel: 177–212.

Good, Mary-Jo DelVecchio. 1992. "Work as a Haven from Pain." In Mary-Jo DelVecchio Good et al., eds., *Pain as Human Experience: An Anthropological Perspective.* Berkeley: University of California Press: 49–76.

Good, Mary-Jo DelVecchio, Paul E. Brodwin, Byron J. Good, and Arthur Kleinman, eds. 1992. *Pain as Human Experience: An Anthropological Perspective.* Berkeley: University of California Press.

Goode, Erica. 1999. "Can an Essay a Day Keep Asthma or Arthritis at Bay?" *New York Times,* April 14.

Goodenough, Ward Hunt. 1957. "Cultural Anthropology and Linguistics." In Paul L. Garvin, ed., *Report of the Seventh Annual Round Table Meeting on Linguistics and Language Study.* Georgetown University Monograph Series on Languages and Linguistics 9. Washington, D.C.: Georgetown University Press: 167–73.

Gordon, David Paul. 1983. "Hospital Slang for Patients: Crocks, Gomers, Gorks, and Others." *Language in Society* 12: 173–85.

Gordon, Deborah R. 1988. "Tenacious Assumptions in Western Medicine." In Margaret Lock and Gordon, eds., *Biomedicine Examined.* Boston: D. Reidel: 19–45.

Gramsci, Antonio. 1971. *Selections from the Prison Notebooks.* Ed. and trans. Quintin Hoare and Geoffrey Nowell-Smith. London: Lawrence and Wishart.

Greenfield, Sidney M. and John Gray. 1988. *The Return of Dr. Fritz: Healing by the Spirits in Brazil.* Video Documentary, Educational Communication Department of the University of Wisconsin-Milwaukee.

Haddox, J. David. 1996. "Appropriate use of the Chronic Pain Specialist and the Role of Conceptual Fluidity." In Mitchell J. M. Cohen and James N. Campbell, eds., *Pain Treatment Centers at a Crossroads: A Practical and Conceptual Reappraisal.* Seattle: IASP Press: 297–306.

Hahn, Robert A. 1995. *Sickness and Healing: An Anthropological Perspective.* New Haven, Conn.: Yale University Press.

Harding, Susan F. 1987. "Convicted by the Holy Spirit: The Rhetoric of Fundamental Baptist Conversion." *American Ethnologist* 14, 1: 167–81.

Harrington, Anne, ed. 1997. *The Placebo Effect: An Interdisciplinary Exploration.* Cambridge, Mass.: Harvard University Press.

Havens, Leston. 1986. *Making Contact: Uses of Language in Psychotherapy.* Cambridge: Harvard University Press.

Hayden, Dolores. 1976. *Seven American Utopias: The Architecture of Communitarian Socialism, 1790–1975.* Cambridge, Mass.: MIT Press.

Heffner, Robert. 1987. "The Political Economy of Islamic Conversion in Modern East Java." In William Roff, ed., *Islam and the Political Economy of Meaning.* London: Croom Helm.

Heirich, Max. 1977. "Change of Heart: A Test of Some Widely Held Theories About Religious Conversion." *American Journal of Sociology* 83: 653–80.

Herdt, Gilbert H., ed. 1982. *Rituals of Manhood: Male Initiation in Papua New Guinea.* Berkeley: University of California Press.

Hershkopf, Isaac S. 1994. "Treatment of Pain Should Be Discussed." *New York Times,* May 30: A14.

Herzlich, Claudine and Janine Pierret. 1987. *Illness and Self in Society.* Trans. Elborg Forster. Baltimore: Johns Hopkins University Press.

Hilbert, Richard A. 1984. "The Acultural Dimensions of Chronic Pain: Flawed Reality Construction and the Problem of Meaning." *Social Problems* 31: 365–78.

Holroyd, K. A., J. E. Holm, F. J. Keefe, J. A. Turner, L. A. Bradley, W. D. Murphy, P. Johnson, K. Anderson, A. L. Hinkle, and W. B. O'Malley. 1992. "A Multicenter Evaluation of the McGill Pain Questionnaire: Results from over 1700 Chronic Pain Patients." *Pain* 48, 3: 301–11.

Honkasalo, Marja-Liisa. 1998. "Space and Embodied Experience: Rethinking the Body in Pain." *Body and Society* 4, 2: 35–57.

International Association for the Study of Pain. 1979. "Pain Terms: A List with Definitions and a Note on Usage." *Pain* 6: 249–52.

"It Pains a Nation of Stoics to Say 'No' to Pain." *New York Times,* April 3, 1994.

Jackson, Jean E. 1986. "On Trying to Be an Amazon." In Tony Larry Whitehead and Mary Ellen Conaway, eds., *Self, Sex, and Gender in Cross-Cultural Fieldwork.* Urbana: University of Illinois Press: 263–74.

———. 1990a. " 'I Am a Fieldnote': Fieldnotes as a Symbol of Professional Identity." In Roger Sanjek, ed., *Fieldnotes: The Makings of Anthropology.* Ithaca, N.Y.: Cornell University Press: 3–33.

———. 1990b. " 'Déjà Entendu': The Liminal Qualities of Anthropological Fieldnotes." *Journal of Contemporary Ethnography* 13, 1: 8–43. Reprinted in John Van Maanen, ed., *Representation in Ethnography.* London: Sage, 1995: 36–78.

———. 1992. " 'After a While No One Believes You': Real and Unreal Chronic Pain." In Mary-Jo DelVecchio Good et al., eds., *Pain and Human Experience: Anthropological Perspectives on the Lived Worlds of Chronic Pain Patients in North America.* Berkeley: University of California Press: 138–68.

———. 1994a: "Chronic Pain and the Tension Between the Body as Subject and Object." In Thomas Csordas, ed., *Embodiment and Experience: The Existential Ground of Culture and Self.* Cambridge: Cambridge University Press: 201–28.

———. 1994b. "The Rashomon Approach to Dealing with Chronic Pain." *Social Science and Medicine* 38, 6: 823–33.

———. 1995. "Chronic Pain, Stigma, and the Concept of Liminality." Paper delivered in symposium on "Chronic Pain, Stigma, and Social Control" at the American Pain Society Annual Conference, Los Angeles.

———. 1997: Entries on "Fieldwork," "Fieldnotes," "Participant-Observation," and "Informants." In Thomas Barfield, ed., *The Dictionary of Anthropology.* Malden: Blackwell.

Jackson, Michael, 1989. *Paths Toward a Clearing: Radical Empiricism and Ethnographic Inquiry.* Bloomington: Indiana University Press.

Jacobus, Mary, Evelyn Fox Keller, and Sally Shuttleworth, eds. 1990. *Body/Politics: Women and the Discourses of Science.* New York: Routledge.

Jacox, Ada K., ed. *Current Concepts of Pain and Analgesia.* New York: Current Concepts, Inc.

James, William. 1963 [1902]. *The Varieties of Religious Experience: A Study in Human Nature.* New Hyde Park, N.Y.: University Books, Inc.

Johnson, Mark. 1987. *The Body in the Mind: The Bodily Basis of Meaning, Imagination, and Reason.* Chicago: University of Chicago Press.

Jones, Maxwell. 1953. *The Therapeutic Community: A New Treatment Method in Psychiatry.* New York: Basic Books.

Kanter, Rosabeth Moss. 1972. *Commitment and Community: Communes and Utopias in Sociological Perspective.* Cambridge, Mass.: Harvard University Press.

Kaufman, Barry Neil. 1976. *Son Rise: One Family's Journey from Hopelessness to the Triumph of Love.* New York: Warner Books.

Keefe, Francis J. 1982. "Behavioral Assessment and Treatment of Chronic Pain: Current Status and Future Directions." *Journal of Consulting and Clinical Psychology* 50, 6: 896–911.

Keefe, Francis J., Amy D. Holzberg, and Pat M. Beaupré. 1996. "Contributions of Pain Behavior Assessment and Pain Assessment to the Developmet of Pain Clinics." In Mitchell J. M. Cohen and James N. Campbell, eds., *Pain Treatment Centers at a Crossroads: A Practical and Conceptual Reappraisal.* Seattle: IASP Press: 79–100.

Keefe, Francis J. and John C. Lefebvre. 1994. "Behaviour Therapy." In Patrick D. Wall and Ronald Melzack, eds., *Textbook of Pain.* 3rd ed. Edinburgh: Churchill Livingstone: 1367–80.

Kennard, David and Robert Clemmey. 1976. "Psychiatric Patients as Seen by Self and Others: An Exploration of Change in a Therapeutic Community Setting." *British Journal of Medical Psychology* 49: 35–53.

Kerns, Robert D. 1996. "Psychosocial Factors: Primary or Secondary Outcomes?" In Mitchell J. M. Cohen and James N. Campbell, eds., *Pain Treatment Centers at a Crossroads: A Practical and Conceptual Reappraisal.* Seattle: IASP Press: 183–92.

Kesey, Ken. 1962. *One Flew Over the Cuckoo's Nest.* New York: Viking Press.

Keyes, Charles. 1985. "The Interpretive Basis of Depression." In Arthur Kleinman and Byron Good, eds., *Culture and Depression: Studies in the Anthropology and Cross-Cultural Psychiatry of Affect and Disorder.* Berkeley: University of California Press.

Kidd, David H. and Richard B. North, 1996: "Spinal Cord Stimulation: An Effective and Cost-Saving Treatment in the Management of Chronic Pain." In

Mitchell J. M. Cohen and James N. Campbell, eds., *Pain Treatment Centers at a Crossroads: A Practical and Conceptual Reappraisal.* Seattle: IASP Press: 173–82.

Kim, Choong Soon. 1990. "The Role of the Non-Western Anthropologist Reconsidered." *Current Anthropology* 31, 1: 196–201.

Kirmayer, Laurence J. 1988. "Mind and Body as Metaphors: Hidden Values in Biomedicine." In Margaret Lock and Deborah R. Gordon, eds., *Biomedicine Examined.* Boston: D. Reidel: 57–93.

———. 1992. "The Body's Insistence on Meaning: Metaphor as Presentation and Representation in Illness Experience." *Medical Anthropology Quarterly* 6, 4: 323–46.

Kirschner, Suzanne R. 1987. " 'Then what have I to do with thee?' On Identity, Fieldwork, and Ethnographic Knowledge." *Cultural Anthropology* 2, 2: 211–34.

Kleinman, Arthur M. 1982. "Neurasthenia and Depression: A Study of Somatization and Culture in China." *Culture, Medicine, and Psychiatry* 6: 117–90.

———. 1988. *The Illness Narratives: Suffering, Healing, and the Human Condition.* New York: Basic Books.

———. 1992. "Pain and Resistance: The Delegitimation and Relegitimation of Local Worlds." In Mary-Jo DelVecchio Good et al., eds., *Pain as Human Experience: An Anthropological Perspective.* Berkeley: University of California Press: 169–97.

———. 1995. *Writing at the Margin: Discourse Between Anthropology and Medicine.* Berkeley: University of California Press.

Kleinman, Arthur M., Veena Das, and Margaret Lock, eds. 1997. *Social Suffering.* Berkeley: University of California Press.

Kleinman, Arthur M., Leon Eisenberg, and Byron Good. 1978. "Culture, Illness, and Care." *Annals of Internal Medicine* 88: 251–58.

Knoll, R. 1975. "Psychoanalysis and Pain." In Benjamin L. Crue, ed., *Pain: Research and Treatment.* New York: Academic Press: 365–69.

Koestler, Arthur. 1941. *Darkness at Noon.* New York: Macmillan.

Kondo, Dorinne. 1986. "Dissolution and Reconstitution of Self: Implications for Anthropological Epistemology." *Cultural Anthropology* 1, 1: 74–88.

Kotarba, Joseph A. 1977. "The Chronic Pain Experience." In Jack Douglas and John Johnson, eds., *Existential Sociology.* Cambridge: Cambridge University Press, 1977: 257–72.

———. 1981. "Chronic Pain Center: A Study of Voluntary Client Compliance and Entrepreneurship." *American Behavioral Scientist* 24: 786–800.

Kotarba, Joseph A. and John V. Seidel. 1984. "Managing the Problem Pain Patient: Compliance or Social Control?" *Social Science and Medicine* 19, 12: 1393–1400.

Kuhn, Thomas S. 1970. *The Structure of Scientific Revolutions.* 2nd ed. Chicago: University of Chicago Press.

Kuper, Leo. 1981. *Genocide: Its Political Use in the Twentieth Century.* New Haven, Conn.: Yale University Press.

Lack, Dorothea Z. 1982. "Women and Pain: Another Feminist Issue." *Women and Therapy* 1, 1: 55–64.

La Fontaine, Jean S. 1985. *Initiation: Ritual Drama and Secret Knowledge Across the World.* Harmondsworth: Penguin.

Langer, Lawrence L. 1997. "The Alarmed Vision: Social Suffering and Holocaust Atrocity." In Kleinman et al., eds., *Social Suffering.* Berkeley: University of California Press: 47–66.

Latimer, Paul R. 1982. "External Contingency Management for Chronic Pain: Critical Review of the Evidence." *American Journal of Psychiatry* 139: 1308–12.

Leavitt, Judith Walzer. 1980. "Birthing and Anesthesia: The Debate over Twilight Sleep." *Signs* 6: 147–64.

Leder, Drew. 1990. *The Absent Body.* Chicago: University of Chicago Press.

Lennon, Mary Clare, Bruce G. Link, Joseph J. Marbach, Bruce P. Dohrenwend. 1989. "The Stigma of Chronic Facial Pain and its Impact on Social Relationships." *Social Problems* 36, 2: 117–34.

Levine, E. M. 1980. "Rural Communes and Religious Cults: Refuges for Middle-Class Youth." *Adolescent Psychiatry* 8: 138–53.

Lévy, Geneviève and Maurice Lévy. 1994. "Foreword." In *The Puzzle of Pain.* Reading, UK: Gordon and Breach: 1–2.

Lewin, Ellen and William L. Leap. 1996. *Out in the Field: Reflections of Lesbian and Gay Anthropologists.* Urbana: University of Illinois Press.

Lewis, Gilbert. 1980. *Day of Shining Red: An Essay on Understanding Ritual.* Cambridge: Cambridge University Press.

Liddy, G. Gordon, 1980. *Will: The Autobiography of G. Gordon Liddy.* New York: St. Martin's Press.

Liebeskind, John C. 1994. "Integrating Behavioral and Biological Approaches to Pain Research." Paper presented at Workshop on Biobehavioral Pain Research: A Multi-Institute Assessment of Cross-Cutting Issues and Research Needs." Bethesda, Md.: National Institutes of Health.

———. 1997. "Introduction: Pain and Nociception: Semantic and Ethical Considerations." Manuscript.

———. 1998. Remarks. In Arthur Barsky, Isabelle Baszanger, Laurence Bradley, Kenneth Casey, C. Richard Chapman, Richard Gracely, Jennifer Haythornwaite, Jean Jackson, Mark Jensen, Francis J. Keefe, John Liebeskind, Henrietta Logan, Patrick McGrath, Deborah B. McGuire, Ronald Melzack, David Morris, Stephen G. Post, Donald Price, Fenella Rouse, Judith Spross, Mark Sullivan, Dennis C. Turk, Lynn Underwood, Father Clement Zeleznik. "Perspectives on Pain-Related Suffering: Presentations and Discussion." *Advances in Mind-Body Medicine* 14, 3: 167–203.

Lippe, Philipp M. 1996. "Pain Medicine: A Conceptual and Operational Construct." In Mitchell J. M. Cohen and James N. Campbell, eds., *Pain Treatment Centers at a Crossroads: A Practical and Conceptual Reappraisal.* Seattle: IASP Press: 307–14.

Lipton, S. and J. C. D. Wells. 1983. "The Pain Relief Clinic: Starting and Organization." *Persistent Pain* 4: 159–71.

Lock, Margaret and Nancy Scheper-Hughes. 1990. "A Critical-Interpretive Approach in Medical Anthropology: Rituals and Routines of Discipline and Dissent." In Thomas F. Johnson and Carolyn F. Sargent, eds., *Medical Anthropology: A Handbook of Theory and Method.* Newark, N.J.: Greenwood Press: 47–72.

Loeser, John D. 1991. "What Is Chronic Pain?" *Theoretical Medicine* 12: 213–25.

———. 1996. "Mitigating the Dangers of Pursuing Care." In Mitchell J. M. Cohen and James N. Campbell, eds., *Pain Treatment Centers at a Crossroads: A Practical and Conceptual Reappraisal.* Seattle: IASP Press: 101–8.

Loeser, John D., Joel L. Seres, and Richard I. Newman. 1990. "Interdisciplinary, Multimodal Management of Chronic Pain." In John J. Bonica, ed., *The Management of Pain.* 2nd ed. Philadelphia: Lea and Febiger: 2107–20.

Long, Donlin M. 1996. "The Development of the Comprehensive Pain Treatment Program at Johns Hopkins." In Mitchell J. M. Cohen and James N.

Campbell, eds., *Pain Treatment Centers at a Crossroads: A Practical and Conceptual Reappraisal.* Seattle: IASP Press: 3–26.

Manning, Nicholas P. 1976a. "Values and Practice in the Therapeutic Community." *Human Relations* 29, 2: 125–38.

———. 1976b. "Innovation in Social Policy—the Case of the Therapeutic Community." *Journal of Social Policy* 5, 3: 265–79.

Maranhao, Tulio. 1984. "Family Therapy and Anthropology." *Culture, Medicine and Psychiatry* 8: 255–79.

Marcus, Alfred C., Teresa E. Seeman, and Carol W. Telesky. 1983. "Sex Differences in Reports of Illness and Disability: A Further Test of the Fixed Role Hypothesis." *Social Science and Medicine* 17, 15: 993–1002.

Marcus, George E. and Dick Cushman. 1982. "Ethnographic Texts," *Annual Review of Anthropology* 11: 25–70.

Marcus, George E. and Michael M. J. Fischer. 1986. *Anthropology as Cultural Critique: An Experimental Moment in the Human Sciences.* Chicago: University of Chicago Press.

Martin, Emily. 1987. *The Woman in the Body: A Cultural Analysis of Reproduction.* Boston: Beacon Press.

———. 1990. "Toward an Anthropology of Immunology: The Body as Nation State." *Medical Anthropology Quarterly* 4, 4: 410–26.

———. 1994. *Flexible Bodies: Tracking Immunity in American Culture from the Days of Polio to the Age of AIDS.* Boston: Beacon Press.

Matthews-Simonton, Stephanie, O. Carl Simonton, and James L. Creighton. 1978. *Getting Well Again.* Toronto: Bantam Books.

Mattingly, Cheryl. 1998. *Healing Dramas and Clinical Plots: The Narrative Structure of Experience.* Cambridge: Cambridge University Press.

McKinlay, John B. 1986. "A Case for Refocusing Upstream: The Political Economy of Illness." In P. Conrad and R. Kern, eds., *The Sociology of Health and Illness: Critical Perspectives.* New York: St. Martin's Press: 484–98.

Mechanic, David. 1972. "Social Psychological Factors Affecting the Presentation of Bodily Complaints," *New England Journal of Medicine* 286: 1132–39.

Melzack, Ronald. 1975. "The McGill Pain Questionnaire: Major Properties and Scoring Methods." *Pain* 1: 277–99.

———. 1989. "Phantom Limbs, the Self and the Brain." *Canadian Psychology* 30: 1–16.

———. 1996. "Gate Control Theory: On the Evolution of Pain Concepts." *Pain Forum* 5, 2: 128–38.

Melzack, Ronald and Joel Katz. 1992. "The McGill Pain Questionnaire: Appraisal and Current Status." In Dennis C. Turk and Ronald Melzack, eds., *Handbook of Pain Assessment.* New York: Guilford Press.

Melzack, Ronald and W. Torgerson, 1971. "On the Language of Pain." *Anesthesiology* 34: 50–59.

Melzack, Ronald and Patrick D. Wall. 1965. "Pain Mechanisms: A New Theory." *Science* 150: 971–79.

———. 1973. *The Puzzle of Pain.* New York: Basic Books.

———. 1983. *The Challenge of Pain: Exciting Discoveries in the New Science of Pain Control.* New York: Basic Books.

Mendelson, George. 1991. "Chronic Pain, Compensation and Clinical Knowledge." *Theoretical Medicine* 12: 227–46.

———. 1992. "Compensation and Pain." *Pain* 48: 121–23.

Menges, Louwrens J. 1981. "Chronic Pain Patients: Some Psychological Aspects."

In Sampson Lipton and John Miles, eds., *Persistent Pain: Modern Methods of Treatment*, vol. 3. New York: Academic Press: 87–98.

———. 1984. "Pain: Still an Intriguing Puzzle." *Social Science and Medicine* 19: 1257–60.

Merleau-Ponty, Maurice. 1962. *Phenomenology of Perception.* Trans. C. Smith. London: Routledge and Kegan Paul.

Merskey, Harold. 1976. "Psychiatric aspects of the control of pain." In J. J. Bonica and D. Albe-Fessard, eds., *Advances in Pain Research and Therapy*, vol. 1. New York: Raven Press: 711–16.

———. 1977. "Psychiatric Management of Patients with Chronic Pain." In Sampson Lipton, ed., *Pain: Modern Methods of Treatment*, vol. 1. New York: Academic Press.

———. 1986. "International Association for the Study of Pain: Classification of Chronic Pain." *Pain* 3 (suppl.): 59–60.

———. 1987. "Pain, Personality and Psychosomatic Complaints." In G. Burrows, E. Elton, and G. Stanley, eds., *Handbook of Chronic Pain Management.* Amsterdam: Elsevier Scientific Press: 137–46.

Merskey, Harold and Nikolai Bogduk, eds. 1994. *Classification of Chronic Pain: Descriptions of Chronic Pain Syndromes and Definitions of Pain Terms.* 2nd ed. Seattle: International Association for the Study of Pain.

Miller, Lawrence G. 1979. "Pain, Parturition, and the Profession: The Twilight Sleep in America." In Susan Reverby and David Rosner, eds., *Health Care in America: Essays in Social History.* Philadelphia: Temple University Press: 19–44.

Mishler, Elliot G. 1984. *The Discourse of Medicine: Dialectics of Medical Interviews.* Norwood, N.J.: Ablex.

Moerman, Daniel E. 1979. "Anthropology of Symbolic Healing." *Current Anthropology* 20, 1 (March): 59–77.

Morris, Brian. 1987. *Anthropological Studies of Religion: An Introductory Text.* Cambridge: Cambridge University Press.

Morris, David B. 1991. *The Culture of Pain.* Berkeley: University of California Press.

Moyers, Bill. 1993. *Healing and the Mind.* New York: Doubleday.

Narayan, Kirin. 1993. "How Native Is a 'Native Anthropologist'?" *American Anthropologist* 95: 671–86.

Natali, Jean-Paul. 1994. "Pain: Beyond all Paradoxes." In *The Puzzle of Pain.* Reading, UK: Gordon and Breach: 3–14.

Newman, Richard I., Joel L. Seres, Leonard P. Yospe, and Bonnie Garlington. 1978. "Multidisciplinary Treatment of Chronic Pain: Long-Term Follow-Up of Low-Back Pain Patients." *Pain* 4: 283–92.

Obeyesekere, Gananath. 1985. "Depression, Buddhism, and the Work of Culture in Sri Lanka." In Arthur Kleinman and Byron Good, eds., *Culture and Depression: Studies in the Anthropology and Cross-Cultural Psychiatry of Affect and Disorder.* Berkeley: University of California Press: 134–52.

Ohnuki-Tierney, Emiko. 1984. " 'Native' Anthropologists." *American Ethnologist* 11: 584–86.

Ong, Ahiwa. 1988. "The Production of Possession: Spirits and the Multinational Corporation in Malaysia." *American Ethnologist* 15, 1: 28–42.

Ortner, Sherry. 1989–90. "Gender Hegemonies." *Cultural Critique* 12: 35–80.

Osterweis, Marion, Arthur Kleinman, and David Mechanic, eds. 1987. *Pain and Disability: Clinical, Behavioral, and Public Policy Perspectives.* Washington, D.C.: National Academy Press.

Painter, John R., Joel L. Seres, and Richard I. Newman. 1980. "Assessing Benefits of the Pain Center: Why Some Patients Regress." *Pain* 8: 101–13.

Palazzoli, Mara Selvini, Luigi Boscolo, Gianfranco Cecchin, and Giuliana Prata. 1978. *Paradox and Counter Paradox.* New York: Jason Aronson.

Parsons, Talcott. 1958. "Definitions of Health and Illness in the Light of American Values and Social Structure." In E. Gartly Jaco, ed., *Patients, Physicians, and Illness: Sourcebook in Behavioral Science and Medicine.* New York: Free Press: 165–87.

Pilowsky, I. 1978. "Psychodynamic Aspects of the Pain Experience." In Richard A. Sternbach, ed., *The Psychology of Pain.* New York: Raven Press: 203–17.

Pinsky, J. J. 1975. "Psychodynamics and psychotherapy in the treatment of patients with chronic intractable pain." In B. L. Crue, ed., *Pain: Research and Treatment.* New York: Academic Press, 1975: 383–99.

Porter, Roy. 1994. "Pain and History in the Western World." In *The Puzzle of Pain.* Reading, UK: Gordon and Breach: 98–119.

Price, Reynolds, 1995. *A Whole New Life: An Illness and a Healing.* New York: Scribner.

Priel, Beatrice, Betty Rabinowitz, and Richard J. Pels. 1991, "A Semiotic Perspective on Chronic Pain: Implications for the Interaction Between Patient and Physician." *British Journal of Medical Psychology* 64: 65–71.

Public Radio International. n.d. "Gray Matters: Pain and the Brain." Typescript of radio broadcast.

The Puzzle of Pain. 1994. Reading, UK: Gordon and Breach.

Randall, W. 1975. "The Role of the Social Worker as a Change Agent in the Pain Center." In Benjamin L. Crue, ed., *Pain: Research and Treatment.* New York: Academic Press: 347–52.

Rapoport, Robert N. 1960. *Community as Doctor: New Perspectives on a Therapeutic Community.* London: Tavistock.

Rawlings, Barbara. 1981. "The Production of Facts in a Therapeutic Community." In Paul Atkinson and Christian Heath, eds., *Medical Work: Realities and Routines.* London: Gower.

Reid, Janice, Christine Ewan, and Eva Lowy. 1991. "Pilgrimage of Pain: The Illness Experiences of Women with Repetition Strain Injury and the Search for Credibility." *Social Science and Medicine* 32, 5: 601–12.

Rhodes, Lorna A., Carol A. McPhillips-Tangum, Christine Markham, Rebecca Klenk. n.d. "The Power of the Visible: The Meaning of Diagnostic Tests for Patients with Chronic Back Pain." Typescript.

Ricoeur, Paul. 1979. "The Model of the Text: Meaningful Action Considered as a Text." *Social Research* 38, 3 (1971). Reprinted in Paul Rabinow and William M. Sullivan, eds., *Interpretive Social Science: A Reader.* Berkeley: University of California Press: 73–102.

Rosaldo, Michelle. 1984. "Toward an Anthropology of Self and Feeling." In Richard A. Shweder and Robert A. LeVine, eds., *Culture Theory: Essays on Mind, Self, and Emotion.* Cambridge: Cambridge University Press: 137–57.

Rosenthal, Elizabeth. 1994. "Panel Tells Albany to Resist Legalizing Assisted Suicide." *New York Times,* May 26.

Roy, Ranjan. 1992. *The Social Context of the Chronic Pain Sufferer.* Toronto: University of Toronto Press.

Sacks, Oliver. 1983. *Awakenings.* 2nd ed., New York: E. P. Dutton.

———. 1984. *A Leg to Stand On.* New York: Harper and Row.

————. 1985. *The Man Who Mistook His Wife for a Hat and Other Clinical Tales.* New York: Harper and Row.

————. 1985. *Migraine: Understanding a Common Disorder.* Berkeley: University of California Press.

Said, Edward. 1978. *Orientalism.* New York: Pantheon.

Sanday, Peggy Reeves. 1990. *Fraternity Gang Rape: Sex, Brotherhood, and Privilege on Campus.* New York: New York University Press.

Sarno, John E. 1976. "Chronic Back Pain and Psychic Conflict." *Scandinavian Journal of Rehabilitation Medicine* 8: 143–53.

Scarry, Elaine. 1985. *The Body in Pain: The Making and Unmaking of the World.* New York: Oxford University Press.

Schaeffer, Phyllis. 1983. "Learning to Be a Chronic Pain Patient." *Aches and Pains* 4: 21–25.

Scheper-Hughes, Nancy and Margaret M. Lock. 1987. "The Mindful Body: A Prolegomenon to Future Work in Medical Anthropology." *Medical Anthropology Quarterly* 1: 6–41.

Schieffelin, Edward. 1976. *The Sorrow of the Lonely and the Burning of the Dancers.* New York: St. Martin's Press.

————. 1985. "Performance and the Cultural Construction of Reality." *American Ethnologist* 12, 4: 707–24.

Schutz, Alfred. 1970. *On Phenomenology and Social Relations.* Ed. Helmut R. Wagner. Chicago: University of Chicago Press.

————. 1971. "On Multiple Realities." In Schutz, *Collected Papers.* Vol. 1, *The Problem of Social Reality.* The Hague: Martinus Nijhoff.

Scott, James. 1985. *Weapons of the Weak: Everyday Forms of Peasant Resistance.* New Haven, Conn.: Yale University Press.

Sharp, V. 1975. *Social Control in the Therapeutic Community.* Farnborough: Saxon House.

Shealy, C. Norman and and Mary-Charlotte Shealy. 1975. "Behavioral Techniques in the Control of Pain: A Case for Health Maintenance vs. Disease Treatment." In Matisyohu Weisenberg and Bernard Tursky, eds., *Pain: New Perspectives in Therapy and Treatment.* New York: Plenum: 22–33.

Sheridan, Mary S. 1992. *Pain in America.* Tuscaloosa: University of Alabama Press.

Shorter, Edward. 1992. *From Paralysis to Fatigue: A History of Psychosomatic Illness in the Modern Era.* New York: Free Press.

Siegel, Bernie S. 1986. *Love, Medicine, and Miracles: Lessons Learned About Self-Healing from a Surgeon's Experience with Exceptional Patients.* New York: Harper and Row.

Singer, M. 1990. "Reinventing Medical Anthropology: Toward a Critical Realignment." *Social Science and Medicine* 30, 2: 179–87.

Snow, David A. and Richard Machalek. 1984. "The Sociology of Conversion." *Annual Review of Sociology* 10: 167–90.

Sontag, Susan. 1977. *Illness as Metaphor.* New York: Random House.

Spence, Susan. 1991. "Case History and Shorter Communication." *Behavioral Research and Therapy* 29, 5: 503–9.

Staats, Peter S. 1996. "Pain is Pain: Why the Dichotomy of Approach to Cancer and Noncancer Pain?" In Mitchell J. M. Cohen and James N. Campbell, eds., *Pain Treatment Centers at a Crossroads: A Practical and Conceptual Reappraisal.* Seattle: IASP Press: 117–24.

Sternbach, Richard A. 1978. "Clinical Aspects of Pain." In Sternbach, ed., *The Psychology of Pain.* New York: Raven Press: 241–64.

————. 1984. "Behavior Therapy." In Patrick D. Wall and Ronald Melzack, eds., *Textbook of Pain.* New York: Churchill Livingstone: 800–805.

————. 1986. "Pain and Hassles in the United States: The Findings of the Nuprin Report." *Pain* 27: 69–80.

Stewart, Donna E. 1990. "The Changing Faces of Somatization." *Psychosomatics* 31: 153–58.

Stoller, Paul. 1989. *The Taste of Ethnographic Things: The Senses in Anthropology.* Philadelphia: University of Pennsylvania Press.

Stoltenberg, John. 1989. *Refusing to Be a Man: Essays on Sex and Justice.* Portland, Ore.: Breitenbush Books.

Streltzer, J. and T. Wade. 1981. "The Influence of Cultural Group on the Undertreatment of Post-Operative Pain." *Psychosomatic Medicine* 43: 392–403.

"Study Says 1 in 5 Americans Suffers from Chronic Pain." 1994. *New York Times,* October 21.

Styron, William. 1990. *Darkness Visible: A Memoir of Madness.* New York: Random House.

Sudnow, David. 1967. *Passing On: The Social Organization of Dying.* Englewood Cliffs, N.J.: Prentice-Hall.

Sugarman, Barry. 1975. "Reluctant Converts: Social Control, Socialization and Adaptation in Therapeutic Communities." In Roy Wallis, ed., *Sectarianism: Analyses of Religious and Non-Religious Sects.* London: Peter Owen.

Sullivan, Mark D. 1995. "Pain in Language: From Sentience to Sapience." *Pain Forum* 4, 1: 3–14.

Swanson, David W. 1984. "Chronic Pain as a Third Pathologic Emotion." *American Journal of Psychiatry* 141, 2: 210–14.

Swanson, David W., Toshihiko Maruta, and Wendell M. Swenson. 1979. "Results of Behavior Modification in the Treatment of Chronic Pain." *Psychosomatic Medicine* 41, 1: 55–61.

Taricco, Alfred. 1996. "Perils of Payors: A Pain Center Paradigm." In Mitchell J. M. Cohen and James N. Campbell, eds., *Pain Treatment Centers at a Crossroads: A Practical and Conceptual Reappraisal.* Seattle: IASP Press: 109–16.

Taussig, Michael. 1980. "Reification and the Consciousness of the Patient." *Social Science and Medicine* 14: 3–13.

Tipton, Steven M. 1982. *Getting Saved from the Sixties.* Berkeley: University of California Press.

Turk, Dennis C. 1996. "Efficacy of Multidisciplinary Pain Centers in the Treatment of Chronic Pain." In Mitchell J. M. Cohen and James N. Campbell, eds., *Pain Treatment Centers at a Crossroads: A Practical and Conceptual Reappraisal.* Seattle: IASP Press: 257–74.

Turk, Dennis C., D. Meichenbaum, and M. Genest. 1983. *Pain and Behavioral Medicine: A Cognitive-Behavioral Perspective.* New York: Guilford Press.

Turner, Bryan S. 1991. "Recent Developments in the Theory of the Body." In Mike Featherstone, Mike Hepworth, and Bryan S, Turner, eds., *The Body: Social Process and Cultural Theory.* London: Sage: 1–35.

————. 1992. *Regulating Bodies: Essays in Medical Sociology.* London: Routledge.

Turner, Candice C. 1987. "A Cultural Model of Chronic Pain Adaptation." Paper presented at the Annual Meetings of the American Anthropological Association, Chicago, November.

Turner, J. and S. Clancy. 1988. "Comparison of Operant Behavioral and Cognitive-Behavioral Group Treatment for Chronic Low Back Pain." *Journal of Consulting and Clinical Psychology* 56: 261–66.

Turner, Victor. 1967. *The Forest of Symbols: Aspects of Ndembu Ritual.* Ithaca, N.Y.: Cornell University Press.

———. 1969. *The Ritual Process: Structure and Anti-Structure.* Chicago: Aldine.

Vincent, Jean-Didier. 1994. "Displayed Pain and Hidden Pleasure." In *The Puzzle of Pain.* Reading, UK: Gordon and Breach: 15–25.

Vonnegut, Kurt, Jr. 1970 (1951). "The Euphio Question." In Vonnegut, *Welcome to the Monkey House.* New York: Dell: 177–92.

Vrancken, Mariet A. E. 1989. "Schools of Thought on Pain." *Social Science and Medicine* 29, 3: 435–44.

Wagner, Roy. 1984. "Ritual as Communication: Order, Meaning, and Secrecy in Melanesian Initiation Rites." *Annual Review of Anthropology* 13: 143–204.

Wall, Patrick D. and Ronald Melzack, eds. 1994. *Textbook of Pain.* 3rd ed. Edinburgh: Churchill Livingstone.

Wallace, Anthony F. C. 1969. *The Death and Rebirth of the Seneca.* New York:Knopf.

Walley, Christine J. 1997. "Searching for 'Voices': Feminism, Anthropology, and the Global Debate over Female Genital Operations." *Cultural Anthropology* 12, 3: 405–38.

Wallis, Claudia. 1984. "Unlocking Pain's Secrets." *Time,* June 11: 58–66.

Ware, Norma. 1992. "Suffering and the Social Construction of Illness: The Delegitimation of Illness Experience in Chronic Fatigue Syndrome." *Medical Anthropology Quarterly* 6, 4: 347–61.

Warwick, Ian, Peter Aggleton, and Hilary Homans. 1988. "Constructing Commonsense: Young People's Beliefs About AIDS." *Sociology of Health and Illness* 10: 213–23.

Weppner, Robert S. 1983. *The Untherapeutic Community: Organizational Behavior in a Failed Addiction Treatment Program.* Lincoln: University of Nebraska Press.

West, Candace. 1984. *Routine Complications: Troubles with Talk Between Doctors and Patients.* Bloomington: Indiana University Press.

Williams, Raymond. 1977. *Marxism and Literature.* Oxford: Oxford University Press: 108–14.

Willis, Paul. 1977. *Learning to Labor: How Working Class Kids Get Working Class Jobs.* New York: Columbia University Press.

———. 1979. "Masculinity and Factory Labor." In John Clarke, Chas Critcher, and R. Johnson, eds., *Working-Class Culture: Studies in History and Theory.* London: Hutchinson: 186–98.

Wilson, R. Reid and Gerald M. Aronoff. 1978. "The Therapeutic Community in the Treatment of Chronic Pain." *Journal of Chronic Diseases* 32, 7: 477–80.

Wissler, Clark. 1921. "The Sun Dance of the Blackfoot Indians." *American Museum of Natural History, Anthropology Papers* 16: 223–70.

Woolf, Virginia. 1947. *The Moment and Other Essays.* New York: Harcourt Brace & Co.

Yablonsky, Lewis. 1965. *Synanon: The Tunnel Back.* Baltimore: Penguin Books.

Young, Allan A. 1980. "The Discourse on Stress and the Reproduction of Conventional Knowledge." *Social Science and Medicine* 14: 133–46.

———. 1982. "The Anthropologies of Illness and Sickness." *Annual Review of Anthropology* 11: 257–85.

———. 1985. "How Ideology Shapes Knowledge." In Shirley Lindenbaum and Margaret Lock, eds., *Knowledge, Power and Practice: The Anthropology of Medicine and Everyday Life.* Berkeley: University of California Press: 108–28.

———. 1995. *The Harmony of Illusions: Inventing Post-Traumatic Stress Disorder.* Princeton, N.J.: Princeton University Press.

Zablocki, Benjamin. 1980. *Alienation and Charisma: A Study of Contemporary American Communes*. New York: Free Press.

Zborowski, Mark. 1952. "Cultural Components in Responses to Pain." *Journal of Social Issues* 8: 16–30.

———. 1969. *People in Pain*. San Francisco: Jossey-Bass.

Zola, Irving Kenneth. 1966. "Culture and Symptoms—An Analysis of Patients' Presenting Complaints." *American Sociological Review* 31, 5: 615–630.

———. 1972. "Medicine as an Institution of Social Control." *Sociological Review* 20: 487–504.

———. 1982. *Missing Pieces: A Chronicle of Living with a Disability*. Philadelphia: Temple University Press.

Index

narrow focus, 2; non-pain specialists as intolerant of "pain patients," 219; over-reliance on technology, 28, 178, 219; pain management as specialty, 40, 186; patients as victims of, 48; vague answers of, 186

Medical gaze, Foucault's notion of, 14, 98, 222

Medication: art of, 182; "candy cart," 22; censorship of patient/doctor discussion, 72; "doctor shopping," 34–35; effectiveness of, 1, 34, 182; "fascist attitude" toward, 72, 227; highly charged topic at CPC, 20, 110; loss of jobs due to, 36; overemphasis on, 28, 41; overmedication, 3; undermedication and vulnerable populations, 187; weaning patients from, 22, 34, 110. *See also* Anti-depressant; Dependency; Doxepin; Drug abuse; Drugs; Pain

Meichenbaum, D., 220

Melzack, Ronald, 26, 171, 217 219, 221, 223, 226, 233, 234, 235, 238, 240, 241

Memory: and imaging pain, 152–56; as sculpting process, 171. *See also* Imaging pain

Mental control images, 155

Mental health, Harvard conference on Latino, 174

Mental stability, 138

Merging with pain, unwelcome, 149

Merleau-Ponty, Maurice, 146, 162, 233, 236

Merskey, Harold, 4, 217, 218, 220, 223, 238

Metaphor: concept of pain, 188; CPC community seen as, 106–8 as expression outside everyday world, 162; eloquence of in pain descriptions, 163; pain as metaphor for distress, 175; of power and authority, 79

Methodological approach. *See* Research

Microcosm, CPC as, 80

Middle Ages, 103, 181

Milieu therapy, 18–19. *See also* Community; Therapeutic community

Military analogies and metaphors, 71, 74, 79, 81, 100, 105, 181

Miller, Lawrence G., 219

Mind: as outside self, 168; over matter strategy of CPC, 168, 240

Mind/body: ambiguous status of pain, 144–45; boundaries threatened by extensive view of pain, 173; connections, willingness to try, 45; dualism, 19, 39–42, 144–45; "in your head pain," 160; integration still not Utopia for chronic pain sufferers, 180; integration, "Brave New World" of, 180; interaction no longer marginal field, 178; separation, Cartesian legacy of, 8; split, 12; views on, 6, 46–48

Minefield, patient interaction as, 94

Minoshima, S., 239

Miracle recovery, suspect nature of, 93–94

Misdiagnosis, 41

Mishler, Elliot G., 223, 229

Misinformation, 49

Misunderstanding of nonsufferers, 157, 164

Models. *See* Biomedical; Chronic Pain; Cognitive; Linear; Medical; Pain; Psychodynamic

Moerman, Daniel E., 182, 240

Moodiness, 42

Moral: opprobrium, 7; responsibility, 45, 138, 173; superiority of "stiff upper lip" approach, 145, 180–81

Morphology, pain-full world's own, 164

Morris, Brian, 230

Morris, David B., 156, 193, 217, 219, 222, 223, 226, 234, 236, 240, 241

Morrow, K., 240

Morrow, T. J., 239

Mortality, disability as reminder, 181

Motivation, 25, 70, 70

Movement therapy, 27, 28

Moyers, Bill, 222

MRIs, 178–79

Multidisciplinary approach, 24, 26–33, 224

Multiply determined, pain as, 174

Mute misery, 176

Mystification as implicit CPC feature, 7–8, 135–42, 167

Naive outlook, 16

Narayan, Kirin, 222

Narcotics: ambivalence toward, 187, 224; avoiding overuse of, 25, 101, 103, 108, 224; cold turkey withdrawal, 103; doctors creating dependency on, 41; questioning legitimacy of treatment with,